READERS' GUIDES TO ESSENTIAL CRITICISM

CONSULTANT EDITOR: NICOLAS TREDELL

Published

Lucie Armitt	George Eliot: *Adam Bede – The Mill on the Floss – Middlemarch*
Simon Avery	Thomas Hardy: *The Mayor of Casterbridge – Jude the Obscure*
Paul Baines	Daniel Defoe: *Robinson Crusoe – Moll Flanders*
Annika Bautz	Jane Austen: *Sense and Sensibility – Pride and Prejudice – Emma*
Matthew Beedham	The Novels of Kazuo Ishiguro
Richard Beynon	D. H. Lawrence: *The Rainbow – Women in Love*
Peter Boxall	Samuel Beckett: *Waiting for Godot – Endgame*
Claire Brennan	The Poetry of Sylvia Plath
Susan Bruce	Shakespeare: *King Lear*
Sandie Byrne	Jane Austen: *Mansfield Park*
Alison Chapman	Elizabeth Gaskell: *Mary Barton – North and South*
Peter Childs	The Fiction of Ian McEwan
Christine Clegg	Vladimir Nabokov: *Lolita*
John Coyle	James Joyce: *Ulysses – A Portrait of the Artist as a Young Man*
Martin Coyle	Shakespeare: *Richard II*
Justin D. Edwards	Postcolonial Literature
Michael Faherty	The Poetry of W. B. Yeats
Sarah Gamble	The Fiction of Angela Carter
Jodi–Anne George	*Beowulf*
Jodi–Anne George	Chaucer: The General Prologue to *The Canterbury Tales*
Jane Goldman	Virginia Woolf: *To the Lighthouse – The Waves*
Huw Griffiths	Shakespeare: *Hamlet*
Vanessa Guignery	The Fiction of Julian Barnes
Louisa Hadley	The Fiction of A. S. Byatt
Geoffrey Harvey	Thomas Hardy: *Tess of the d'Urbervilles*
Paul Hendon	The Poetry of W. H. Auden
Terry Hodgson	The Plays of Tom Stoppard for Stage, Radio, TV and Film
William Hughes	Bram Stoker: *Dracula*
Stuart Hutchinson	Mark Twain: *Tom Sawyer – Huckleberry Finn*
Stuart Hutchinson	Edith Wharton: *The House of Mirth – The Custom of the Country*
Betty Jay	E. M. Forster: *A Passage to India*
Aaron Kelly	Twentieth-Century Irish Literature
Elmer Kennedy–Andrews	The Poetry of Seamus Heaney
Elmer Kennedy–Andrews	Nathaniel Hawthorne: *The Scarlet Letter*
Daniel Lea	George Orwell: *Animal Farm – Nineteen Eighty-Four*

Sara Lodge	Charlotte Brontë: *Jane Eyre*
Philippa Lyon	Twentieth-Century War Poetry
Merja Makinen	The Novels of Jeanette Winterson
Matt McGuire	Contemporary Scottish Literature
Timothy Milnes	Wordsworth: *The Prelude*
Jago Morrison	The Fiction of Chinua Achebe
Carl Plasa	Tony Morrison: *Beloved*
Carl Plasa	Jean Rhys: *Wide Sargasso Sea*
Nicholas Potter	Shakespeare: *Antony and Cleopatra*
Nicholas Potter	Shakespeare: *Othello*
Nicholas Potter	Shakespeare's Late Plays: *Pericles, Cymbeline, The Winter's Tale, The Tempest*
Steven Price	The Plays, Screenplays and Films of David Mamet
Andrew Radford	Victorian Sensation Fiction
Berthold Schoene–Harwood	Mary Shelley: *Frankenstein*
Nick Selby	T. S. Eliot: *The Waste Land*
Nick Selby	Herman Melville: *Moby Dick*
Nick Selby	The Poetry of Walt Whitman
David Smale	Salman Rushdie: *Midnight's Children – The Satanic Verses*
Patsy Stoneman	Emily Brontë: *Wuthering Heights*
Susie Thomas	Hanif Kureishi
Nicolas Tredell	F. Scott Fitzgerald: *The Great Gatsby*
Nicolas Tredell	Joseph Conrad: *Heart of Darkness*
Nicolas Tredell	Charles Dickens: *Great Expectations*
Nicolas Tredell	William Faulkner: *The Sound and the Fury – As I Lay Dying*
Nicolas Tredell	Shakespeare: *Macbeth*
Nicolas Tredell	The Fiction of Martin Amis
Matthew Woodcock	Shakespeare: *Henry V*
Angela Wright	Gothic Fiction

Forthcoming

Thomas P. Adler	Tennessee Williams: *A Streetcar Named Desire – Cat on a Hot Tin Roof*
Pascale Aebischer	Jacobean Drama
Brian Baker	Science Fiction
Stephen J. Burn	Postmodern American Fiction
Sarah Haggarty & Jon Mee	William Blake: *Songs of Innocence and Experience*
Nicolas Tredell	Shakespeare: *A Midsummer Night's Dream*
Michael Whitworth	Virginia Woolf: *Mrs Dalloway*
Gina Wisker	The Fiction of Margaret Atwood
Gillian Woods	Shakespeare: *Romeo and Juliet*

Readers' Guides to Essential Criticism
Series Standing Order
ISBN 978-1-4039-0108-8
(outside North America only)

You can receive future titles in this series as they are published by placing a standing order. Please contact your bookseller or, in the case of difficulty, write to us at the address below with your name and address, the title of the series and the ISBN quoted above.

Customer Services Department, Macmillan Distribution Ltd
Houndmills, Basingstoke, Hampshire RG21 6XS, England

The Novels of Kazuo Ishiguro

MATTHEW BEEDHAM

Consultant editor: Nicolas Tredell

palgrave
macmillan

First published 2010 by
PALGRAVE MACMILLAN

Palgrave Macmillan in the UK is an imprint of Macmillan Publishers Limited,
registered in England, company number 785998, of Houndmills, Basingstoke,
Hampshire RG21 6XS.

Palgrave Macmillan in the US is a division of St Martin's Press LLC,
175 Fifth Avenue, New York, NY 10010.

Palgrave Macmillan is the global academic imprint of the above companies
and has companies and representatives throughout the world.

Palgrave® and Macmillan® are registered trademarks in the United
States, the United Kingdom, Europe and other countries

ISBN 978-0-230-51745-5 hardback

ISBN 978-0-230-51746-2   ISBN 978-1-137-08062-2 (eBook)
DOI 10.1007/978-1-137-08062-2

This book is printed on paper suitable for recycling and made from fully
managed and sustained forest sources. Logging, pulping and manufacturing
processes are expected to conform to the environmental regulations of the
country of origin.

A catalogue record for this book is available from the British Library.

A catalog record for this book is available from the Library of Congress.

10 9 8 7 6 5 4 3 2 1
19 18 17 16 15 14 13 12 11 10

Contents

presentation of the Anglo-American tensions as they appear in the novel, Bo J. Ekelund's reading of the novel's various genres, and James Lang's complication of historical interpretations. Postcolonial analyses of the novel include Susie O'Brien's contrast of the old values of England and the new values of the United States and Molly Westerman's attempt to extend the work done by narrative theorists by adding a layer of postcolonial analysis.

Surveys the various interdisciplinary responses to Ishiguro's third novel, including Lillian Furst's use of the anatomy of memory errors proposed by psychologist Daniel L. Schacter, John J. Su's reading of nostalgia that leads to a discussion of the *ethos* embodied in Stevens's journey, Kwame Anthony Appiah's use of the novel to make a case for the moral power of individualism, David Medalie's investigation of the difficulty of discussions of dignity, and legal scholar Rob Atkinson's comparison of Stevens's relationship with Lord Darlington to that of a lawyer and client to illustrate the ethical difficulties in serving.

Investigates the powerful, and divided, response to Ishiguro's fourth novel before outlining the world that the novel creates and the propensity to respond to the novel in terms of dreams and nightmares. After introducing Ishiguro's 'appropriations' technique, this chapter turns to Cynthia Wong's postmodern framing of the novel and Pierre François' psychoanalytic reading.

Through a discussion of the varied responses to Ishiguro's fifth novel, this chapter highlights the novel's similarities to Ishiguro's earlier novels and his use of the 'appropriation' technique. After outlining the discussions of the novel's narrative and prose and Banks's character, the chapter considers the novel as a detective story, Alexander M. Bain's essay on the portrayal of the failure of the international community, and the roles of memory and children in the novel.

Surveys the range of positive responses that greeted Ishiguro's sixth novel, including discussions of the novel's instigation of ethical debates and its portrayal of childhood. The novel then turns to two scholarly responses: Rebecca Walkowitz's reading of the novel as a critique of individuality, and Bruce Robbins's consideration of the 'banality' of Ishiguro's themes.

Considers recent work that has been done on Ishiguro's novels and Ishiguro's work in film before turning to gaps in the response to his novels and a discussion of his status as an 'international' writer.

Introduction

One of the world's most important contemporary writers, Kazuo Ishiguro (born 1954) has produced a body of work that has been rewarded with several top literary prizes and consistent critical praise. His first novel, *A Pale View of Hills* (1982) received the Winifred Holtby award 'for the best regional novel of the year'. *Artist of a Floating World* (1986) received even more critical attention and won the prestigious Whitbread Book of the Year award. It was, however, his third novel, *The Remains of the Day* (1989), which received the equally prestigious Booker Prize, that solidly established Ishiguro's reputation. He was 34 years old. Since then his reputation has continued to grow in both English-speaking and non-English-speaking countries. His work has been translated into more than thirty languages. Additionally, he has screenwriting credits on three major motion films, including, most famously, *The Remains of the Day*, which received eight Academy Award nominations. But he remains a novelist and since *Remains* has produced three more novels, each demonstrating an artist pushing against the limits of what a novel can portray, and each displaying his masterly control of prose and narrative. This Guide examines the immense critical response to these six novels so that readers can better understand how Ishiguro has been read and what work remains to be done.

Ishiguro's biography serves as an important starting point to the readings of his work. Since the appearance of his earliest novels, his ethnicity has been a prominent concern, addressed in an almost standard paragraph in all reviews that notes that Ishiguro was born in Japan but raised since the age of five in England. This issue of his ethnicity is accentuated, and some might argue justified, by Ishiguro's use of Japanese characters and Japanese settings in his first two novels. In an oft-quoted interview with Alan Vorda and Kim Herzinger, Ishiguro offers a theory based on his ethnicity for the attention he received early in his career. After Salman Rushdie (born 1947) had won the 1981 Booker Prize with *Midnight's Children*, the search was on for 'other Rushdies'. Ishiguro's first novel had the good fortune to appear at this time: 'I received a lot of attention, got lots of attention, got lots of coverage, and did a lot of interviews. I know why this was.

It was because I had this Japanese face and this Japanese name and it was what was being covered at the time'.[1]

Ishiguro has pointed out, repeatedly, how ill-conceived the attempts to read his work as the work of a Japanese writer are. He maintains that the calm surface of his first two books was simply an expression of his natural voice, and that he 'wasn't trying to write them in an understated, a Japanese way'.[2] Speaking with Dylan Krider, Ishiguro explains what he does and does not know about Japan:

> ■ I was brought up by Japanese parents. I think I understood very deeply how a Japanese family works and about parent/child relationships, marriages, and so on. But I wasn't qualified to comment on the economic situation in Japan or what Japanese people did or didn't do in the '80s. These books were very much my own creations, and as a novelist, I was wanting to write about universal themes, so it always slightly annoyed me when people said, 'Oh, how interesting it must be to be Japanese because you feel this, this, and this', and I thought, 'Don't we all feel like this?'[3] □

In an informative interview with Gregory Mason, Ishiguro notes that his Japanese is 'like a five-year-old's'. On the subject of literary tradition, Ishiguro replies, 'I feel that I'm very much of the Western tradition. And I'm often quite amused when reviewers make a lot of my being Japanese and try to mention the two or three authors they've vaguely heard of'. When he mentions the Russian novelist Fyodor Dostoevsky (1821–81), the Russian playwright and short-story writer Anton Chekhov (1860–1904), and the English novelists Charlotte Brontë (1816–55) and Charles Dickens (1812–70) as influences, Mason, nevertheless, asks him about Japanese influences. Ishiguro mentions the novelists Junichiro Tanizaki (1886–1965), Yasunari Kawabata (1899–1972), Masuji Ibuse (1898–1993), and Natsume Soseki (1867–1916), but then adds that the most relevant Japanese influence in his work is probably the Japanese films of directors such as Yasujiro Ozu (1903–63) and Mikio Naruse (1905–69).[4]

Rather than basing discussions of his work on his biography, Ishiguro's work is better approached through an understanding of his style and his narratives. For example, although numerous critics, such as Rocio Davis[5] and Mark Wormald,[6] have connected Ishiguro to Rushdie, it is a superficial connection of limited use. Ishiguro accurately describes how dissimilar his writing style is from Rushdie's:

> ■ My style is almost the antithesis of Rushdie or [Timothy] Mo [born 1950]. Their writing tends to have these quirks where it explodes in all kinds of directions. Rushdie's language always seems to be reaching

out – to express meaning that can't usually be expressed through normal language. Just structurally his books have this terrific energy. They just grow in every direction at once and he doesn't particularly care if the branches lead nowhere. He'll let it grow anyway and leave it there and that's the way he writes. I think he is a powerful and considerable writer.[7] □

The language that Ishiguro uses for his own writing takes the opposite tack, hiding and suppressing meaning. He favours a 'spare, tight structure because I don't like to have this improvised feeling'. The possible similarity between Rushdie's writing and his own, Ishiguro proposes, is that the younger writers of the time are aware that 'Britain is not the center of the universe'.[8]

Ishiguro's introduction to Nobel Prize winner Yasunari Kawabata's short novels, *Snow Country* (1935–7) and *A Thousand Cranes* (1949–52), on the other hand, offers a valuable starting point for reading Ishiguro's fiction:

■ Kawabata was a writer who quite deliberately aspired to a 'classical' tradition of Japanese prose writing pre-dating the influence of European realism – a tradition which placed value on lyricism, mood and reflection rather than on plot and character. Read either of these novels for a tangible, developing plotline – adopt a 'what-happens-next?' attitude – and one is bound to reach the end with the feeling one has missed the point. Kawabata needs to be read slowly, the atmospheres savoured, the characters' words pondered for nuances.[9] □

One could hardly ask for better direction for reading Ishiguro's own fiction. Clearly in his signalling of aspects of Kawabata's writing he finds important, he has also signalled aspects that he cultivates in his own work.[10]

The response to Ishiguro's work has been not only voluminous but also complex. Given this complexity and the variety of readings that Ishiguro's work inspires, a guide to the responses of reviewers and scholars fills a necessary gap to help readers understand not only the subtleties of Ishiguro's writing but also the main lines of argument his work generates. Consequently, this book aims to outline the initial critical response to Ishiguro's novels, the key critical positions that have developed since, and the arguments that support these positions.

Each of this Guide's eight chapters presents the response to one of Ishiguro's novels, although the response to *Remains*, due to its immensity, is presented in three chapters. After introducing Ishiguro's first novel, *A Pale View of Hills*, I summarise the influential reviews that appeared following the novel's publication. These reviews lead to a discussion of the critical essays that tackle this novel. The primary issues of discussion are Ishiguro's relationship to Japan, his ability to convey emotions through his manipulation of narrative, and the role of memory in this novel. Ishiguro's second novel, *An Artist of the Floating World*, received much more attention than his first, and this chapter charts the response of reviewers before discussing Ishiguro's relationship with Japan, his skilled handling of narrative, and his investigation of the fallibility of memory. Chapter Three, the first of three chapters focused on Ishiguro's third novel, *The Remains of the Day*, notes the response of the reviewers before turning to work on Ishiguro's use of narration, perhaps most importantly, Kathleen Wall in '*The Remains of the Day* and Its Challenges to Theories of Unreliable Narration' (1994). The fourth chapter continues the discussion of *Remains* by following the trajectory of readings based on the historical aspects of the novel, which, in turn, leads to discussions of the novel by postcolonial theorists. Chapter Five, the third chapter dedicated to *Remains*, begins with conversations about the role of memory in the novel and continues by investigating one of the novel's most important themes: the ethics of service, an issue that has been approached from a variety of angles.

Frustrated by critics who attempted to categorise him as a realist and attempting to push his writing in a new direction, Ishiguro replied with his fourth novel, *The Unconsoled* (1995). Almost as long as his three previous novels combined and much more challenging to read, the novel has divided critics. Chapter Six investigates this mixed response and then outlines attempts to interpret this difficult novel. Chapter Seven turns to Ishiguro's fifth novel, *When We Were Orphans*, beginning again with an analysis of the novel's reception based on the reviews it received and using those responses to outline the themes readers have found in the novel. The final chapter looks at the reception of Ishiguro's most recent novel, *Never Let Me Go*, and two of the early scholarly responses the novel has inspired.

The novels of Kazuo Ishiguro demand that readers look honestly at the past, to consider what they hold valuable, and to question how they live their lives. Evaluating the responses to his work provides insight into how critics have responded to these challenges, how they have developed and extended his work, and what has yet to be discussed. These responses demonstrate, then, how Ishiguro, and other writers, might best be read. Perhaps more importantly, however, evaluating these responses reveals how readers can not only better understand the intricacies of Ishiguro's fiction but also gain a clearer perception of the stakes involved in his fiction, nothing less than how best to live life.

CHAPTER ONE

Bad Memories: *A Pale View of Hills* (1982)

Kazuo Ishiguro's first novel, *A Pale View of Hills* (1982), was well received: it was greeted with almost universally appreciative reviews and won the Winifred Holtby Memorial Prize of the Royal Society of Literature. Set in England during the early 1980s, *A Pale View of Hills* recounts the meeting of a mother and daughter. The mother, Etsuko, is a Japanese woman who at the time of the novel's present lives in England. Her daughter, Niki, is the product of Etsuko's second marriage to a now-deceased Englishman named Sheringham. Niki's visit repeatedly leads Etsuko to think back to the time shortly after the bombing of Nagasaki when she was living with her first husband, a Japanese man named Jiro, and pregnant with her first daughter, Keiko, who committed suicide sometime after moving to England. Although this brief summary may suggest a tangled narrative, the novelist and children's author Penelope Lively (born 1933) found the novel's style intriguing and thought the novel powerful despite its simplicity. At the same time, she found it 'unsettling and a little baffling'. She sums up its effect as 'one of extraordinary tension, of implied griefs and evils'.[1] Similarly, Edith Milton finds Ishiguro's novel dark and mysterious.[2] Michael Wood calls it 'a small masterpiece'.[3]

A NEW WRITER WITH A JAPANESE NAME AND FACE

The critical reception of Ishiguro's first novel introduced several issues to which readers continually return when responding to his novels. In keeping with Ishiguro's theory that he satisfied the desire for 'other Rushdies',[4] early reviewers were eager to concentrate discussions of his fiction on his Japanese roots. As well, the detail with which Ishiguro has described Japan in his first two novels has led critics to another prevalent concern with Ishiguro's work: its value as social and historical commentary. Reviewers and critics have also directed considerable attention to the reticence of Ishiguro's protagonists. Finally, the issue of memory, a topic seemingly present in all of Ishiguro's fiction, is another key issue in discussions of this novel.

Throughout the early reviews writers repeatedly return to Japanese stereotypes to find language to discuss Ishiguro's work. In one of the first reviews of *Pale View of Hills*, the poet Anthony Thwaite (born 1930) begins by pointing out how he wants to use a Japanese term *yugem*, 'a suggestive indefiniteness full of mystery and depth', to describe Ishiguro's writing, but admits that given Ishiguro's biography, doing so does not seem appropriate, an inappropriateness that he is apparently ready to overlook. For Thwaite the novel does seem a Japanese novel although this assessment appears based on Ishiguro's setting the flashbacks in Japan and Ishiguro's Japanese name and face.[5] The novelist and short-story writer Francis King (born 1923) begins by pointing out that Ishiguro has grown up speaking English; however, he then describes Ishiguro's work as typical of Japanese literature because of 'its compression, its reticence and in its exclusion of all details not absolutely essential to its theme. It might, one feels, be some apprentice work by Kawabata or Sushaki Endo [1923–96], its dialogue rendered slightly stilted by translation'.[6] In his 'Two Worlds Japan Has Lost Since the Meiji' (1982), Jonathan Spence goes so far as to pair a review of Ishiguro's novel with a book that relies heavily on a Japanese woman novelist Higuchi Ichiyo (1872–96), writing at the end of the nineteenth century. The 'two worlds' that the title refers to are the periods of the 1880–90s, and then the time of Ishiguro's novel, before and after World War II. In the second half of the review, when Spence turns to Ishiguro, he finds that 'The cadences of Ishiguro in the 1980s recall Ichiyo's of a century before', and then offers a long well-chosen quotation of Etsuko describing the dusk in pre-war Nagasaki (*PVH* 120).[7] But the penultimate paragraph of the review is a troubling one. Spence proposes that Ichiyo would have appreciated Ishiguro's novel: 'She would have noted how a whole society was being put together under her eyes from sudden comments and apparently random phrases'.[8] Spence adds that she would have understood the suffering the novel portrays, especially the suffering of young Mariko, a young girl often abandoned and generally neglected by her mother, the only person the young girl seems to have in her life. This speculated understanding, however, is based almost entirely on the perceived 'Japaneseness' of the somewhat unlikely pairing of the twentieth-century British male Ishiguro and the nineteenth-century Japanese female Ichiyo. Ishiguro's fiction, for many, marked his Japaneseness, so much so that after the first two books, he was the person that the English media would call on when they needed a comment on Japanese topics.[9]

On a similar note, in *Kazuo Ishiguro* (2000), Barry Lewis notes the frequency with which reviewers refer to Japanese art in their efforts to describe Ishiguro's style.[10] Lewis outlines the various stereotypes Westerners associate with Japan and suggests that Ishiguro seems caught between being Japanese and British. Ishiguro, Lewis suggests, does not exaggerate any differences between the two cultures, but at the same time, he does want to retain the distinction between them. Lewis offers Ishiguro's introduction to two novels by Yasunari Kawabata as proof of the difficult balance Ishiguro maintains.[11] There, Ishiguro argues that although Kawabata's context might be different, his characters are similar to people everywhere and concerned with issues that concern people everywhere. Lewis reads Ishiguro as proposing that a different sort of reading is required, which leads Lewis to a constructive distinction that distances himself from critics who have seized on Ishiguro's Japaneseness as a shortcut to critical discussion: 'the interesting question about Ishiguro's writing is not "Is it Japanese?" but "How Japanese is it?"'[12] One Japanese influence to which Ishiguro admits is Japanese films: 'I'm probably more influenced by Japanese movies. I see a lot of Japanese films. The visual images of Japan have a great poignancy for me, particularly in domestic films like those of Ozu and Naruse, set in the postwar era, the Japan I actually remember'.[13]

ISHIGURO'S JAPAN THROUGH THE LENS OF OZU AND KUROSAWA

Mason has followed up on Ishiguro's claim of filmic influence in his essay, 'Inspiring Images: The Influence of the Japanese Cinema on the Writings of Kazuo Ishiguro' (1989). It is one of the most important and informative essays that has been written on Ishiguro's first two novels. While most references to Japanese elements in Ishiguro's work rely on vague resemblances and superficial understandings of Japanese authors, Mason provides a detailed comparison that helps illuminate Ishiguro's unique and resonant style. Specifically, Mason studies the narrative techniques Japanese cinema has offered Ishiguro, a study which leads Mason to consider the influence of Yasujiro Ozu and Akira Kurosawa (1910–98), directors who developed the domestic genre, the *shomin-geki*, and thereby provided an alternative to the previous tradition in Japanese film, replete with militarism and ritual suicide. *A Pale View of Hills* does share some remarkable parallels with various Japanese films from this era and genre. Mason sees Etsuko 'embattled in her search for independence and dignity', a familiar heroine found in films such as Mikio Naruse's *When a Woman Ascends the Stairs* (1960). Alongside Ishiguro's pairing of Sachiko (Etsuko's double) and a guilt-ridden Etsuko, Mason posits a parallel use of a double and a central figure consumed with guilt in *The Heart* (1955), directed by Kon Ichikawa (1915–2008). The novel's ghostly atmosphere filled with mothers, daughters, and old ladies suggests the influence of *Ugetsu* (1953), directed by Kenji Mizoguchi (1898–56). So similar are the atmospheres that Mason suggests the film critic Basil Wright's comment on *Ugetsu* might be written by a reader of *A Pale View of Hills:* that the reader of the novel might begin 'to realise that it involves things which are not what they seem', and that 'there may be mirror realities in reflection or opposition'.[14]

Ozu and Ishiguro also make similar use of visual details to manipulate plot. Citing various film critics, Mason demonstrates that Ozu felt that too much action prevented a film from allowing full exposition of its characters, and observes that 'Ozu often attends to seemingly irrelevant physical and spatial details such as passageways, hat racks, or teakettles. He lingers on these spaces or objects to subvert the linear trajectory of the narrative and to challenge its dominance as an all-consuming focus of viewer interest'.[15] Ishiguro's fiction works in a similar way:

■ Ishiguro employs analogous devices to retard and disperse the impetus of his narratives in order to reveal subtle and surprising aspects of character. In *A Pale View of Hills*, the narrative contains gaps, apparent contradictions, and later emendations. Rather than proceeding in a horizontal line, events appear to be vertically stacked.[16] □

Mason's work not only helps illuminate Ishiguro's conception of the Japan he depicts in his first two novels, a place to which he had not returned since leaving at age five; his detailed analysis also helps readers better understand how Ishiguro's fiction works.

Mason's essay develops another thread from his interview with Ishiguro by recalling that the *shomin-geki*, or domestic drama, is Ishiguro's primary Japanese influence. The characteristics of the domestic genre are certainly present in these first two novels in the form of 'the classic *shomin-geki* domestic configuration of conflict between parents and children in an extended family setting with certain comic overtones'. Specifically, Mason notes the predecessor to the 'boisterous, sometimes disrespectful'[17] Mariko in Ozu's *Good Morning* (1959); the tender relationship between Ogata and Etsuko recalls the situation in Ozu's *Tokyo Story* (1953); and the visit of Jiro's drunken colleagues and the scenes set in the noodle shop are similar to scenes in his *Early Spring* (1956).[18] Such scenes generate the mood and images of the *shomin-geki*, an ambience aptly described by the Japanese phrase, *mono no aware* ('the sadness of things'). It is a mood present in many Japanese films, especially Ozu's, and Mason finds evidence of it in Ishiguro's work and his take on the past:

■ More than just a setting, the cultural upheaval and reorientation of postwar Japan furnishes Ishiguro a rich metaphor for a world in transition. From a rare Western perspective, familiar with but removed from traditional Japanese experience, he is able to explore the psychological and ethical dilemmas common to both cultures.[19] □

This view of domestic life agrees with Ishiguro's perception of Japanese life as normal rather than extraordinary, or notably, that the quiet endurance of the tribulations of life is not particular to Japanese only.

Both *A Pale View of Hills* and Ishiguro's next novel, *An Artist of the Floating World*, combine aspects of Eastern and Western world views: 'Fortified by the textural realism of the *shomin-geki*, and sharpened with Western irony, Ishiguro explores themes that possess a Japanese resonance but with a Western incisiveness'. Remembering that Ishiguro cites Dostoevsky and Chekhov as two of his most important influences, Mason points out Dostoevsky's influence in Ishiguro's probing of 'deep psychological dissonances, the struggles between the urges to hide and to rebel, to temporize and to confess'. Chekhov's influence reveals itself in Ishiguro's portrayal of 'strong currents of emotion moving beneath a seemingly quiet surface, and an oblique forward movement of plot, to reveal and confront moral issues', and further in Ishiguro's use of irony 'that is both judgmental and humorous'.[20] These subtleties, however, are often overlooked given the ease with which Ishiguro's work can be appropriated by critics most concerned with his portrayal of society and history.

ISHIGURO'S NOVELS AS SOCIOLOGICAL
AND HISTORICAL PRIMERS

Asked by Dylan Krider about the amount of research that he had to do for the first two books, Ishiguro explains that he frequently went to Japanese films, but adds that he had to rely on memory.[21] The exchange is notable for what Ishiguro's answer omits: research. Ishiguro's reliance on Japanese films and memory, rather than research, defies the realist precision that some of his reviewers find in the novel's evocation of social and historical contexts. James Campbell, in a positive review, focuses immediately on the 'conflict between the traditional and modern worlds' as one of Ishiguro's themes.[22] Similarly, King, like Lively, emphasises the gap between generations as one of the themes of the novel: not only are there difficulties between mothers and daughters, but the Ogata-San and Jiro plot also reveals a secondary conflict between the generations.[23]

Reviewers have also noted the importance of the historical moment. Spence reads the novel as a comment on the Japan of the time, explaining that the 'Pale Hills' are not just the slopes that rise above Nagasaki: 'they are also evocations of a fading life, of a Japanese world where one's own dead children and their sufferings blur with the impact of other people's dislocated lives'.[24] Fumio Yoshioka, too, sees the novel as tracing the difficulties of the historical period:

■ Ogata-San's visit, which turns out to be much longer than he originally contemplated, sets up another scene in which the fragility of spurious dutifulness and decorum is mercilessly exposed to view. What should be a heartwarming reunion for a war-torn family ends up in dissolution of human bonds which are, once lost, unlikely to be regained.[25] □

Peter Wain makes one of the more radical claims about the social and historical aspects of the novel when he asserts that the subplot, which focuses on the father and son, Ogata and Jiro, is 'the core of the novel', a claim that Wain makes no attempt to support except to point out a similar theme, presumably of an older man looking back on the past, in Ishiguro's next two novels.[26] Cynthia Wong asserts that the novel is about 'exploring the peculiar atmosphere of a society reconstructing itself', a point she connects with the conception of a 'common odyssey', propounded by the French thinker Michel Foucault (1926–84).[27] The Japanese in the novel, she argues, seek solace in the institution of the family, a connection supposedly supported by the Ogata-San plot, but the novel reveals that the massive transitions of the post-war period destabilise the family, ultimately leading the young away from the family home. Consequently, the bombing of Nagasaki inflicts not only physical destruction but also the destruction of perdurable values serving as familial bonds, a destruction which in turn splits generations.[28] Edith Milton finds grounds for a similar reading. She sees Sachiko observing the abandonment of ancient customs in the rush to capitalist pragmatism and self-interest. Like many of those around her, Sachiko veers away from the nationalism that led Japan into the war, towards the American values of progress, a change that leads her to the 'pathetic illusion of the good life in the form of Frank the American, a cruder and lesser version of poor Madame Butterfly's caddish Pinkerton' (in the opera *Madame Butterfly* (1904) by the Italian composer Giacomo Puccini (1858–1924)). But Ishiguro is not just bemoaning the changes that have overtaken the old culture; the past was not perfect, as the Ogata plotline demonstrates. The future, Milton suggests, belongs to Niki, the hybrid who lacks attachments or loyalties but is honest and free from prejudice.[29] Such readings not only provide interesting contextual glosses to the understanding of the novel, they also enable a better understanding of Ishiguro's characters and their motivations.

ISHIGURO'S NOVELS AS SOCIOLOGICAL AND HISTORICAL PRIMERS – COUNTERPOINT

Other critics have focused more directly on the individuals in the novel. 'Private Desolations', a short review by the novelist Paul Bailey (born 1937), counters those asserting the centrality of the novel's context. He begins by explaining his title: Ishiguro is not intending to 'do' Nagasaki; instead he wants to lead the reader into the 'private desolations' people feel. Rather than history or politics, Bailey points out, 'Ishiguro very cleverly shows a person exploring the unhappiness of her own past by concentrating on other people'.[30] Thwaite's appreciative review, 'Ghosts in the Mirror', also concludes that this story is more about Etsuko than anyone else and in fact, Etsuko may be transposing her story onto Sachiko.[31] Even Nicholas de Jongh, despite his interest in the bombing of Nagasaki, points out that the novel does not make moral judgements. It just observes.[32]

Ishiguro has, in fact, claimed discomfort when his books are taken as realistic, heavily researched accounts. When asked about the obligation writers have to represent a place accurately, Ishiguro replies,

■ I'm not sure that I ever distorted anything major, but my first priority was not to portray history accurately. Japan and militarism, now these are big, important questions, and it always made me uneasy that my books were being used as a sort of historical text.[33] □

Responding to Mason's questioning of the difference between Etsuko's apparent timidity in Japan and the actual boldness of her actions, Ishiguro agrees that this is one of the gaps in the novel, but adds that he is 'not interested in the solid facts. The focus of the book is elsewhere, in the emotional upheaval'.[34]

Lewis provides a compelling reconciliation of the novel's historical grounding and Ishiguro's professed indifference to facts. He describes some of the historical references, such as the *kujibiki* stand where Mariko tries to win a basket for her kittens and sees the scene as 'evocative of a way of life fast disappearing under the post-war onslaught of American colonisation'. Lewis, however, questions these 'historical snapshots', and claims that the novel 'as a whole under-mines its own authenticity' by 'echoing Giacomo Puccini's *Madam Butterfly*',[35] an opera which presents the usual kind of exotic Japan complete with 'exotic costuming, its sets of fake cherry blossoms and sliding rice-paper screens'.[36] Shaffer also notes the connection to *Madame Butterfly* and adds to Lewis's comments by connecting Ishiguro's Frank to 'Eveline', one of the short stories in *Dubliners* (1914) by James Joyce (1882–1941), which portrays another Frank in a similar plot, adding the irony that neither Frank appears to be frank.[37] Shaffer's additional note on these connections makes Lewis's argument even more convincing: 'Its overt intertextual nods towards Puccini hint at the novel's constructedness, preventing the reader from interpreting its depicted world too literally'.[38] The socio-his-torical position is a weak one, one that the novel may gesture towards but in ways that reveal the position's speciousness when the details are taken too literally.

IN THE AFTERMATH OF THE BOMB

The falseness of the socio-historical position is particularly important to acknowledge before turning to one of the novel's largest peculiar-ities: the absence of reference to the atomic bombing of Nagasaki in 1945. Since much of the novel is set in Nagasaki a few years after the atomic bombing, many readers have assumed that it plays a large role in the novel. Campbell, for instance, reads the bombing of Nagasaki as the novel's background.[39] Milton too suggests that the nuclear bomb, although absent, lies at the nucleus of the novel visible only in the shattered lives it has altered. While its absence is part of this novel's strategy that leaves its most important information unsaid, 'those blanked-out days around the bomb's explosion become the paradigm of modern life'.[40] De Jongh too reads the bombing as a key part of the novel. Even though it is never discussed directly, the consequences of the war 'are like unseen or hidden protagonists'. At the same time, de Jongh quotes Ishiguro as saying that he did not want the novel to be about the horrors of nuclear destruction, but about the recovery.[41]

Lewis observes that the bombing of Nagasaki is mentioned just twice in the novel and that both of these mentions are unemphatic.[42] The absence is made even more peculiar, Lewis adds, by Ishiguro's foregrounding of the bombing in an earlier short story, 'A Strange and Sometimes Sadness' (1981).[43] Yoshioka speculates that this perhaps unexpected shift of emphasis alters readers' perception of the narrative:

■ Emphasis is continuously placed on the days after, not the days of, the atomic holocaust. Accordingly, the focus of depiction is fixed on people and not on the horrendous incidents; on the devastated minds and lives of the survivors and not on the colossal devastation of the war and the atomic bomb.[44] □

Michael Wood addresses this question by diagnosing the absent bomb as a consequence of Etsuko's repression:[45] her denial, Lewis adds, of what happened in Nagasaki and what happened to Keiko. Wood's explanation, however, does not go far enough in Lewis's opinion. Consequently, Lewis sets out to investigate the wider context of the bomb, and after a perhaps too sweeping discussion determines that Ishiguro, having been born years after the bombing and having grown up far from Nagasaki 'cannot be a spokesman for the unspeakable'. Instead, Ishiguro has crafted 'a silence more eloquent than words'.[46]

Shaffer confronts other critics, such as Wong and Milton, who put too much weight on the bombing. He cites Wong's argument that 'What begins for Etsuko as a personal post-mortem, inquiring into her daughter's death, evolves into a tale about Nagasaki after the bombing'[47] and suggests that Milton overreaches when she writes, 'Sachiko and Etsuko become minor figures in a greater pattern of betrayal, infanticide and survival played out against the background of Nagasaki, itself the absolute emblem of our genius for destruction'.[48] Shaffer concludes: 'the focus of Ishiguro's first novel is more on individual psychology – specifically, on the way in which people use other people's stories to conceal yet, paradoxically, to reveal their own – than it is on national history and the role individuals play in public affairs'.[49] Shaffer's comments lead to some of the most interesting analysis of the novel, work on its narration and psychology.

RETICENCE

One aspect of the novel's narration that has drawn the attention of critics is its reticence. Readers have remarked on the novel's 'control and economy',[50] called it 'brief, elliptical, and spare', and observed that it works 'largely by inference'.[51] Wain, having surveyed the variety of comments and interpretations the novel's reticence has inspired, concludes that the novel leaves 'more questions unanswered than answered'.[52] For example, one of the key questions that readers want answered is why Etsuko left Japan. At one point Etsuko addresses this question but will only say that she left a long time ago and does not want to spend any more time thinking about it. She believes that her motives for leaving were just, so there is no point in revisiting that move (*PVH* 91). Norman Page thinks that she does provide her motives in a 'persistent act of self-explanation and self-justification'.[53] It is a compelling argument, but he fails to provide the reasoning for it. It is perhaps one of the novel's symbolic lacunae that she does not *literally* enunciate her motives. Wong acknowledges the reticence but places it alongside the role of memory in the novel:

■ Ishiguro's deceptively simple manner of presenting Etsuko's retrospective narrative is complicated by the determination to let silence itself speak. In turning toward the dreaded past, Etsuko conveys a tale that is the disclosure not of a tangible secret, but of a private shame associated with the memories now on the verge of becoming public.[54] □

The novel's reticence has bothered some critics, such as James Campbell and Paul Bailey. Campbell's review is appreciative although he declares the one fault that 'Some characters are rather faceless, and the dialogue is vapid in places', and he too sees a lack of 'incidental detail'.[55] While Bailey obviously enjoyed the book, he did provide the famous line, 'at certain points I could have done with something as crude as a fact'. Bailey, who calls the novel 'bravely reticent' and 'courageous in its self-effacement' also points out that Keiko's withdrawal from the family is the most traumatic event in the novel, and while he finds it clever that Ishiguro has left it out, he wants to read more about Etsuko's deceased English husband, Sheringham, 'who would appear to have been a man of some intelligence'.[56] Notably, there is no support provided for this claim; in fact, if, as some have proposed, Etsuko and Keiko are represented by Sachiko and Mariko, it could be argued, as Petry does, that Sheringham is represented by the American Frank,[57] an equation that would cast doubts on Bailey's speculations. It appears that Bailey simply wants a different novel.

Lewis defends Ishiguro against the criticisms of Campbell and Bailey suggesting that the absences may be Ishiguro's deliberate narrative choices rather than lapses, and that the two critics may have misunderstood the novel's silences:

■ Within the Japanese culture in which the book is set, indirect communication is an important feature of everyday life. The dialogue, far from being vapid, portrays the clipped spoken content of a typical discourse. Its meaning is not simply in the words that are uttered, but in the pauses and prevarications punctuating the exchange. □

Additionally, Lewis notes, in passing, the similarity of Ishiguro's use of conveying meaning through the pauses with the dramatic technique of Harold Pinter (1930–2008), a similarity of increased interest given that Pinter wrote the first screenplay of *The Remains of the Day* (even if that attempt was ultimately discarded).[58] On a similar note, Lively is particularly impressed by Ishiguro's rendering of the conversations between Etsuko and Sachiko, an observation of style that forces readers to look at the novel's underlying structure.[59]

ETSUKO AND/OR SACHIKO

One of the crucial issues confronting the novel's readers, an issue that critics have queried since the earliest reviews, is the question of the relationship between Etsuko and Sachiko. King, having noted that Etsuko and Sachiko have acted in similar ways by forming relationships with foreign husbands, reads the parallel literally: both have harmed their daughters by pursuing Western lovers.[60] Nicholas de Jongh also sees the parallels between the two as markers of a past that cannot be forgotten.[61] Yoshioka's comments on the novel's dual structure help to explain the difficulty of sorting out the relationship between the two characters. He observes how the two are not parallel: they remain distinct, but as the novel progresses their lives start to overlap each other until by the novel's end they become as 'indistinguishable' as 'mirror images'. It is an accurate description of the subtle process to which readers are subjected. Yoshioka is on less solid critical ground, however, when he proposes that the blurring of the boundaries that usually separate individuals lessens the severity of their personal miseries, a difficult argument for which he can provide no support.[62]

Closely parsing the novel's text, Shaffer finds that there are 'hints' to support the idea that Etsuko uses the parallel narrative to comment on her own treatment of Keiko. Building on Yoshioka's reading of Etsuko and Sachiko as dissolving into each other, Shaffer identifies the important slippages that mark the blurring and notes that eventually readers discover 'that Sachiko and Mariko function less as "real" individuals than as individuals onto whom Etsuko can project her own guilt for neglecting and abusing Keiko'.[63] Given Etsuko's unreliability, readers are compelled to ask if Sachiko and Mariko are real people or manifestations of Etsuko's guilt. Shaffer offers, 'it is probably the case that Sachiko, like Mariko's mysterious woman visitor, is neither exactly as she appears to be nor "entirely imaginary", (43)' but somewhere in between;[64] however, his evidence is, at times, highly suppositious. For example, in attempting to argue that Etsuko feared becoming a parent, Shaffer asserts, 'Etsuko may only be pretending "to be delighted" that a child is on the way (49); instead, like Frank, she may actually be "scared of" the child (86).'[65] In such cases Shaffer does not offer evidence but merely possibilities, and, somewhat carelessly, does not consider the evidence to the contrary.

Shaffer is more persuasive in arguing that Etsuko uses Sachiko's story to comment on her own history when he turns to the novel's climax, the slipping pronouns scene when Etsuko at first appears to be speaking to Mariko, but after a shift of the pronouns, seems instead to be speaking to Keiko (*PVH* 172–3). In the previous scene, Etsuko had set out to find Mariko, so when she meets a little girl in the next scene, readers are reminded of earlier scenes in which Etsuko went out and found Mariko. After promising the little girl that her move will be successful, Etsuko uses 'we' rather than 'you' which indicates that Etsuko and the child will be going on the trip together, and suggests that the child is not Sachiko's daughter Mariko, but her own daughter Keiko. As Shaffer points out, Ishiguro has proposed in an interview that this slip of the pronouns is the point where the narrative reveals itself:

> ■ [T]he meanings that Etsuko imputes to the life of Sachiko are obviously the meanings that are relevant to her (Etsuko's) own life. Whatever the facts were about what happened to Sachiko and her daughter, they are of interest to Etsuko now because she can use them to talk about herself. So you have this highly Etsuko-ed version of this other person's story; and at the most intense point, I wanted to suggest that Etsuko had dropped this cover. It just slips out: she's now talking about herself. She's no longer bothering to put it in the third person.[66] □

The scene presents Etsuko promising her daughter that they will return to Japan if life in England does not work out. Keiko's suicide, the event that lies outside the narrative but serves as its impetus, suggests that it is a promise that Etsuko did not keep. Shaffer follows up on the stakes of this transformation by drawing a direct equation between Etsuko and Sachiko, arguing that 'it is now Etsuko who is the mother guilty of negligent child rearing',[67] a statement that the novel does not support if the negligence refers to Sachiko's repeated abandoning and poor treatment of her daughter, but one that might apply if, as Shaffer goes on to suggest, Etsuko took Keiko to England even though she knew her daughter would be unhappy there.

Although Shaffer does not cite it, this reading is supported by Mason's analysis of the Inasa Hills episode, a scene Etsuko recounts near the middle of the novel. Etsuko, pregnant with her first child, Keiko, and looking for some respite from the dreariness of Nagasaki, goes on a short outing with Sachiko and Sachiko's daughter Mariko (*PVH* 103–24). Near the very end of the novel, Etsuko describes a photo of Nagasaki's harbour with the Inasa Hills in the background that is in a calendar that she has just given Niki and mentions a trip she once took there. Asked to explain the trip's importance to her, Etsuko describes how happy Keiko was that day (*PVH* 182). Readers, of course, had until that point been under the impression that Keiko was still an unborn child being carried by Etsuko on the day of that trip. Mason sums up the effect: 'The disoriented reader is left to reorder the chronology of events, to reevaluate the actions, and to reassess the very identities of the protagonists'.[68] Instead of telling the story we expect, Ishiguro explains, Etsuko 'tells another story altogether, going back years and talking about somebody she once knew. So the whole narrative strategy of the book was about how someone ends up talking about things they cannot face directly through other people's stories'.[69] Confronted by troubling aspects of her past, Etsuko can only tell her story by telling the story of another.

Given Etsuko's manipulations of her story, Shaffer embarks on a psychoanalytic discussion of defence mechanisms of the ego: specifically, projection and rationalisation.[70] Projection describes the unconscious rejection of what is emotionally unacceptable to the self and its attribution, or projection, onto another. Rationalisation, similar to its everyday meaning, describes the creation of elaborate explanations for one's behaviour which allow one to escape anxiety about one's actions and continue with the behaviour. Etsuko, Shaffer argues, 'is clearly guilty of scapegoating – of using her "Sachiko narrative" to deflect her personal guilt onto another. It is not she who has "sacrificed" a daughter, who is guilty, figuratively speaking, of infanticide, but someone else'.[71] In this scheme, Niki is the 'rationalizing voice, explaining away the fact that Etsuko deserted her first daughter'.[72] But Shaffer does not provide support for the idea that Etsuko deserted Keiko. Etsuko, he notes, feels guilty for taking Keiko from Japan, but taking her from Japan does not equal the crime of deserting her. Etsuko's guilt does, however, require more analysis.

GUILTS AND GHOSTS

One approach to the novel, put forward not only by Shaffer but also earlier by Gabriele Annan in her insightful review, 'On The High Wire', is to read it as a ghost story, a reading that helps illuminate Etsuko's guilt. Annan, for example, reads Niki's departure as based in part on 'Keiko's unseen ghost' keeping her awake. Although she is careful to point out that Etsuko would not have behaved as cruelly as Sachiko behaves towards Mariko, Annan proposes that Etsuko feels guilty for having taken Keiko to England. Ishiguro, Annan argues, has fitted Etsuko with a mask of self-deception that does not slip, and is able to build tension by gradually revealing, 'clue by clue', the misjudgements she has made. Moreover, Annan adds, this plotline about private guilt is complemented by a subplot on public guilt – the Ogata story, where the artist with imperialist values is discredited.[73]

Shaffer expands on Annan's reading. The 'never-articulated fear that Keiko's ghost haunts' Etsuko's English house is proof for Shaffer that Etsuko and Niki both feel guilty: 'The reason for Etsuko's buried guilt is obvious', and Niki's guilt 'may be attributed both to "survivor's guilt"' and to the fact that she purposefully absented herself from her sister's funeral'.[74] Unfortunately, the support for his claim that the novel is a ghost story is not fully developed: he relies heavily for proof on the discomfort the women feel in the proximity of Keiko's room and a small sound each hears coming from the room. Since he has just argued that Etsuko's observations are unreliable, this reliance on her observations seems injudicious. Notably, he does not attempt to incorporate Mason's observation on the similarities of the novel with Mizoguchi's ghost story *Ugetsu*.[75]

Shaffer's analysis is stronger, however, when he turns to the dreams that Etsuko has of the little girl in the park (*PVH* 47). Etsuko later realises that the dream is related not to the little girl, but to her remembering Sachiko. Shaffer, in turn, postulates that despite Etsuko's denials, the dream is related to Keiko, and the little girl is not on the swing but hanging from a noose.[76] Shaffer puts together the ghost story idea and the dream to lead to Ishiguro's comment that the novel 'is largely based around her guilt. She feels a great guilt, that out of her own emotional longings for a different sort of life, she sacrificed her own daughter's happiness'.[77]

Lewis, having determined that the novel's topic is not what Japan refers to in the text, but 'how the text refers to Japan', reads the novel as based on displacement, as do Rocio G. Davis and Gary Corseri, and in doing so, he adds another useful interpretive dimension. Surprisingly, given his fondness for psychoanalytic readings, Lewis does not use the term displacement to refer to a defence mechanism, like projection and rationalisation, that describes the unconscious process by which an individual refocuses the shameful feelings for one entity to a more acceptable one (the classic example being the situation in which the worker after being bullied by his boss, someone to whom he cannot express his anger, returns home and becomes angry with his family, a safer target for his anger). Rather, Lewis appears to use the term more literally, as in *things out of place*. Consequently, he finds 'geographical displacement' in people being out of place, 'cognitive displacement' brought on by Etsuko's fractured memories, 'psychological displacement' in the relationship between Etsuko and Sachiko, and 'familial displacement' due to Keiko's suicide.[78] Displacement, Lewis argues, helps to contextualise the ghost story readings. Although there is a strong tradition of ghost stories and suicide in Japanese literature, Ishiguro's work does not use that tradition; instead, Ishiguro's work is structured more like European literature, such as *The Turn of the*

Screw (1898) by the English-based American novelist Henry James (1843–1916). To prove this claim Lewis examines *A Pale View of Hills* using Gustav Freytag's components of dramatic plot: 'initial situation, conflict, complications, climax, and resolution'.[79] This analysis leads him to the points in the novel where the identities of Etsuko and Keiko blur with those of Sachiko and Mariko, and in these slips, he finds 'displacement between the outer and inner narratives'. Most importantly, Lewis argues that this displacement destabilises the text beyond the point of recuperation leaving readers with only shifting interpretive possibilities:

■ Either: (a) Etsuko is confusing different sets of memories; or (b) Etsuko is merging memory and fantasy; or (c) Etsuko is projecting her guilt about forcing Keiko to leave Japan on to her memories of Sachiko in a similar situation; or (d) Etsuko is projecting her guilt about the above on to a *fantasy* of a woman called Sachiko and her child.[80] □

This list serves as a useful map through other readings of the novel.

IMAGERY

Left with these interpretative difficulties, several critics have looked to Ishiguro's imagery for exegetic assistance. Milton, for example, asserts that 'themes and images echo and repeat in a contrapuntal arrangement of increasing power'. Milton also points out the images to which critics keep returning: the kittens drowned by Sachiko, the long-dead woman who reappears throughout the novel, the small bit of rope twisted around Etsuko's sandal, and the girl 'dangling from a swing'.[81] Lively sees Mariko as 'a premonitory symbol' for Keiko and perceives that the imagery around Mariko hints at 'some macabre fate'.[82] Yoshioka focuses on the images that cluster around the 'two dominant trains of death-imagery which thread through the story: one envisages a girl hanging in the air, while the other is related with a river'. The significance of the recurring rope imagery, he asserts, becomes greater given the context of Mariko's childhood:

■ The whole city of Nagasaki is alerted by a series of child murders, the last of which has just recently left a little girl hanging dead from a tree. The frightening sight is linked, in the chronological confusion of Etsuko's reveries, with her indelible vision of Keiko suspended in the air for days on end in a desolate room.[83] □

While Milton, Lively, and Yoshioka provide a start to understanding the image of the rope, Lewis provides a more complete study.

For Lewis the rope is a motif that 'binds together' different parts of the novel.[84] Most obviously, the suicide of Keiko features the rope she uses to hang herself. Less obviously, Etsuko's guilt manifests itself in the dream of the little girl on the swing, swinging on a rope (*PVH* 95–6). Lewis places the neglect of the oft-abandoned Mariko in the same image bundle. On one occasion, when Etsuko finds her sitting in the grass, Mariko is frightened by a piece of rope tangled around Etsuko's ankle (*PVH* 83–4). Perhaps most importantly, this incident is repeated during the change-of-pronoun scene, prescient timing because it is this scene that suggests that Etsuko was not talking to Mariko but rather to Keiko (*PVH* 172–3). A little girl, who the reader has been led to believe is Mariko but now seems instead to be Keiko, is again frightened by a piece of rope around Etsuko's ankle (*PVH* 173). Most importantly, the child's fear of the rope that Etsuko is holding becomes apparent only after Etsuko promises the little girl that if the move abroad is unsuccessful, they can return to Japan. The child's connecting of the rope and the promise, which seems to have been broken, strongly suggests that the present-time Etsuko may retain a considerable amount of guilt for Keiko's suicide; thus, she cannot speak of how she had forced Keiko to come to England but only of how Sachiko may or may not have forced Mariko to go to America. Lewis, therefore, sees the rope in 'Etsuko's guilt, the dream of the little girl on the swing, the neglect of Mariko and the suicide of Keiko'.[85]

As is apparent from the earlier discussions of defence mechanisms, the novel's indeterminacy has served as a powerful lure for Freudian readings. Shaffer, who provides one of the most extensive readings of the novel's imagery, perceives the novel as having roots in both the ancient Greek myth of Styx and modern psychology, and in his tracing of these roots he points out some of the more important image clusters. First, he attempts to forge a connection between Ishiguro's river and the ancient Greek myth of Styx. It is an effort which not only usefully parses the novel's descriptions of the river and its environs but also incorporates the image of the long-dead woman, equating her to the river goddess Styx. Shaffer is certainly correct in adumbrating the dark mood that Ishiguro has created around his river, but given the precision of Ishiguro's prose, readers might question how much is added to the analysis by bringing in the comparison to the myth of Styx. It seems an unnecessary critical step.

Shaffer then ties this equating of the river to death to modern psychoanalytic theory. He reads a character who fears the river as fearing death, and a character attracted to the river, such as Etsuko, as attracted to death.[86] Freudian theory, Shaffer asserts, helps explain this attraction: 'Freud postulates the existence of a death-wish, a sado-masochistic urge to self-destruction, that is triggered when an individual's aggression cannot find satisfactory outlet in the external world.' For Shaffer, Freud's speculation helps to explain why Mariko and Keiko are aggressive 'towards themselves and their mothers'.[87] Going further, Shaffer then introduces the concept of masochism to explain the troubled relationship of Sachiko and Mariko. Mariko, Shaffer avers, not only takes pleasure in pain, but also acts based on her desire for punishment from Sachiko. Since suicide, in Shaffer's psychoanalytic reading, is the ultimate masochistic act, he surmises that what he takes to be Mariko's symbolic suicide, is really Mariko's desire to kill her neglectful mother. Shaffer's reading also proposes that Sachiko has '"murderous" intentions toward Mariko': the proof of which is in Sachiko's drowning of Mariko's cats.[88] Shaffer then carefully catalogues the connections in the novel between cats and children, especially between cats and Mariko, before concluding, 'Sachiko treats Mariko less like her "baby" than like a "filthy little" animal or a "dirty little" creature worthy only of abandonment or worse.' Consequently, Sachiko's drowning of the kittens is, for Shaffer, a 'figurative murder of her daughter'[89] (although he later calls it a 'symbolic murder' which is closer to what he seems to mean).

While Shaffer's investigation of an important set of images in the novel is useful, his choice of psychoanalytic criticism is unfortunate. It is a difficult path made more difficult by Shaffer's previous argument that Etsuko has constructed Sachiko and Mariko so that she can project her guilt onto them.[90] In fact, once we are reminded of this earlier argument, the psychoanalytic interpretation of Sachiko and Mariko appears rather pointless: if Mariko and Sachiko are constructions of another character's imagination, what is the point of trying to psychoanalyse them as though they were independent individuals? Such an analysis would seem only to have value in an assessment of Etsuko, although the value of such an assessment is debatable.

Shaffer's next interpretive jump is a large one. Having constructed Sachiko's symbolic murder of Mariko, Shaffer casts about for a way to transfer this dynamic to Etsuko and Keiko. The answer is, apparently, the tomatoes that Etsuko was attempting to grow. Etsuko's neglect of the tomatoes is, for Shaffer, an indication of how she has treated Keiko. Not content to draw the line at neglect, Shaffer next attempts to demonstrate that Etsuko is 'figuratively speaking, the murderer of Keiko'. Notably, nothing in this paragraph relies on Freud. Here we are back to basic images that others have pointed out: the variations on a girl swinging by a rope and the rope around Etsuko's ankle.[91] It should be noted, however, that while Shaffer's steps are often too big and his conclusions too audacious given the reserve with which Ishiguro writes, his close reading of the novel's language provides several useful glimpses into aspects of Ishiguro's imagery.

Mark Wormald annotates another important image in the novel by looking back to the scene of the daytrip to Inasa. He points out two brief passages, watching the cable cars in the distance and Etsuko's buying of binoculars for Mariko (*PVH* 104), and suggests that both offer 'curious failures of perspective'.[92] These failures, Wormald notes, anticipate the larger confusion to come: a woman notices that Etsuko is pregnant (with Keiko) (*PVH* 118), but in the novel's frame, Etsuko has told Niki that Keiko 'was happy that day' (*PVH* 182). Wormald concludes,

■ [W]e glimpse through the quietly distorting medium of Etsuko's prose childhood and adult passions looming and losing themselves in each other with primitive passion. Ishiguro is, of course, using those binoculars too, to contrive a brilliant, eerie moment, in a novel that proved merely the first layer in a palimpsest composed of similarly sliding perceptions and perspectives.[93] □

Seeing across vast distances, we are warned, is fraught with difficulty. Undoubtedly, it is a particularly keen difficulty when surveying temporal distances that can only be traversed through memories.

RECONCILING THE INDIVIDUAL AND THE COLLECTIVE

Cynthia Wong considers what Etsuko's narrative, regardless of its factual shortcomings, offers readers. She contends that first-person narration allows Etsuko to tell her story in order to forget the difficulties of her past. She sees Ishiguro's narrators, here and in other novels, as remembering 'in order to forget; they reconstruct the past in an effort to obliterate it'.[94] It is an argument that demonstrates the insufficiency of readings that simply label Etsuko unreliable:

■ The reader cannot truly validate the incompatible details of Etsuko's past and future without undermining conventional aspects of the narrative itself; only by casting doubt on Etsuko's veracity can the reader probe the veiled truth in a manner set forth by the narrative itself. □

Instead, Wong argues, we have to allow 'for complexities without eradicating narrative authority' and not overlook the obvious point that Etsuko was not the only person damaged by war and its aftermath. To place so much emphasis on her unreliability, therefore, risks overlooking the value of an account of a woman mentally harmed by war. Rather than categorise her narrative as 'one woman's confused ranting', an assignation that downplays the bombing and its consequences, her fractured memories remind readers of the ubiquity of the suffering. The important point, Wong suggests, may not be finding the boundary between Etsuko and Sachiko but observing that Etsuko remembered Sachiko despite the turmoil in which they lived.[95] Wong counters readings that Etsuko is simply mad and reaffirms the meaningfulness of the novel's context, a context that reasserts itself in the narrative by silencing any mention of the bombing. This silence, which confirms how unspeakable such events can be, is countered with only one discursive event: Etsuko's attempt to resolve the pain of the silence between mother and daughter by talking with Niki, a meeting which constitutes the entire present of the novel. Focusing on the harm experienced by a few individuals allows Ishiguro to achieve 'a fuller portrait than what factual records such as a body count, for instance, might reveal'.[96]

Wong, consequently, offers a reconciling of socio-historical readings with Ishiguro's interest in individuals, thereby illuminating the difficulty of Etsuko telling either aspect of the story. Etsuko can make this painfully awkward attempt to address the incomprehensibility of her daughter's suicide only by telling the story of her life in post-war Nagasaki. Her attempt to evaluate the recent history of her daughter produces a larger historical backdrop, and while this history includes unspeakable events, 'it is in the effort to find expression that one deflects the torment of life onto language'. The story of Nagasaki is told through Keiko's suicide, a death that suggests the parallel of the meaningless deaths attributable to the bombing, but 'Just as horrific in the tale are the shattered lives being salvaged amidst the wreckage'. And amidst that salvaging, Etsuko's shattered narrative creates the novel's effect: 'its seemingly straightforward narration compounded by the subtle suggestions of much deeper implications'. Ultimately, it is a story that cannot be told unswervingly; Etsuko's narrative method, replete with abrupt shifts to the past, allows readers to begin 'to understand that what remains below the surface of her speech and admission of pain struggles not for expression but silence'. Sachiko's story is not one that Etsuko wants to tell but, rather, has to tell 'to represent the grief enveloping her own life – and by extension, the lives of those remaining after Nagasaki – as a silent and ineffable tale'.[97] Telling one's story, Wong appears to argue, is not always a simple matter of reliable or unreliable narration, but involves finding the available means to communicate.

CONCLUSION

Near the end of his interview with Ishiguro, Mason asks about Ishiguro's preoccupations and Ishiguro replies that much of what has previously concerned him, 'parental responsibility, or even exile', no longer interests him.[98] He does return to those topics precisely in *The Unconsoled* and *When We Were Orphans*, but he concludes this interview with a comment that explicates much of *A Pale View of Hills* while also predicting each of his following novels:

> ■ [T]hings like memory, how one uses memory for one's own purposes, one's own ends, those things interest me more deeply. And so, for the time being, I'm going to stick with the first person, and develop the whole business about following somebody's thoughts around, as they try to trip themselves up or to hide from themselves.[99] □

It is the psychology of his characters that interests Ishiguro who while talking with de Jongh indicates the direction of the next two novels: 'I was concerned with how people evaluate their lives and ask themselves what they have done with it and whether it's been worthwhile and whether they fell into self-deception and delusion' [*sic*].[100] Ishiguro's concern here and in the novels to come is how his characters respond to the lives they have lived. It is a comment that looks back to *Pale View*, but equally, one that foreshadows the troubled artist of Ishiguro's second novel, Masuji Ono, who is forced to evaluate a life lived in a floating world.

CHAPTER TWO

A Troubled Artist's Art: *An Artist of the Floating World* (1987)

Ishiguro's second novel, *An Artist of the Floating World*, looks back to his first, *A Pale View of Hills*, and anticipates his third, *The Remains of the Day*. While his first novel used Japan in the aftermath of World War Two for its flashback sequences, in his second novel, this period serves as the narrator's present. The character Ogata, the father-in-law in the subplot in *A Pale View of Hills*, assumes centre stage in *An Artist of the Floating World*, although he is now the artist Masuji Ono (a character often compared to Stevens, the narrator of Ishiguro's third novel). Like the narrator Etsuko in his first novel and Stevens in his third, Ono, the narrator of *An Artist of the Floating World*, is compelled to look back on his life, a look back that extends well beyond the build-up to World War Two. Confronted by the marriage negotiations of one of his daughters, Ono embarks on an evaluation of his career to ensure that it does not prevent his daughter from marrying. Writing in the novel's present, Ono presents the reader with four entries – dated October, 1948; April, 1949; November, 1949; and June, 1950 – but as Ono relates this narrative he is consistently drawn back into the past, to the difficulty that he had with his father, to his apprenticeship in an art studio that features cheap copies of stereotypical images of Japan, to his time in the 'floating world', and to his success as a painter of nationalist propaganda. Always floating on the edges of his life story, however, is the growing certainty that Ono's narration might be unreliable: more precisely, that Ono is leaving some important information out of his account of his life.

The novel's reception provides an important frame to interpretations of the novel, revealing many of the issues that have since occupied the novel's readers. Again, the Japanese setting plays a key role in readings of the novel, sometimes pulling interpretations towards a socio-historic reading. Some have considered the novel's structure, especially its cinematic qualities, while others have investigated the language used in the novel and its odd ability to convey what might seem like a Japanese sensibility by means of a peculiar English. The narrator Ono, however, has received the most critical attention. Critics have investigated his manipulations, his faulty memory, and his denials, and questioned his motives for what he does and does not tell us.

THE INITIAL RESPONSE

Nominated for the Booker Prize and winning the Whitbread Award, Ishiguro's second novel was very well received. Nigel Hunt's favourable review of the novel articulates the deep connection between the language of the novel and its themes: 'Beautifully written, Ishiguro's book presents his themes clearly but without sacrificing any of the integrity of his story. The features of his system reach us in a way which enables us to feel something of the place between the pages.'[1] Though science-fiction scholar Patrick Parrinder (born 1944) focuses primarily on the social aspects of the novel – the Americanisation of Japanese culture and the generation gap – he too calls it 'beautiful and haunting'.[2] Writer Geoff Dyer (born 1958), while praising Ishiguro's precise yet leisurely prose, perhaps captures the novel's intricacies most fully by discerning how its 'uncertain reminiscences' coax 'nuances out of hinted ambiguities', a strategy akin to the one Ishiguro used in his first novel. Dyer also notes the compelling contrast between the artist in the novel and the artist of the novel: 'While Ono abandons the "fragile lantern beauty" of the floating world for a strident, political art of thick black outlines and bold calligraphy Ishiguro impresses by how much history he can contain within – and between – his frail lines.'[3] Kathryn Morton, equally appreciative, notes the strong impact the book has on readers, observing that it 'stretches the reader's awareness, teaching him to read more perceptively'.[4] It is a comment that extends to the whole of Ishiguro's *oeuvre* but it was first noticed with this novel.

ANOTHER JAPANESE SETTING

As with his first novel, Ishiguro's ethnicity commanded substantial attention in the reviews of this work. Michele Field, for example, spends the first third of her review sorting out the question of his nationality.[5] Anne Chisholm seems to think that Ishiguro is Japanese and reads the novel as 'instructive' in presenting the change happening in Japanese society.[6] Such responses always run counter to Ishiguro's own assessment of his knowledge of Japanese society. Asked by film critic Christopher Tookey (born 1950) why he writes about Japan, Ishiguro acknowledges 'that Japan triggers off images, memories and thoughts in me' but concedes a lack of concern about Japan's reality and abdicates the responsibility of explaining Japanese society to westerners. In fact, he sends an implicit warning to those compelled to take his novels as accurate portrayals: 'The Japan in my books probably more-or-less corresponds to post-war Japan, but I'm not bothered if it doesn't match exactly.'[7] His intention is not to produce a novel akin to the stereotypical Orientalist paintings done in Master Takeda's studio for tourists.

Despite Ishiguro's consistent avowals in interviews that he is not producing a socio-realist novel, critics have continued to construct readings based on stereotypical understandings of Japan. Rocio Davis, for example, attempts to compare Ishiguro's narrative technique to Japanese poetry, but offers no evidence in his analysis to support his generalities. Davis also briefly looks at the dialogue in the novels before comparing Ishiguro to Haiku poets.[8] Bruce King, too, reads Ishiguro's style as a Japanese trait: 'His instincts are for the nuanced, the understated, elegant but significant gesture, similar to the deft brushwork of Japanese paintings.'[9] Asked about the setting of *An Artist*, Ishiguro replies that the city is imaginary, that he did not want to do the research that putting it in a real city would require because there was no point to doing so: he wanted to work freely, not produce a documentary. Also, while Nagasaki was the city that he knew best, he did not want it to become 'another bomb book'.[10] Consequently, Ishiguro claims he did very little research, putting the novel's 'Japan together out of little scraps, out of memories, out of speculation, out of imagination'.[11]

Another problem Ishiguro faced was how to evoke a foreign language in English. Norman Page suggests that one part of Ishiguro's solution is his use of 'English dialogue that is quite unlike contemporary speech in the English-speaking world in its extreme and sometimes archaic formality'.[12] Ishiguro replies to this concern about portraying Japanese voices in English, explaining 'the prose has to conform to the characterization of the narrator', as in the case of Ono:

■ he's supposed to be narrating in Japanese; it's just that the reader is getting it in English. In a way the language has to be almost like a pseudotranslation, which means that I can't be too fluent and I can't use too many Western colloquialisms. It has to be almost like subtitles, to suggest that behind the English language there's a foreign language going on. I'm quite conscious of actually figuring these things out when I'm writing, using a certain kind of translationese. Sometimes my ear will say: 'That doesn't quite ring true, that kind of language. Fine if this were just English people, but not here.'[13] □

For King, Ishiguro's pseudotranslation works very well:

■ One of the delights of this novel is the notation of Japanese speech. Ishiguro shows how conventions of politeness and fear of showing disrespect lead to artificial behaviour, absurd conversation and failure of communication. The characters avoid shaming each other by denying that anything of a critical nature is intended; yet their subtle hints can be the cause of suicide.[14] □

This description needs to be balanced, however, with a story that novelist Clive Sinclair (born 1948) tells about novelist Malcolm Bradbury (1932–2000) meeting the Japanese translator of *A Pale View of Hills*. Bradbury suggests to the translator that it must have been a much easier book to translate because, in Bradbury's mind, the novel has intrinsic Japanese qualities. '"On the contrary", replied the translator, "it is very hard because it is such an English book."' Ishiguro responds to this story by pointing out that he writes like a Western novelist: that his books have 'have strong plots and three-dimensional characters'; whereas Japanese novels more closely resemble a diary with a hazy, ruminating narrator, little plot, and underdeveloped characters. His books, then, he claims, are Japanese in only a superficial sense: structurally they are Western. His translator, a real Japanese, knew immediately that he was not Japanese.[15]

The attempt to tie the novel's themes too closely to the setting misreads what Ishiguro is trying to achieve. When Gregory Mason points out the dramatic parallel between Ono's mentor's treatment of Ono, and Ono's treatment of his own pupil, Ishiguro replies that this similarity reveals a universal theme: 'In a way, I'm using Japan as a sort of metaphor. I'm trying to suggest that this isn't something peculiar to Japan, the need to follow leaders and the need to exercise power over subordinates, as a sort of motor by which society operates.' Ishiguro is not asking readers to view this relationship of power as something unique to Japan, 'but as a human phenomenon'.[16] For some critics this invitation has obviously been overlooked, but it is readily found in the novel's conclusion, which as Mason deduces runs contrary to stereotypes: Ono does not commit suicide. For Ishiguro, however, the lack of a suicide does not render the ending 'un-Japanese'. In fact, in his early short story 'A Family Supper', (1983) he uses a similar ploy to play with readers' expectations. Ishiguro treats people as people, and in his experience Japanese are 'like everybody else. They're like me, my parents. I don't see them as people who go around slashing their stomachs.'[17]

NARRATION

The Japanese setting of the novel has also been invoked to discuss the novel's narration. Bradbury, for example, begins a useful commentary by outlining the novel's concealments:

■ The novel [...] is a work of fine shadings, a novel of concealments in which the hidden secrecies of a cunningly constructed narrative merge with the practiced concealments of a mannered and civil culture. By choosing to present the story as Ono's own narration, Ishiguro sets the narrative in a world of high stylization and complex aesthetic awareness.[18] □

The structure of Ishiguro's narrative leads Bradbury to connect his description with generalised notions of Japanese culture:

■ The result is a world that is topographically designed and abstractified, so that every instant of the verbal composition feels like a certain kind of Japanese art. Ishiguro hence forces us to read exactly, aesthetically, as few modern British writers do. The story hides behind itself, forcing the reader persistently to unlock it, since the strange distances of politeness, respect, deference and reserve that dominate Japanese social and expressive practice allow little to be said but much to be implied.[19] □

King finds a similar connection between the novel's method of presenting information and Japanese culture:

■ Explanation is usually indirect, glanced at, in conformity to the conventions of Japanese politeness. At times Ishiguro parodies such conventions – even the narrator claims to be uncertain what has been said to him – but the basic method is the indirect polite circling around a subject, the significance of which only becomes clear later. Did the narrator gain his house, of which he is proud, through his prestige as an artist, or (as seems more probable) through his political power?[20] □

Notably, King pushes past the appearance of convention to see how Ishiguro plays with this indirectness. Doing so leads King to an important but almost always overlooked point: that Ono's success in the 'auction of prestige' for his home was almost certainly more a matter of his political than artistic influence. It is a small point but one with large ramifications because it helps us evaluate the question that confronts Ono: is he released from the fate of the composer Mr Naguchi or the President of Jiro Miyake's company because he was not really a famous artist at all or because he was a good artist caught up in a bad movement? (*AFW* 55) To understand this dilemma requires a closer look at what the narration provides and withholds.

Lewis presents the most useful reading of the novel's narration, and he does so by discussing the novel through a filmic lens. Lewis justifies this reading by pointing out the narrative's incompleteness, subject to Ono's editing of his tangled, fractured memories, and introduces several pages of film editing terms, explaining how they are exemplified in the novel.

He begins with one of the most common methods of joining two episodes: the flashback. Lewis offers the example of Noriko telling her father about a chance meeting she had with Jiro Miyake, a man with whom she had been involved a year previously. Hearing of this meeting, Ono recalls his own meeting with Jiro one year earlier while the couple were still involved with each other, and he begins to wonder if the opinions he expressed during the conversation that day – regarding the suicide of the President of Jiro's company – were connected to Jiro's ending his relationship with Noriko. These paired flashbacks put Ono's contemplation of his role 'within the context of Noriko's broodings about the Miyakes', bringing together 'the guilt and shame of father and daughter'.[21]

Next, Lewis turns to flashback's opposite, flashforward. To present events from a future part of a narrative told by a first-person narrator is not technically possible in a text bound by the terms of realism; Lewis, however, sees a power similar to that invoked by the flashforward when characters or themes are introduced in an early part of the narrative while their significance does not become apparent until later, a kind of foreshadowing. For example, Ono's account of a memory of Kuroda at the end of the war introduces Kuroda (*AFW* 77), but the significance of this character is not demonstrated until later.[22]

One of the less convincing translations of film editing techniques to narration is Lewis's adaptation of the dissolve. Dissolve, the fade-out from one scene into a fade-in to another scene, allows the filmmaker to join two scenes regardless of how separate they are in time and space. For example, Lewis offers the sequence in which Setsuko arrives at Ono's house leading Ono's thoughts to return to his father's house and his father's burning of Ono's paintings before returning to Setsuko and her request. With these transitions, Lewis claims, 'Ishiguro [...] elides Ono's determination – despite his father's antagonism – to forge a career as an artist.'[23]

Better is Lewis's outlining of Ishiguro's use of jump cuts. Lewis focuses on jump cuts as the eliminating of extraneous action from a continuous shot, as in the elimination of the middle part of a shot of someone crossing a room. Jump cuts are part of elliptical editing, shot transitions that omit parts of an event causing an ellipsis in the plot. Lewis offers the example of Ono's time at the Takeda studio, an apprenticeship of several years which can be condensed into five short scenes. Similarly, Ono's stay at Mori-san's villa can be divided into two short sequences. Lewis uses these examples to demonstrate the 'nimbleness' of Ishiguro's narrative.[24]

Lewis's discernment of a cross cut is particularly insightful. Although the cross cut is usually used to alternate between shots of two or more lines of action occurring in different places, usually simultaneously, Lewis uses it somewhat differently. He finds the alternation between lines of action, but sees them as separated by time rather than space. Consequently, he is able to find a cross cut in *Artist* when the Migi-Hidari bar is portrayed during its period of popularity and matched with a portrayal of the bar in the state of decline that it has undergone in Ono's present (*AFW* 74–5 and 76). The significance of this cut, Lewis claims, is its role in portraying the accrual of 'resonances by the accumulation of Ono's experiences'.[25] Lewis continues his examination by turning to the match cut: the matching of two shots by their visual similarity. The most famous example of this type of cut occurs in *2001: Space Odyssey* (1968) by Stanley Kubrick (1928–99) when a bone thrown up into the air by a prehistoric man is matched with an orbiting space craft, a reference, Lewis proposes, to the advance of technology. Lewis indicates a few of these matches: for example, the boys in the shanty district of Nishizuru are matched with the figures in Ono's painting 'Complacency', although their looks change from the criminal to the samurai, and then the boys appear again in the painting 'Eyes to the Horizon', but now as soldiers (*AFW* 168). Lewis suggests that these matched cuts illuminate 'the regression of Ono's views from humanitarian concern to hostile nationalism'.[26]

Lewis also finds the equivalent of establishing shots in the novel. Usually establishing shots are long-range shots that establish the location of the action, commonly a shot of the skyline of a city before the camera moves into the city's streets. In a novel, Lewis suggests, its repetition 'can act as a girding for the rest of the narrative', and he finds this repetition in scenes at the Bridge of Hesitation.[27] In fact, three of the four parts – October, 1948; April, 1949; and June, 1950 – open at the bridge. This repetition leads to the final film technique that he considers, overlap: when the sound from one scene overlaps with the next scene. Lewis finds overlap in the scenes that portray Ono as being unable to recall the exact participants and words in various conversations (for example, *Artist* 56).

Part of what makes Lewis's use of film editing terms in a discussion of Ishiguro's work so useful is that Ishiguro does seem to eschew linear plots: instead, he relies heavily on the kind of meaning created by juxtaposing two scenes. Asked by Mason about the digressions in the plot, Ishiguro replies that he does not believe that a plot has to be linear. On the contrary, he believes that there are other criteria, such as tone, that can determine the order in which elements of the story can be presented. This, he adds, is how people talk and think, drifting from one point to another. He later asserts, 'What's important is the emotional aspect, the actual positions the characters take up at different points in the story, and why they need to take up these positions.'[28]

These rhetorical considerations remind us that this novel is entirely composed of a first-person narration, and as Hunt points out, this narrative method allows Ono to reinterpret his memories and prohibits readers' access to 'incidents and their relevance which he does not wish to consider at the moment'.[29] Rebecca Walkowitz notes especially Ono's repetition of phrases and the difficult questions that are raised by what Ono omits. For example, Ono is surprisingly reticent on the topic of his late wife and son. These omissions lead to an important characteristic of the novel's narration:

■ The telling of stories turns out to be the subject as well as the strategy [...] As 'reliable' and 'unreliable' narration is usually distinguished, one is either the master of a narrative, one who possesses knowledge, or one *is* the narrative, the object of knowledge itself. In *Artist,* however, the narrator's inability or unwillingness to maintain these distinctions, to make it clear for the reader whose experiences he is describing, produces a life of several histories and several perspectives.[30] □

To consider the narration further, then, requires an investigation of the novel's narrator, the painter Masuji Ono.

Masuji Ono: An Artist of the Past

Most commentators on the novel focus their efforts on Ono. Brian Shaffer, Cynthia Wong, and Margaret Scanlan all dedicate extensive commentary to an evaluation of the artist. Shaffer provides an important introduction to Ono that examines his shifts and his motivations for those shifts. He begins by suggesting the Bridge of Hesitation as an expression of Ono's psychological state: '[H]e is a "conscience-troubled" man, though he would deny it, who hesitates between owning up to his past mistakes and covering them up; between moral responsibility and psychological expedience; between uncovering and further hiding his lingering guilt.'[31] This psychological state is reflected in Ono's storytelling, which Shaffer views as 'a series of defense mechanisms in order to avoid his past. In particular, he exhibits repression and projection to the extent that he lies to himself, rationalizes past activities, comments upon himself (through others), and selectively filters the past'.[32] Ono has constant troubles with his memory: for example, he admits to being unable to recall what happened with Jiro Miyake only a week after the meeting (*AFW* 54) and frequently notes that the words he is quoting are *probably* not the 'precise' words used (*AFW* 69, 72).[33] Ono displaces and projects his fears and wishes as when he insists that Ichiro wants to go to the cinema although it is clearly his own wish to go (*AFW* 37–9).[34] He also suffers from denial: he denies

his role in the failure of Noriko's marriage negotiations.[35] Instead he
readily believes that the Miyakes have pulled out of the marriage to
his daughter because the Miyake family's status wasn't high enough
(*AFW* 18–9 and 80). Shaffer also argues that Ono denies he is an
artistic 'has been', based on his refusal to show Ichiro his paintings;
but while this detail and Shaffer's subsequent examination of Ono's
use of 'tidying' does support the argument that Ono denies that his
role as a propagandist was wrong, it does not support the idea that he
is a 'has been'. Finally, Ono also denies the changes going on in Japan,
changes apparent in the novel's provision of the Hirayama boy's sad
situation as a comparison to Ono:

> ■ [L]ike the Hirayama boy, Ono is exposed as lacking in vision, opportunistic,
> pandering to crowds, and incapable of changing his tune. Like the boy, he is
> shown to mimic patriotic themes and slogans, and to be incapable of under-
> standing why his message no longer falls on sympathetic ears. Thus, Ono
> is depicted as closely resembling the boy, even if he sees himself in starkly
> opposite terms, as the quintessential freethinking, critical artist-citizen.[36] □

After outlining the conflicts of which Ono is a part – conflicts between
teacher and student, Ono and his father, Ono and Mori-san[37] – Shaffer
separates Ono's career into three artistic stages: the early stage in which
he produces stereotypical Oriental paintings for tourists at the Takeda
firm; the crucial seven years with Mori-san; and his time as a painter of
propaganda posters for the nationalists. From his final stage, Ono looks
back on the earlier two periods as 'shallow and decadent'.[38] He evolves
within his third period, moving from social concern to unquestioning
fascism. Encouraged by Matsuda and bolstered by his experience in
the Nishizuru district, Ono begins to believe that painting should not
serve commercial or aesthetic ends but rather political ones:

> ■ Ono's shifting conception of art's proper engagement with worldly con-
> cerns is revealed no more clearly than in his evolving portrait of Japan's
> current crisis and triumphal destiny. The first version of this painting is
> entitled *Complacency* and the second is called *Eyes to the Horizon*.[39] □

It is just such a conceptual shift, however, that leads to the betrayal
of his student Kuroda, a key scene in the novel often alluded to but
never depicted. Ono's refusal to discuss this scene, a part of his filter-
ing, is the one shift in point of view that Ono does not make. Ishiguro
explains the changes in his narrator:

> ■ [T]he structure [...] is dictated less by plot than by the changes in the
> main character's state of mind. For example, in the opening section, his

position is that he's not ashamed of anything he's done; but gradually his point of view shifts and he starts owning up.[40] □

In the end, the novel is sceptical of all three periods of 'art in the service of purely commercial, aesthetic, or political ends'.[41]

After the war, when Ono realises that the tide of thought has turned against him, he suggests 'that even if he was wrong, at least he was influential: that it is more important to have made one's mark than to have been a right-minded nonentity'.[42] Ono pretends that he is not concerned about prestige,[43] but he admits to being wrong in supporting the Nationalists as long as he can be thought of as influential. His influence, however, is put into question by slips in his narrative which reveal that his reputation was not as large as he has led readers to believe.[44] Ishiguro expresses his interest in such characters: 'I'm very interested in people who have a great desire to do something of worth, something to distinguish themselves, but who maybe in the end find that they don't have it in them to be more than ordinary.'[45] Ono was, in fact, ordinary.

Ono's narration is replete with manipulations and elisions that seek to belie this ordinariness. As Ishiguro has pointed out, Ono's diary entries allow Ono to make slight changes he can modify as he goes.[46] One of the best examinations of Ono's techniques is provided by Wong. Ono's focus, Wong argues, is on his struggles to become a prominent artist and maintain his position as family patriarch. The story is not the document of an artist coming to understand his life, but the adjustment of facts that will allow Ono to see himself as the person he believes he is:

■ [W]hat occurs instead of discovery is the narrator's own version of life made more palatable in the very act of telling it. Indeed, though he does not 'lie' about his past in any conventional sense, he is anxious that some details from that period do not emerge.[47] □

Ono may profess to want to understand his life but he is deceiving himself and, Wong claims, unaware that he is deceiving himself, although this claim that he is unaware seems specious. Wong bases it on Ono's admissions of his faults as a storyteller:

■ At the same time he proclaims to be telling the truth, he calls attention to his own distortions; Ono's slips may be read as accidental, or as moments when his façade shows through. Literally, Ono leaves traces for the reader's detection of his insincerity, while he remains ambiguous about his own knowledge of those slips.[48] □

For example, Wong points out how Ono opens his account with an effortful foregrounding of his status but then pretends that it is not important and attempts to push the information he has just presented into the background. Scanlan perceives similar qualities in Ono's opening, reading his descriptions of struggles with his businessman father as his attempt to become 'the hero of a Western portrait of the artist'.[49] Wong sees Ono, initially, as attempting to be objective and forthcoming, but then, referring to the instances in which Ono breaks off his narrative and blames his bad memory, suggests that he might be trying to suppress rather than reveal uncomfortable details. She quotes Ono on self-portraiture (*AFW* 67) suggesting that this is one of Ono's revealing slips:

■ Intent on preserving his reputation now that the war has tarnished it, Ono unwittingly reveals that he does not truly recognize himself as the person he is reconstructing. Whether he accepts the futility of conveying to others the same fictionalized self that he envisions, Ono warns the reader that his own accounts may be questionable and may not correspond to the way others saw his character. □

Wong suggests that when Ishiguro lets his characters unknowingly reveal their flaws, those characters are able to salvage dignity, 'a quality important to the author's vision of how people accept and deal with failure in their lives'.[50] When readers meet Ono, Wong argues, Ono is starting to understand that the daughters are talking about him, so he begins to look at his past to reassure himself and his audience of his status. The motivation for Ono's reconstruction of his past is not, however, to protect his family but to bolster his pride. She notes that when Ono takes 'precautions' it is 'to remember the person he felt he was and had become'.[51] Seeing that he no longer fits the role that he remembers playing, Ono mourns his lost self.

Wong finds some proof for her reading of Ono in the strategies he uses to tell his story. Ono has put his story together in non-chronological fashion with himself at the centre, but it is a divided centre. Ono tells Shintaro that he ought to own up to the past, but Wong asks, what would owning up to the past mean? As the title of the novel suggests, 'Ono is suspended between two states, one that denies causing shame to Japan and one that responds to the effects of misguided principles.'[52] For example, Ono finds the suicides of men acknowledging their wrongdoing during the war a wasteful gesture. In reference to Ono's fractious relationship with his daughter Noriko, Wong points out that Ono can discuss only *his* interactions with her: she might be entirely pleasant with everyone else: 'The gaps in the narrative, then, may be read as Ono's blindness to other people's dimensions at a time when he is so desperate to salvage his own dignity.'[53] Wong does not, it seems, consider that the gaps may be part of Ono's manipulation of the reader.

As it is for other readers, for Wong the key scene is Ono's betrayal of Kuroda. Given the many allusions to Kuroda, readers can deduce that Ono thinks about Kuroda all the time, but he apparently does not feel remorse for his betrayal, a lack evident when after seeing Kuroda in a rundown neighbourhood Ono blandly observes that his former student has aged. Wong reads Ono's attitude towards Kuroda as a salvaging of his dignity, for 'Also unspoken is Ono's jealousy that his own student has far surpassed him in his artistic career. Confronting him again under the guise of smoothing over the past for Noriko's sake represents another moment when Ono acts as if he is the wronged man.'[54]

Ono cannot, in fact, acknowledge how the nationalist movement he served is implicated in the deaths of his wife and son. He devotes very little space to his dead wife and son: their deaths are mentioned only in passing. This omission, Wong argues, protects him from connecting his advocacy of war with his son's death while fighting that war, and from connecting his pride in the Sugimura house with his wife's death from a bomb that struck the house. Surprisingly, Wong does not point out that Ono's support for the war plays a more direct part in his wife's death through the plain connection that it was because of the war that the house was bombed, but this omission does not mitigate her point that, 'given Ono's seeming commitment to family, failure or refusal to say more about their absence is in accord with Ono's narrative strategy'.[55] Wong concludes by stating that Ono's story might draw us in and cause us to sympathise with him, but we have to see all the lies he tells and thus he cannot be redeemed.

On a similar trajectory, King reads Ono's manipulations as Ono protecting himself from accusations regarding his behaviour during the war. King, however, sees Ono as a skilled rhetor:

■ He pretends to be an old fool, but this is a protective mask – many of his nationalist acquaintances commit suicide as a form of apology to society – which allows him first to avoid, then adapt to the attitudes of postwar society. Eventually and with subtlety he indicates his sorrow for past behaviour in such a way as to lose nothing.[56] □

Moreover, King suggests that Ono has craftily followed whoever is in power by adapting. Given Ono's control over the narrative, this analysis certainly demands attention. As Peter Mallet points out, one of the ways that Ono differs from Stevens, in *The Remains of the Day*, is in how the narrators reveal their characters: we learn about Ono not through what he tells us about himself, as Mallet proposes we do with Stevens, but through 'the reactions of other characters to him'.[57] While this comparison seems to underestimate vastly the degree of Stevens's dissembling, the imperative here is to recognise that Ono's is the only voice we hear directly. One area for future analysis, consequently, is to determine whether or not Ishiguro has allowed Ono to misspeak in ways that might support King's argument for a more Machiavellian Ono. The comparison of Ono and Stevens is noted by a few critics, such as Page, who begins by citing how much Stevens and Ono have in common. Page finds 'responsibility for past actions in both the private and public spheres',[58] the main theme here and in *Remains*. In fact, he finds many similarities between Ishiguro's second and third novels. The difference, he asserts, is that one is in English and one in Japanese. Margaret Scanlan, however, develops the comparison over the length of her essay. Framing her analysis with a discussion of 'the death of humanism', Scanlan focuses on the instability of Ono's identity. She begins her examination of the significance of Ishiguro's narrative method by comparing Ono and Stevens:

■ [Ishiguro's] narrators, both old men looking back from the postwar period to their involvement with fascism in the 1930s, in some ways resemble the unreliable narrators of older fiction. But Ishiguro uses them to explore the extent to which identity is socially constructed, and the consequent instability of selves formed in a traditional culture when that culture dies. Identity in these novels is not an essence but instead depends on a social context that has changed so radically as to leave characters floating in an unfamiliar world. Through his first-person narrators, Ishiguro dramatizes the connections between public history and an 'I' dependent for definition on its circumstances, suggesting that the unconfident and marginalized self of the posthumanist world view is drawn to find authority in totalitarian politics.[59] □

Both narrators acknowledge that their stories might be marred by the distortions imposed by uncertain memories. Memory may fail because of age, but it may fail so that Ono does not have to remember betraying Kuroda.

Scanlan, however, points to another possible reason for the failure of memory: society has lost its memory: 'Ono is especially conscious that Japan seems to have lost its own memory, that people around him are wilfully discarding values maintained proudly during the war.'[60] Scanlan then switches from the novel to an analysis of Japanese linguistics, citing anthropologist Dorinne K. Kondo on the instability of the first-person singular pronoun (the 'I') in Japanese, and this instability of the pronoun leads Scanlan to William Bohnaker's assertion of the flexibility of the Japanese psyche.[61] Ono too demonstrates this flexibility. His training has been rigidly controlled to ensure that he stayed within the approved styles:

■ These structures of authority are the structures of his identity as a painter – his success in following one style, his courage in breaking with another; the maxims of his great teacher and their transmission, with a few necessary emendations to his own students; his teacher's praise; his students's [*sic*] adulation; his winning of the Shigeta Foundation award. Indeed, he is well aware that much of what might seem to constitute his personal identity has been acquired from other people. □

As the novel opens, readers find that Ono must look back and evaluate his past against the values of the present society:

■ Now most of the people around him are adopting American values: His grandson plays at being the Lone Ranger, until recently a forbidden activity; corporate presidents and once-famous musicians commit suicide to apologize for their part in the war while the occupiers execute generals and a mentally retarded man is beaten up by neighbors tired of hearing him shout old fascist slogans. His paintings are hidden away; he has no students; no one cares for the prizes he regards as uncontaminated measures of worth.[62] □

The instability of Ono's identity is seen when he collapses scenes together as he does with the scene of Moriyama (*AFW* 177–8) and his memories of a parallel scene with Kuroda.[63] Ono uses what Scanlan labels 'a trick of attributing to his teacher words that might actually have been his own'.[64] Scanlan notes the larger significance: 'Repetition of situation and even words blurs these scenes together, not only in Ono's mind, but in the reader's.'[65] As well, Scanlan reads the presence of more than one character nicknamed 'the Tortoise' as proof of the loss of fixed identities. Ono is able to use this loss to deceive.

■ Confronted with a painful situation, he is likely to abstract it, generalize about it; when he talks about other people, he frequently appears to be talking about himself. This trick, of course, is a familiar psychological defense, but in Ono's case it seems to point to a more fundamental confusion of himself with the people he discusses.[66] □

Ono is never more confused than in regards to his contribution to the militarisation of Japan. We read Ono making insincere self-deprecations but are led to believe that Ono was an important artist, a belief which becomes increasingly dubious as the novel progresses. Late in the novel, after the *miai*, a meeting between a potential couple and their parents, the unreliability of his memory cannot be overlooked. Lewis unpacks the consequences of Ono's admission at the *miai*, the bewilderment of those present, and the success of the event:

■ It could be that Ono's guilt is not registered by the others at the *miai* for the simple reason that he reveals no specific names or crimes. He assumes, almost certainly incorrectly, that Saito is familiar with the propaganda work that he did in support of the militaristic regime immediately before and during the war. He also does not mention the betrayal of his former pupil Kuroda, the unwholesome facts of which are withheld from the reader, too, until after the *miai*. Given this vagueness, it is little wonder that Ono's listeners are underwhelmed by his revelations. Another option is that Ono has vastly overestimated his importance in the scheme of things. There are many signs that he is a vain, self-serving man who is desperate to be admired by others for having made a contribution to something.[67] □

Scanlan outlines the critical moment when Ono's contribution is put in doubt:

■ [A]t the end, his daughter tells him that all of this self-dramatization is unnecessary, for his contributions to the war effort were scarcely on the scale of the composer Mr. Naguchi's: 'Father's work had hardly to do with these larger matters of which we are speaking. Father was simply a painter. He must stop believing he has done some great wrong' [*AFW* 193]. In this speech, Setsuko undermines the one point on which many readers may have been willing to take Ono at his word, his view that his propaganda paintings played a key role in militarizing Japan.[68] □

Lewis concurs, concluding that Ono has exaggerated his part and that 'ultimately he was just a minor functionary who is now burdened with an inappropriate sense of guilt'.[69] Mallett too deduces a much more ordinary ending:

■ Ono may not always have the correct perception of reality and truth, but he does show everything, including incidents from his past and reactions of others to him which are far from favourable, so that at the end of the novel *we* see the truth: that he was, like Stevens, just an ordinary man who was trapped into behaving in the way he did by the times in which he lived and the values that were current.[70] □

Rather than the sly rhetor that King finds narrating the novel, Mallett proposes that Ono is so forthcoming that he allows us to see a truth that may not even be recognisable to himself, an irony enabled by the use of the unreliable narrator.

For Mallett and Scanlan, there is no epiphany here. Ono simply moves on and 'back into life'.[71] Ono recalls his happiness thinking about how he had succeeded and Moriyama had failed, and by the end of the novel, Ono 'has learned to appreciate Americanization and hence to merge his perspective with that of the group'.[72] Scanlan's point is well observed. One of the novel's key sequences is Ono's slow realisation of the reversal that has occurred around him. The weight of this realisation, however, is only fully recognisable when one understands Ono's character. Mason helps with this understanding by connecting Ishiguro's work to the filmmaker Yasujiro Ozu.[73] Like Ozu, Ishiguro's choice of characters is derived from the tradition of a type of domestic drama film, the *shomin-geki*. Lewis defines the *shomin-geki* and connects it to Ishiguro's work.

■ Although essentially realistic in tone, this type of film often has comic overtones and a desentimentalised mix of smiles and tears. The typical hero or heroine is someone who is ready to give up at the intractability of the world, but then finds the strength to continue by compromising with the way things are. They do so with passive acceptance, and not through the grand emotions of valour and rapture. This concentration on the small victories and defeats of ordinary people as they grapple with their everyday lives is also mirrored in Ishiguro's work.[74] □

This description fits Ono well. He too grapples with what he sees as a new perception of the behaviour of the nationalists during the war and a new outlook on the suddenly ubiquitous American culture. Ono continually confronts the realisation that he was simply a product of his time, and that that time is now over, a reading supported by Ishiguro: when Mason asks the identity of the reader that Ono addresses and the narrative situation, Ishiguro replies that the opening was simply a device to create a mental world. He was trying to show Ono's parochial perspective, which of course leads to his downfall. It is an important facet of this novel to examine 'the inability of normal human beings to see beyond their immediate surroundings, and because of this, one is at the mercy of what this world immediately around one proclaims itself to be'.[75] The novel provides further support for this conclusion. King, for example, outlines the importance of change in the novel:

■ The theme of change is expressed throughout the novel in descriptions of the growth and decay of various urban areas, changes in painting and building styles, as well as in the career and attitudes of the narrator. The novel reflects Japanese culture over half a century, from the supposed decadence of the early 1900s through the nationalism of the thirties to the Americanised new society of the postwar years. Changing notions of art mirror politics and manners.[76] □

This theme of change, suggested in the novel's title, provides the deepest insight into the novel's world.

CONCLUSION – THE FLOATING WORLD

Most critics have read Ono, as Mallet does, as similar to Stevens: 'a man trying to justify the life he has led and find some dignity in it'.[77] The justifications are, however, hard for Ono to find, as is the dignity, in part because of the shifting terrain on which Ono takes his stands. Ishiguro alludes to this state, positioning Ono as caught between historical periods and between generations: 'It's the story about the old man who's overtaken by history, so that the things he was once proud of become things he's ashamed of; and about his relationship to the younger generation, how he doesn't fit in.'[78] A few years later, Ishiguro supplements this idea with a comment that could be explaining Stevens or Ono:

> ■ I'm interested in people who, in all sincerity, work very hard and perhaps courageously in their lifetimes toward something, fully believing that they're contributing to something good, only to find that the social climate has done a topsy-turvy on them by the time they've reached the ends of their lives.[79] □

The shifts that Ono encounters seem diametrically opposed. King lays out the binary nature of the world in which Ono finds himself: 'If the old order is tyrannical and unrepentant, the younger generation is necessarily selfish. The choice seems to be between the living death of the past, which provides protection and guidance, and the new American democratic way, which offers opportunities and insecurity.'[80] Ono floats from the old perspective to the new.

The shifts that Ono must negotiate should not, however, suggest that Ishiguro has developed a realistic portrayal of Japan and its shifting values at the conclusion of World War Two. The instability of the novel's world, its flux, does not narrow the novel's locale to Japan, as many critics have supposed. Instead the instability allows the difficulty of the novel's moral order to be floated elsewhere. Asked by Mason about Ono's mood at the end of the novel, Ishiguro offers a long, detailed reply proposing that Ono realises the mess Japan has made but believes that in a few years it will recover because a nation's life is longer than a man's, and that Ono has used various strategies to save his dignity; so although he is constantly stripped of this dignity, in the end he somehow holds onto it. One of these techniques is Ono's making concessions that he himself cannot see. Ishiguro points out that he used the diary method to allow Ono to write from four different emotional positions, a range, Ishiguro notes, which has created some irony:

> ■ [T]here are no solid things. And the irony is that Ono had rejected that whole approach to life. But in the end, he too is left celebrating those

pleasures that evaporated when the morning light dawned. So the floating world comes to refer, in the larger metaphorical sense, to the fact that the values of society are always in flux.[81] □

The difficult questions that the novel raises about values remain underdeveloped areas in the criticism of this novel. Morton's series of questions provide a glimpse into the difficult work to be done on this issue and perhaps the best way to conclude the discussion of this novel:

■ What do the superlatively polite but insistent elder daughter and the sassy younger one see when they look at their father? To what are his former friends and colleagues reacting when on the one hand they flatter and on the other snub him? Which honorifics are – or were – deserved, which were merely formal and which may even be a means of avoidance? What does life add up to when society's values change? Is it enough to have meant well at the time? And what course does the honourable man take whose well-intentioned actions as a war propagandist have led others to suffer?[82] □

The critical response to *Artist* supplies the critical scaffolding to answer these questions, but the novel's delicate ambiguities and ironies require further investigation and discussion. The response does, however, prepare readers for Ishiguro's next protagonist, the English butler Stevens, a character subject to turns of fate similar to those endured by Ono and pursuing some of the same questions.

CHAPTER THREE

The Remains of the Day (1993): Reception and Narration

Ishiguro's third novel, *The Remains of the Day*, was both a change and a repetition of his previous novel, *An Artist of the Floating World*. While his protagonist, Stevens, an English butler, might seem at first glance to be completely incomparable to his earlier protagonist, the artist Ono, and while Darlington Hall is around the world from Ono's floating world, the two novels, at their cores, are similar. Both follow a man in the latter stages of his life looking back and trying to reconcile his past with his present. As well, both novels draw on first-person narration to tell their stories and to reveal narrators unwilling to tell their stories fully. This chapter, the first of three focused on Ishiguro's third novel, evaluates the responses of the reviewers before turning to the key essays that have addressed Ishiguro's use of narration in the novel.

THE INITIAL RESPONSE

The novel received an excellent reception. Michiko Kakutani of the *New York Times* calls it 'an intricate and dazzling novel'.[1] Terrence Rafferty begins by pointing out that it seems to be by a veteran novelist and then expands on the novel's craftsmanship: 'Modest in tone, ironic, reflective, and utterly precise in its effects [...] a novel that fulfills its author's intentions as flawlessly as a "classic" short story from the college anthologies', but is most interested in 'the whiff of melancholy that rises from its formal brilliance – an intimation of the futility of perfection'.[2] Philosopher Galen Strawson (born 1952), writing for the *Times Literary Supplement*, expresses similar admiration for Ishiguro's prose style: 'It is a strikingly original book, and beautifully made. Reading it, one has an unusual sense of being controlled by the author. Each element is unobtrusively anticipated, then released in its proper place.'[3] Several critics noted the novel's ability to mix what William Hutchings has called the 'comic and poignant'.[4] Finally, Merle Rubin begins to match the prose style to the story that it tells: 'Delicate, devastating, thoroughly ironic, yet never harsh, this is a novel whose technical achievements are matched by its insightfulness.'[5] There is a resounding critical agreement on the masterfulness of Ishiguro's prose. In fact, three critics point to similarities with Henry James, especially, James's 'The Beast in the Jungle' (1903).

Other critics sought comparisons with Ishiguro's earlier work. Geoff Dyer finds *Remains* less impressive than *Artist* 'whose scheme and form it repeats almost exactly'.[6] Mark Kamine remarks on the similarity with the two earlier novels, but in terms of technique: he points out how they all take their time and build towards grand disclosures, demonstrating 'Ishiguro's narrative deftness': 'Slowly and carefully he lays bare the butler's inner thoughts, intertwining past and present, truth and evasion, seeming at times to meander yet inevitably closing in on the series of admissions at the novel's heart.'[7] Other critics, however, clearly wanted Ishiguro to write about Japan. Annan, who sees *Remains* as more naïve and more flawed than the first two novels, describes Stevens as having a 'Japanese soul'. This is apparently because 'the butler runs on loyalty, devotion, propriety, and pride in his profession'. What Annan really wants is for Ishiguro to write about Japan, and she ends by returning to her fixation: 'Compared to his astounding narrative sophistication, Ishiguro's message seems quite banal: Be less Japanese, less bent on dignity, less false to yourself and others, less restrained and controlled.'[8] There is, unfortunately for Annan, no mention of Japan in the novel. She has captured some of the themes – although her construal of a message of honesty, warmth, and openness as banal is worrying. Hermione Lee too cannot read the novel without connecting it to Japan. Although she begins by pointing out what an unlikely topic the butler is, she then turns to the ideal qualities of a butler before showing how everything turns against Stevens, as it does with Ono. She mentions the historical setting and how the Suez crisis, like the bombing of Nagasaki, is never directly mentioned and then, oddly, argues that the novel is really a Japanese novel in disguise, that Stevens is a kind of *ronin* or faithful servant left without a master. Anthony Thwaite also reads Stevens as a ronin: 'the masterless retainer who is still tied by firm bands to the master'.[9] It is a suggestion that no one would make if the author's name were Beedham or Thwaite, a point supported by Gurewich when after tracing the possible connections to Japan he adds, 'Yet – the proof of his mastery – had he chosen to publish the book under an assumed Anglo name, one would never suspect.'[10] Interestingly, Thwaite goes on to make a more apt comparison, revealing more of Stevens by putting him beside another character who broods over his muddled dignity and what the past might have offered had one made better choices, the deferential Prufrock of T. S. Eliot (1888–1965):

■ Politic, cautious, and meticulous; Full of high sentence, but a bit obtuse.[11] □

While the more mischievous might then ask if Thwaite also sees Prufrock as a *ronin*, the comparison of Stevens and Prufrock is suggestive.

The early reviews were quick to establish Stevens's difficulties. Lawrence Graver is able to read Stevens as Stevens, not as some sort of Japanese double:

■ Ishiguro's command of Stevens' corseted idiom is masterly, and nowhere more tellingly so than in the way he controls the progressive revelation of unintended ironic meaning. Underneath what Stevens says, something else is being said, and the something else eventually turns out to be a moving series of chilly revelations of the butler's buried life – and by implication, a powerful critique of the social machine in which he is a cog.[12] □

Strawson concisely describes Stevens's inability in love, his inability to even acknowledge the love between himself and Miss Kenton: 'He avoids it by brilliant inconsequentiality, by the perfect inarticulateness of irrelevant wordiness.'[13] Kamine continues this discussion by further describing Stevens's emotional state: 'He has been unprotestingly obedient throughout his life, and he now finds himself full of regret and struggling to give voice to his feelings. His tale is an account of Stevens confronting his moral and emotional emptiness.'[14] Rafferty adds another dimension by briefly suggesting that the background holds more than is suggested in the early reviews: 'we're never free of the uneasy feeling that he's intended to *represent* something about the English soul – its repressive decorum, its love of order and authority, its cozy self-regard, its reverence for the past.'[15] Graver understands that while Ishiguro's novels are set during momentous historical times, Ishiguro's concern is for the people of his fictions and what they discover about themselves. He quotes Ishiguro:

■ What I'm interested in is not the actual fact that my characters have done things they later regret. [...] I'm interested in how they come to terms with it. On the one hand there is a need for honesty, on the other hand a need to deceive themselves – to preserve a sense of dignity, some sort of self-respect. What I want to suggest is that some sort of dignity and self-respect does come from that sort of honesty.[16] □

Alice Bloom makes an interesting distinction on this point. She considers whether Stevens has trouble writing about what has happened or whether Stevens knows what has happened: 'In the painful review of his long life, he faces *telling about* (not knowing; I disagree with the reviews that claim he never faced up to things) his beloved Lord Darlington who conspired with the Nazis.'[17] These early comments are suggestive of the critical debates that later scholars have developed.

The earliest reviews were also attuned to the novel's language. Stevens's contortions of language are particularly profitable. Kamine sees them as illuminating Stevens's rationalisations: 'The novel is rich with examples of the contortions it is possible to go through to rationalize past errors.'[18] Rafferty notes Stevens's inexpressiveness and neutrality: 'his verbal style is elaborately inexpressive, or means to be: we recognize immediately the contorted language of rationalization, the studied neutrality of someone taking great pains to avoid the truth'.[19] And again, Kamine, connects the secretiveness and deceitfulness of Ishiguro's narrators to Stevens's self-deceit, concluding 'Stevens labours to construct a wall against his regrets by imagining himself one of the world's greatest butlers – but in the end it is self-deceit he serves more than any proprietor of Darlington Hall'.[20] Ishiguro's use of the deceitful first-person narrator leads to extensive comment on Ishiguro's narration.

NARRATING *REMAINS*

Ishiguro's use of first-person narration in his first two novels was crucial in allowing him to achieve the powerful effects of those novels, and as several reviewers have pointed out, in *Remains* his narrative strategy allows him to develop a character and novel with depth and power. Critics have made extensive use of *Remains* to introduce different modes of narration and in doing so have exposed layers of the narration that might otherwise have escaped notice. Margaret Scanlan, in 'Mistaken Identities: First-Person Narration in Kazuo Ishiguro', demonstrates Ishiguro's new use of unreliable narration and how the narration helps reveal aspects of Stevens's character. The novel's structure, language, and play with knowledge is introduced by Deborah Guth in her 'Submerged Narratives in Kazuo Ishiguro's *The Remains of the Day*' (1999). Perhaps the most useful of the essays on narration, Kathleen Wall's 'The Remains of the Day and Its Challenges to Theories of Unreliable Narration', through a close analysis of the narration, demonstrates the originality of Stevens's narration and its constricting of attempts to find one true account of events. Like Wall, James Phelan and Mary Patricia Martin in 'The Lessons of

"Weymouth": Homodiegesis, Unreliability, Ethics, and *The Remains of the Day*' (1999), also examine the uniqueness of Ishiguro's narration but extend their analysis to include a discussion of Stevens's ethics. Finally, Andrew Teverson, in 'Acts of Reading in Kazuo Ishiguro's *The Remains of the Day*' (1999), provides an excellent analysis of Ishiguro's narrative by focusing on moments when characters are observed reading. As in all these essays, Teverson makes a strong case for the careful textual analysis of Ishiguro's work.

Margaret Scanlan: A New Use for an Old Narration

As noted in Chapter Two, Scanlan connects Ishiguro's narrative method to the social context of his narrators Stevens and Ono, from *An Artist of the Floating World*, 'both old men looking back from the postwar period to their involvement with fascism in the 1930s'. Despite the similarities they may have with unreliable narrators of old, Scanlan reads Ishiguro as putting them to a new use.[21] That is, the traditional cultures provide so much structure that the individual is not able to form a strong identity, so when that traditional culture breaks down, the individual has nothing left on which to base his identity. Ishiguro's fiction allows readers to see individuals such as Stevens, who is always following someone else's rules, encounter this abyss and the shelter they take in totalitarianism.

Unreliable narration also helps Ishiguro develop his character. Scanlan notes that Stevens, like Ono before him, does not have much confidence in his story: he has uncertain memories and knows that he may distort as he narrates. Maybe his memories fail because of age, but they may also fail so that he can let go of painful memories. Stevens also has techniques for avoiding painful memories, such as his use of the first person: 'he transforms the first person into the third person, disguising a painful assessment of his life as an abstract exploration of the question "What is a great butler?"'[22] Scanlan notes Stevens's pronoun use: 'Stevens indeed frequently avoids the first person, substituting an evasive *one* when his emotions are in danger of breaking through. The great heartbreak of his life, his estrangement from Miss Kenton, hides behind this locution, as when he describes how, meaning to condole with her for the loss of her aunt, he ended by rebuking her for failing to supervise the new maids'.[23] Finally, Scanlan points out how the use of the unreliable narrator allows for a mocking of epiphanies:

> ■ Stevens's epiphany occurs at the end of his reminiscence about the evening his father died, when he had kept away from the deathbed for all but a few minutes to pass his tray and attempt to placate a hypochondriacal

guest complaining about his infected blisters. Ignoring the tears that suggest the survival of some inner emotional self, he recalls only his success at keeping up the role. Remembered, this evening evokes joy, seems a victory rather than the defeat his narrative suggests it was.[24] □

Scanlan fails, however, to see Stevens's reading of his own unreliabity.

Deborah Guth: Distortions Reflected Clear

In one of the most helpful discussions of the novel, Deborah Guth argues that Stevens does eventually see what he has lost. She begins, however, with an analysis of what the novel says without actually saying, how Stevens's own narrative slips away from his grasp. This explanation of Ishiguro's technique begins with his introduction of the two concepts Stevens uses to discuss his life's work: greatness and dignity. After establishing these key terms, however, Ishiguro surreptitiously establishes a gap between Stevens's definition of these terms and their illustration by the events of the novel: 'the hidden narrative dismantles those very terms Stevens is trying to justify and progressively undermines the basis as well as the purpose of his life'. Guth is particularly interested in the technique that allows this deconstruction: 'by realigning apparently insignificant or unexplained details, [the narrative] uses the same events to generate quite different meanings, clearly at odds with Stevens' own narrative agenda'.[25] For example, Stevens presents Lord Darlington as a great humanist, but also tells us about Darlington's dismissal of the Jewish maids, Darlington's meetings with fascists, and his own denials of Darlington. Consequently, the 'greatness' of his employer is cast into doubt.

At the beginning of his journey Stevens reflects on the greatness of the English landscape (*RD* 28) and connects this greatness to the greatness of English butlers. Guth describes the unnaturalness of Stevens's conception of dignity, pointing out how it encompasses Stevens's ignoring the death of his father and even counting the evening of his father's death a great success. Parallel to this evening is Stevens's encounter with Harry Smith who is forthright and challenges Stevens's views. This challenge causes Stevens to respond first like the gentleman he is pretending to be, but when he remembers how he was mocked by Lord Darlington's guests he is better able to see himself as Harry Smith's ordinary man being humiliated for his lack of opinion: 'And if a large part of this humiliation lies in his having repeatedly to admit his inadequacy, its real bitterness – and his own true slavery – derives from his collusion in this game'.[26] His 'dignity', Guth proposes, is merely the ability to suffer indignity.

Alongside the meditations on greatness and dignity, a second major narrative begins to emerge: his unacknowledged love affair with Kenton. Guth distinguishes a critical difference in how these narratives function, focusing primarily on their handling of memory. In the greatness and dignity narrative, 'the interaction between apparent and latent levels follows an arc leading first the reader and later Stevens himself to awareness'. In contrast, in the Kenton narrative, 'the text enacts memory as an ongoing act of repression, repeating in recall the same erasure of emotion that characterised the relationship itself, and cunningly allowing one aspect to emerge in order better to camouflage the other'.[27] It is a relationship that emerges through a latent narrative, 'shaped mainly through a series of "clues": ambiguous comments and silences which cumulatively imply the presence of unexpressed emotion'.[28] These clues form a plot line though they are not presented objectively to the reader: 'the completely submerged, in fact absent narrative of Stevens' feeling for her is characterised by a series of enigmas, gaps and dislocations: ripples on the surface of the text'. This narrative is further complicated by Stevens's description of a series of four turning points which, Guth points out, do not initially make sense to the reader. Despite his thoroughness elsewhere, Stevens does not articulate 'the central point around which the information is organised'. The reader, consequently, can only acknowledge these incidents unable to comprehend exactly what Stevens is referring to and its larger significance. This difficulty is worsened by Stevens's constant questioning of whether these incidents should even be classified as turning points.[29] It is only, she proposes, when they say goodbye at the bus stop that the turning points make sense.

Guth also extrapolates from the scene in which Kenton and Stevens observe Stevens's father practicing his walk over a spot where he had fallen (*RD* 50) to examine the importance of repetition in the novel. While the father replays his failure physically, Stevens repeatedly returns to his failures mentally, 'trying to discover how or when he alienated Miss Kenton and pushed her into the arms of a man she didn't love'. These repetitions, however, are repeatedly blocked, 'for even as he narrates his search he suppresses the key to its significance and ends up with a text that exists to hide the meaning he is trying to prise from it'.[30] But it is in the repeated return to memory that Stevens creates meaning: 'Stevens' memories imaginatively repeat his former life in order to recreate its meaning, weaving and unweaving as he simultaneously re-enacts the suppressions on which that construction was based.' Guth provides a long list of the cases of repetition supporting her claim that 'repetition emerges both as the structuring principle of Stevens' life and as a textual strategy for its exposure'. The reader, therefore, is left with the job of 'going back over Stevens' text in order to unscramble the clues, reconstruct the hidden narrative and arrive at an integrated understanding'.[31]

Contrary to Scanlan's claim that the novel mocks epiphanies,[32] Guth argues that at the end Stevens does see what he has lost. The ending's tragedy is his, perhaps, too late a discovery, after a life of dedication and self-denial, of what has been missing from his life: 'the individual self he thought had no value, the ability to love a woman, to sit on a common bench and watch the sun go down without ritual or ceremony attached, without ennobling purpose or grand rhetorical flourish'.[33] Guth's essay, then, is crucial for readers of the novel interested in a close analysis of its language and structure and awareness of how knowledge is attained. Through Stevens's restraint, she realises, Ishiguro has developed a narrative that tells itself through inflection and subverts its narrator. It is, she proposes, 'an endless *jeu de miroirs* in which reflection and repetition reveal distortion and distortions are reflected clear'.[34]

Kathleen Wall: A New Kind of Unreliable Narration

Kathleen Wall also focuses on the novel's narration to provide an excellent reading of *Remains*. She explains the challenges of understanding reliability and describes how Stevens is trying to comprehend his situation. She begins by noting the unique nature of the unreliable narration in this novel:

> ■ the novel challenges our usual definition of an unreliable narrator as one whose 'norms and values' differ from those of the implied author, and questions the concept of an ironic distance between the mistaken, benighted, biased, or dishonest narrator and the implied author, who, in most models, is seen to communicate with the reader entirely behind the narrator's back.[35] □

Earlier conceptions of unreliable narration, Wall proposes, were not clear about how the reader could close the distance between what the author could be ascertained as believing normal or valuable and the narrator's language and actions. *Remains*, Wall proposes, compels readers to consider *why* Stevens is unreliable and how his motives condition the implied author's choices about the narration. Wall argues, then, that the novel demonstrates unreliability 'in the structural elements controlled by the implied author and in the ways that Ishiguro expects us to interact with the text'.[36] Specifically, by investigating the narrative discourse, differences between scenes and Stevens's commentary on those scenes, the order of the narrative, and the tendency of readers to naturalise texts, Wall focuses attention on the narrator's mental processes, demonstrates the difficulty of terms such as 'reliable' and 'unreliable', and ultimately, reveals the difficulty of sorting out the truth.

First, Stevens's use of language reveals his unreliability. Wall points to his highly elevated diction which she proposes separates him from the modern reader although it is unclear how she connects this point to Stevens's unreliability. Her argument is stronger when she, like Scanlan, notes that Stevens often refers to himself as 'one' rather than 'I', especially when he attempts to distance himself from an emotion or judgement.[37] This distancing is readily evident when Stevens speaks of his father: 'I realize that if one looks at the matter objectively, one has to concede that my father lacked various attributes one may normally expect in a great butler' (*RD* 34). Wall cites 'professional' as another instance in which Stevens's language use betrays 'unreliability', claiming that he uses the word to excuse actions that seem devoid of emotion or to mask actions that are not professional but the result of his feelings.[38] For example, he repeatedly refers to his trip to see Kenton as a professional venture, only slowly allowing himself to perceive his personal interest in seeing her again. Wall also seizes on Stevens's defensiveness as evoked in phrases such as '"Let me be perfectly clear," "I should say", "I should point out", "let me make it immediately clear", "I feel I should explain"'. The connection between such phrases and Stevens's unreliability is evident: Stevens is defending against questions that he thinks the narratee might ask, questions that hint at anxieties that he has not expressed and has possibly repressed.[39] These various verbal markers reveal some of Stevens's preoccupations, and from them readers can determine the issues on which he may be biased.

Second, Wall investigates the difference between how we read a scene and Stevens's interpretation of that scene. He reports feeling one way, but he behaves as if he felt differently. Sometimes we have to deduce his emotions from observations that other characters make because Stevens fails to report them. He sees himself and others as having particular motives but those motives do not match the way he and others act or behave. These discrepancies are largely due to Stevens's construal of dignity. It is a somewhat odd topic, Wall asserts, for a travel narrative, especially since Stevens seems to have defined it to mean repressing any non-professional feelings, a definition that so privileges the professional over the personal that even though he wants to comfort Kenton after hearing the news of the death of her aunt, he ends up upbraiding her for some work done by maids in her charge.[40] He simply has no language for the personal topics such as love and grief.[41] We see a similar response to the death of his father: Stevens tries to withhold emotion but readers are alerted to the conflict when Cardinal and Lord Darlington are both compelled to ask Stevens if he is all right. In fact, Stevens is asked if he is all right three times within fifteen lines, a scene that is repeated somewhat when Stevens receives the news of Kenton's engagement and Cardinal, again, notes that he looks 'unwell' (*RD* 220). Notably, Wall points out, in both cases Stevens turns these sad events into triumphs (*RD* 110 and 227). Moreover, readers intending to grasp Stevens's psychological state must learn to privilege the pattern formed by his responses to these repeated moments of conflict over Stevens's own reporting. In doing so, readers acknowledge the implied author, the agent in charge of developing these discrepancies and manipulating these patterns.[42] It is through these scenes that Ishiguro lets us better see Stevens's psychological state rather than through what Stevens says about his situation.

Wall also uses the idea of 'Naturalization',[43] a term she defines as 'using what we know about human psychology and history to evaluate the probable accuracy of, or motives for, a narrator's assertions.'[44] For example, we use our historical knowledge to see that Lord Darlington's recommendation of Italy and Germany is ill-fated. Here the author is speaking over the voice of Stevens although we have to remember that Stevens is looking back and able to comment with the benefit of hindsight. We also use psychology to understand Stevens's motives and behaviour: Wall offers the example of Stevens remembering the warning of his father's demise as coming from Kenton rather than Lord Darlington, a mistake that protects him in the short term because he sees Kenton as biased against his father. Perceiving her bias, he can discount her warnings and, in turn, the realisation that his father's health is failing.

These are all somewhat standard tactics of the unreliable narrator, but Wall then makes the connection that while it is Stevens who misremembers, it is also Stevens who figures out his mistakes.[45] Wall finds another interesting nuance when Stevens is thinking over the letter he received from Kenton (*RD* 48): Stevens attributes disappointments to Kenton that are probably his own.[46] The text supports this supposition when Kenton denies the assertions he makes about her life (*RD* 236). Wall also points out that we cannot totally trust Kenton either, for she might also be guilty of accusing Stevens of behaviour that actually describes her own: her accusation on the evening of Herr Ribbentrop's visit that Stevens has been stomping about because he objects to her leaving for a date with Benn (*RD* 215–16) might instead reflect her own displeasure in dating Benn or in Stevens's lack of response. And thus Wall arrives at a critical point in her commentary on this novel: 'In creating a text that is, at some points, thoroughly indeterminate, Ishiguro foregrounds the problem of "truth", perhaps challenging us never to figure out "what really happened", and hence to take only an ironic pleasure in reaching what few conclusions come our way.'[47] The novel is, in part, an investigation into what it means to know.

'Order' and 'Duration' provide readers with more information with which they can assess the narration. Wall cites Seymour Chatman to point out that authors are revealed by the way they structure a work and by the events their characters encounter.[48] For example, Wall notes the time frame of the novel: it is supposed to be a travel narrative, but Stevens keeps getting pulled back into the past. This imbalance is so great that we can see the narrative as 'a re-examination and justification of his life as Lord Darlington's butler and of the values that to a large degree determined and constructed that life'. Stevens, of course, does not return to just any event in the past; readers need to attend to the motivations for and order of his flashbacks because it is in these places that the implied narrator helps us see the events that trouble Stevens, those that lack resolution, and the conclusions that he avoids.[49]

Our understanding of the past is not fully revealed by what Stevens says about the past: we must also consider why Stevens looks back to the past and the order in which he looks back. Stevens himself sometimes admits that he has digressed (*RD* 67). Wall provides an example from the third day of his travels when Stevens is in Mursden. Because Mursden was the source of silver polish, Stevens is led to think of how the excellent state of the silver helped put Lord Halifax in a better frame of mind leading up to an important meeting with von Ribbentrop. This memory, in turn, leads to Stevens saying 'a few words concerning Herr Ribbentrop', (*RD* 136) words that are meant to defend Lord Darlington against charges of anti-Semitism. Realising that he has drifted, Stevens tries to bring himself back to the silver, but in an absolute non-sequitur, he goes on to discuss how butlers judge their employers to assess their own standing. He again notes that he has deviated from his original point and acknowledges that the past is difficult given the small errors that have crept into his work. Wall reads through the associations and explains the drift of Stevens's thinking, a sequence that Stevens himself may not have charted:

■ Made uncertain about his current value as a butler by the number of small mistakes, he must justify his past value by recalling the impact of his silver polishing on international affairs and by asserting, further, that his value as a professional is assured by that of the master he has served. Yet because Stevens offers such a justification even when he knows that Lord Darlington's career has been a 'waste', he merely reveals here his tendency to compartmentalize his knowledge into bearable segments and, further, the strength of his drive to protect himself from any contradictions that will undermine the values on which he has constructed his life.[50] □

By tracing the connections between Stevens's reminiscences, Wall demonstrates not only the subtlety of Ishiguro's narrative, but also another facet of Stevens's defence against the onslaught of the past.

Narrative order also emphasises events in the scene in which
Stevens runs out of gas. During this scene he continually returns to
the time Lord Darlington dismissed the two maids and his conversations at that time with Kenton. This flashback is interrupted by his
returning to the present to talk about his difficult evening at the
Taylor home (RD 159), but he then retreats to the past to discuss the
time Kenton caught him with a sentimental romance and the period
a month earlier when she started to date. This recollection leads him
to consider the events leading up to that change and the realisation
that perhaps he should not have cancelled the evening cocoa meetings. He concludes he is being so introspective because of the difficulty of the day, but these digressions are all a prelude: the main
act is an account of the conversation with Harry Smith who argues
vehemently for a conception of dignity radically opposed to the one
that Stevens has used to guide his life. Ishiguro uses narrative order
and Stevens's admission of his avoidance to emphasise the importance of the conversation with Smith. The unreliability here is, Wall
argues, 'mixed'. Stevens seems to be starting to become aware of his
manipulations as is seen in his admission that he is avoiding the meeting with Smith, although he still does not explain why he would do
so. Despite Stevens's lack of awareness of his motives, Wall detects in
the progression from the previous example to this one that Stevens is
becoming slightly more reliable.[51]

This slight improvement in reliability, in fact, marks a major
change in Stevens. He begins to see that which he previously could
not, and ultimately, the meeting with Harry Smith causes a deconstruction of Stevens's concept of dignity. In contrast to Stevens's
silence and blind faith in his employer, Harry Smith construes dignity
in terms of having the right to speak one's opinion.[52] Initially, Stevens
tries to defend his notion of dignity (RD 201), but Wall's exegesis
of this monologue demonstrates Stevens's defensiveness and unease:
Stevens notes Darlington's failures and must recognise that he cannot
justify his own life by praising the man he served. Stevens's questioning of Lord Darlington suggests his questioning of himself.

This progression of Stevens's thinking over the course of the trip has
been nicely demonstrated by Karl Jirgens who juxtaposes a series of quotations by Stevens from different parts of the narrative.[53] Although Jirgens
offers these quotations in support of a logically flawed effort to demonstrate how Stevens was duped by the Nazis, this contrasting of quotations
does reveal the changes through which Stevens's thinking progresses:
Stevens begins satisfied with the work he has done for Lord Darlington
(RD 126); a day later he qualifies his satisfaction to point out that while
Lord Darlington's efforts may have been a waste, Stevens did his best
(RD 201); next, Stevens sees that while Lord Darlington may have been

mistaken, at least he made his own mistakes, while Stevens must question his dignity after acknowledging that he has not even made his own mistakes (RD 243); and finally, moments later, Stevens consoles himself by suggesting that men such as he have very little choice (RD 244).

The concept of unreliable narration is not straightforward in this novel. The narration is complicated by aspects of Stevens's character which have not received much critical attention: for example,

■ Stevens is not an entirely unreflective man, merely one who has found it necessary to bracket off large areas of feeling, experience, and desire because of the huge investment he has made in a certain image of himself and of his place in life. □

Wall supports this claim by recalling his reassessment of Kenton's letter.[54] First, he proposes that he cannot possibly be misreading the letters (RD 48), but later he acknowledges that he may have exaggerated (RD 140), and finally, he sees that he reads meaning into the letters that the text does not support (RD 180). In his return to the past, Wall argues, Stevens learns, and this learning helps him better evaluate his past and allows him to attempt to close 'the critically ironic distance between implied author and narrator, between narrator and implied reader'. Stevens is not trying to deceive and blithely ignore the contradictions of his account. He is trying to get at the truth of his life. The novel's narration is significant, then, in its reconfiguring of the role of the unreliable narrator and challenging our conception of the truth unreliable narrators offer. Particularly important for Wall is the challenge this novel issues to the 'approach to unreliable narrators that focuses on a fixation with an authoritative version of events that the implied reader cleverly constructs in spite of the narrator's purposeful or unconscious obfuscation'. Ishiguro banishes hopes of 'one true account' with a narrator whose awareness of his contradictions and missteps is hard to determine, a narrator whose lack of self-knowledge precludes a more accurate telling of his story. Stevens may want to tell his story accurately but the attempt at absolute reliability is futile here: 'The Truth' is not always an easy matter. Consequently, Wall concludes by suggesting that analyses of unreliable narrators grounded on the project that readers have not been given the truth 'and that our task is to figure out "what really happened"' require re-evaluation. As Wall point out, there are '"fashions" in unreliable narration': what was a 'norm and value' of James or Joseph Conrad (1857–1924) is not necessarily a norm today.[55]

James Phelan and Mary Patricia Martin: Beyond Unreliable Narration

James Phelan and Mary Patricia Martin also look back to Wayne Booth's work in *The Rhetoric of Fiction* (1961) as a point of departure.

Like Wall they supply another catalogue of narrative techniques and in doing so provide readers with further insights into the complexities of Stevens's unreliability. Phelan and Martin, however, focusing for the most part on the meeting between Stevens and Kenton near the novel's conclusion, also consider the ethical dimensions of unreliable narration. Stevens, they propose, may be realising the problems with his ideals and the sacrifices he has made, and this creates a challenge for Ishiguro: 'Ishiguro's difficult task is to communicate the psychological complexity, emotional richness, and ethical difficulty of Stevens's climactic realisation by means of Stevens's generally reticent and often unreliable narration'.[56] They begin to explain how Ishiguro overcomes this obstacle by examining why a passage from Stevens's meeting with Kenton (*RD* 233–4) is unreliable but quickly add the interesting distinction that 'unreliable' is not an accurate representation of Stevens's narration: 'Stevens's narration here is an accurate and honest report of his motives *as he understands them*. Or to put the point another way, the passage is reliable *as far as it goes*; the problem is that it doesn't go far enough.'[57] Reading the passage as both reliable and unreliable, Phelan and Martin note that 'unreliable' is not subtle enough to capture the passage's complexity.

To address this lack, Phelan and Martin provide distinctions to 'unreliable'. Stevens could be 'underreporting' or 'underreading'. Underreporting would mean he is not admitting what he and the reader know to be true, an unreliability related to ethics. Underreading would mean he does not read what we do about his personal interest, not an unreliability of ethics or events but a previously unnoticed axis of knowledge and perception. For example, we could suppose that his denial of his emotions, part of a career-long commitment to dignity, has left him unaware of what he is feeling. However, once we acknowledge Stevens's admission of a broken heart, we must also acknowledge that he does have awareness of his feelings for Kenton: 'Because Stevens the narrating-I speaks in the present tense – that is, at the time of the narration, after the anagnorisis [the moment of the self-discovery of the true identity] of Stevens the experiencing-I – the standard approach would now lead us to conclude that he is not underreading but underreporting. Although he says, "I am aware", he clearly leaves out much that has entered his awareness by the time of the narration'.[58] At this point of the narrative, then, Stevens appears to be 'underreporting'.

Given the deep discrepancy between what Stevens says in response to Kenton and what he feels, Phelan and Martin discuss 'the ethics of reading'. This consideration of ethics leads Phelan and Martin to question whether or not Stevens should have told Kenton what he was feeling. On the one hand, doing so would show him acting honestly. On the other hand, it would have been an abuse of his new self-knowledge – it is not possible to return to the earlier days of their relationship. Interestingly, each co-author reads this complex scene differently, a difference that underlines 'the multifarious relations among the narrative texts and our responses to them'.[59]

Phelan and Martin look back, momentarily, to the scene in which Stevens corrects an earlier account about standing outside Kenton's room (*RD* 226–7). His previous misremembering is clearly a repression of feeling and that he can now recall this episode correctly demonstrates that his journey is leading him to admit where he has gone wrong in the past. Phelan and Martin stress how close Stevens and Kenton are at this time to becoming romantically involved and how this scene activates our desire for Stevens to act. Understanding the scene in this way 'allows us to regard the final meeting in "Weymouth" as Stevens's finally deciding to knock on Miss Kenton's door, a recognition that in turn increases our desire for them to make a satisfactory emotional connection'. At this point the co-authors diverge to produce two readings. First, Martin argues that Stevens should have shared his feelings with Kenton in Weymouth and that his failure to do so 'frustrates our desire':

■ Kenton has again opened herself to Stevens, and he ought to reply in kind; his feelings would not be a burden for her; she would welcome – and he owes her – the acknowledgment of their mutual regret for the life they now realize might have been. Consequently, the pain of Stevens's broken heart is doubled. And Miss Kenton's tears as she boards her bus are the objective correlative of the reader's unfulfilled desire.[60] □

This call for Stevens to act is contrasted with Phelan's reading that Stevens does enough:

■ Stevens's knocking and Miss Kenton's answer give a twist to the reader's desire: although the emotional connection is not complete, something new has happened between them. Although Miss Kenton does not know all that Stevens is feeling, she does understand what it means for him to knock, however tentatively, and she can feel the tenderness with which he treats her throughout the scene. Her tears, then, signify her own recognition that if he'd acted this way twenty years before, her life would be different. In that important respect, her knowledge catches up with ours.[61] □

The important similarity in the readings, they realise, is that in both, our hopes for Stevens are crushed and he is left heartbroken. Phelan and Martin do, however, find consolation for Stevens and readers in the novel's conclusion.[62]

Following the meeting with Kenton, Stevens meets a retired butler on the pier at Weymouth. It is a meeting that Phelan and Martin find highly unlikely, and one that highlights our role as readers, readers unsatisfied with Stevens's ending. Phelan and Martin suggest that the scene is 'apart' from other scenes in the novel, point out that it is told in the present tense, and argue that the conversation is unusually intimate for Stevens. Phelan and Martin connect these observations to their observation of Stevens's addresses to his narratee at various points in the novel[63] leading them to propose that the retired butler Stevens encounters 'is a figure of the narratee'.[64] The butler, 'minimally characterized', assumes the role of 'stand-in, first, for the authorial audience, and, second, for the flesh-and-blood readers'. Since the butler is standing in for us, we can feel some satisfaction when Stevens seems to take the advice the butler offers, advice that we readers might also like to offer.[65] Unfortunately, Phelan and Martin seem to have overlooked the novel's last paragraph in which Stevens looks forward not to the rest suggested by the retired butler but to getting back to the work of bantering, an important distinction. They do, however, point out that Stevens's newfound belief in bantering as the essential skill in establishing human warmth demonstrates that he still needs to improve his ability to share emotions: 'Bantering can convey warmth but it does not equal the warmth generated by the intimate and frank disclosure of thoughts and feelings among people who trust each other'.[66]

Like many readers, Phelan and Martin ultimately arrive at Ishiguro's humanity. Through Stevens's realisation of the need for human communication, such as bantering, Ishiguro illustrates the value of human warmth. As in the earlier novels, Ishiguro uses his protagonist to share 'his concerns about lives not lived, sacrifices made for the wrong reasons, whole dreams irredeemably lost'. Notably, however, it is a sharing that requires readers to work through Ishiguro's narrative strategies to read his characters more fully and to sort through their ethical dilemmas.[67]

Andrew Teverson: Acts of Reading

Taking a different focus, Andrew Teverson adopts a more specific stance to unreliable narration by examining occasions of reading within the novel to demonstrate that Ishiguro forces us to become good readers, so that we do not make the mistakes that Stevens makes. This is necessary, he argues, because in works such as Ishiguro's 'the reader is given greater freedom to interpret the situations for himself or herself: feeling textures, analysing moods and shaping events'.[68] He begins with two examples from the prologue: Kenton's letter and Stevens's reading of his travel guide. Stevens, at this early stage of the novel, reads Kenton's letter finding what he hopes to find:

■ He is, in this sense, a 'bad' reader, because he is not willing to use the text to get outside of himself and see things from another perspective, but only uses it to strengthen his own biases and confirm what he wants to believe.[69] □

Stevens first reads the travel guide, he claims, to see the country without having to travel it, but in particular, to get a sense of the place where Kenton has gone (*RD* 11–12). Teverson points out that

■ Stevens is reading this guide in an insincere manner by refusing to admit the true intentions behind his act of reading. Stevens is evidently motivated to read about Devon and Cornwall because he misses Miss Kenton and wants to feel closer to her. □

Stevens's travel guide is also significant because it is approximately twenty years out of date, and Teverson proposes that Stevens does not understand the changes that may have occurred in England:

■ The England of 'great houses' that Mrs. Symons' book reflects and that Stevens has founded his identity upon has passed away, and it has been replaced by an England characterized by men such as Harry Smith whose democratic political ideals are inimical to Stevens' way of life.[70] □

On a related note, Lord Darlington is also a bad reader.[71] He fakes reading the *Encyclopaedia Britannica*, (*RD* 60) an act of *not* reading which leads Teverson to two important notes on the history of this encyclopaedia: first, that it was founded for Brits to capture the immensity of British knowledge; and second, that by 1899 the encyclopaedia had been bought by Americans. To fake reading this encyclopaedia, then, signals Lord Darlington's lack of understanding of 'exactly what Britain has become or what its status in the world is. It also suggests that he is hiding behind outdated and unexamined notions of British ubiquity and British power'.[72]

Reading also provides one of the key moments of the novel: Kenton's interruption of Stevens while he reads a romantic novel. Kenton, Teverson proposes, has a vested interested in Stevens being a better reader. If he were a better reader, he would perhaps better understand her advances. Stevens does not comprehend the strange mood that ensues in this scene, and this failure leads Teverson to his larger point in this section: the reader of this novel is encouraged to 'abandon conventional generic expectations of satisfactory romantic outcomes'.[73] (It is a point that has been alluded to elsewhere: Jirgens reads the novel as parodying the eighteenth-century novel.[74] In a much earlier review, David Gurewich is surely closer to the right time period when he notes that the 'deliberate plotting is strictly in keeping with the nineteenth-century genre that Ishiguro studiously follows'.[75] Unfortunately, Gurewich misses out on Ishiguro's parodic intentions.) Similarly, if one were to understand Stevens as on a quest, the reader's expectations of this genre would be dashed as well.[76] The crushing of expectations is particularly important in Teverson's argument:

> ■ Because the meaning of Stevens' narrative [...] is only available to the reader if the reader *reads around* his words, and because the reader has to be prepared to eschew Stevens' narrative position in order to gain a greater perspective upon events, he or she is forced to adopt a much freer relationship with narratives that is not blindly dependant upon formulaic and generic precedents. As a result, he or she is much less likely to accept any narrative viewpoint as 'normal' or 'natural' but is more likely to interrogate and investigate narrative viewpoints to discover what kind of buried mythologies they contain. In addition, he or she is also less likely to believe that any singular perspective will suffice as a full explanation of events, but will conclude that events can only be explained in many different ways, from several different perspectives.[77] □

Ishiguro's playing with readers' expectations is part of a training of the reader to better understand his novel. Teverson demonstrates how his analysis of these small scenes of reading is tied to the novel's larger themes and interests. Notably, his argument for an ongoing investigation of narrative viewpoints arrives at a position similar to Wall's dismantling of authoritative accounts but by an entirely different route. It is a reading useful not only to Ishiguro scholars but to all aspiring literary scholars.

CONCLUSION

In his first novel with no reference to Japan, some reviewers found Ishiguro's past content and ethnicity impossible to resist. Fortunately, most reviewers were able to recognise the achievement *Remains* represents, and several initiated discussions on key moments and questions of the novel. Reviewers' praise of the novel's craft, for example, has been confirmed by excellent criticism such as Guth's teasing out of the novel's structure and language and work that reassesses and refines the concept of the unreliable narrator as in essays by Scanlan, Wall, and Phelan and Martin. Teverson not only demonstrates good scholarship in his tight analysis of moments of reading but also urges us to read better and provides some indication of the stakes involved in doing so. Issues such as the novel's approach to history and memory received little critical attention when *Remains* first appeared; however, as the next chapter will show, scholars have recently found these topics particularly fruitful.

CHAPTER FOUR

The Remains of the Day 2: Historical and Postcolonial Readings

Set in England in 1956 with flashbacks to a grand English estate in the years between World Wars One and Two and replete with appearances by key political figures of the time, *The Remains of the Day* plainly invites historical discussion. Several commentators have responded to this invitation, providing useful background information and interpretations that read the novel through a historical lens. This second chapter on the responses to *Remains* follows the trajectory of these readings, a trajectory that begins with the unsaid. As in *A Pale View of Hills*, a novel that despite the setting of its flashbacks amidst the aftermath of the atomic bombing of Nagasaki, mentions the bombing only twice, in *Remains*, the Suez Crisis, a major international conflict that dominated newspaper headlines in England, stays hidden in the background of the novel's fictional present, unnoticed by its first-person narrator, Stevens. The crisis erupted on 26 July 1956 when Egypt's President Nasser (1918–70), frustrated by the withdrawal of funding by Britain and the USA for the Aswan Dam, nationalised the Suez Canal, leading the USA and the co-owners of the canal, France and Britain, to first, impose economic sanctions, and shortly thereafter, conceive a plan for international control of the canal, which Nasser duly rejected. When further negotiations failed, France and Britain secretly backed an Israeli invasion of Egypt, which began on 29 October 1956, then joined the war themselves the next day. Although a military success, public condemnation of the war and American pressure rendered it a diplomatic failure, and on 9 January 1957, British Prime Minister Anthony Eden (1897–1977) resigned. John Sutherland's short chapter on the novel provides a clear and comprehensive explanation of this crisis and its timeframe. After outlining the Anglo-American context of the crisis, John P. McCombe, in a widely cited article, investigates the role of these strained tensions as they appear in the novel. Taking a much broader view of the novel's history,

Bo J. Ekelund's provocative, but flawed, reading focuses on the various genres that Ishiguro uses to allow Stevens to relate his narrative and argues, consequently, that the failure to understand the connotations that these genres import into the novel constitutes a misrecognition of the history portrayed in *Remains*. James Lang, in perhaps the most compelling of these readings, complicates historical interpretations by introducing the distinction between public and private histories and the theory of historical 'backshadowing'. Each of these readings, then, offers a unique perspective on the role of history in the novel, providing readers with a sense of the novel's rich historical texture.

Alongside these historical readings, postcolonial theorists have also found an entry point to readings of *Remains* in its historical elements and sought, with widely varying levels of success, to develop postcolonial analyses of the novel. In the two most useful such essays, Susie O'Brien addresses the contrast the novel establishes between the old values of England and the new values of the United States while Molly Westerman begins well by continuing the work done by narrative theorists but falters when she attempts to introduce a layer of postcolonial analysis. These theorists provide suggestive readings that occasionally advance the scholarship on *Remains*, but their failures in reading are equally suggestive, pointing as they do to the difficulty of interpreting Ishiguro free of preconceptions concerning his ethnicity.

HISTORICAL READINGS

John Sutherland, What Stevens Doesn't See

John Sutherland's short chapter from his collection, *Where Was Rebecca Shot?: Curiosities, Puzzles, and Conundrums in Modern Fiction* (1998), clearly details the connections between the Suez Crisis and Stevens's motoring trip. Sutherland works out the date of Stevens's trip by starting with the subtitle to the prologue which puts the date at July 1956, then adding the information in Stevens's first paragraph on the months of Farraday's proposed five-week trip, August and September, and finally, looking at the novel's end, subtracting the one week that Stevens tells us remains before Farraday returns: 'Stevens's six days, therefore, are at the end of August or the beginning of September, 1956.' Many have pointed out that England at this time was in the midst of the Suez Crisis and that Stevens's failure to mention these events is an unimaginable oversight, especially in light of his boasting in Moscombe of his connection with foreign affairs. Readers of Ishiguro's first two novels, however, might not be surprised by this oversight given Ishiguro's previous choices to set stories near or against large historical events and then not mention them. As Norman Page observes, he 'foregrounds private experience and allows domestic and even trivial events to represent, by synecdoche, historic happenings on a world stage'.[1] Having collated the details of the Suez Crisis, Sutherland observes an important irony:

> ■ Eden was driven in his mad Suez adventure by the demons of Munich – the sense that there must be no 'appeasement'. His favourite rallying call was that Nasser was Hitler all over again. But, unlike 1938, this was an occasion on which diplomacy, international co-operation – 'appeasement', if you like – was exactly the right policy to have adopted. Lord Darlington's policies of discussion and détente, so tragically wrong in the 1920s and 1930s, would have been precisely right in autumn 1956.[2] □

Sutherland does not follow up on this point, but it is important to note that his observation of Eden's motivation does help contextualise Darlington's error. Like Eden, Darlington was, according to Senator Lewis, 'decent, honest, well meaning' (*RD* 102). It is an important contextualisation that refutes the one-dimensional characterisations of those scholars who quickly categorise Lord Darlington a 'crypto Fascist'[3] without understanding the complexities of the situation and the benevolence behind Lord Darlington's motivation (*RD* 73–5, 87). For readers of Ishiguro, to assign characters to basic categories is to miss some further understanding of human character, an argument consistently illuminated by scholarship on Ishiguro's work.

John P. McCombe, 'Anglo-American Tensions'

Despite Ishiguro's insistence on his lack of interest 'in researching history books',[4] in this essay McCombe investigates Ishiguro's use of history, intending to 'explore the ways in which Stevens's journey illuminates a particularly tense moment in Anglo-American relations'. He reads 'the implications of the crisis for Britain's changing relations with the United States'[5] as similar to the changes that Stevens is going through and determines that 'Understanding the political and cultural tensions that existed at this time between Britain and America helps us to understand the ambivalence toward US political and cultural hegemony that is central to Ishiguro's narrative.'[6]

The strongest part of McCombe's paper is his connecting of events of the novel's fictive present to the Suez Crisis. After providing a considerable amount of background on the crisis, he summarises how the crisis illuminated Britain's geo-political standing:

> ■ Britain was far from a major player in the day's simmering Middle East tensions. Before the canal's nationalization, [...] both Egypt and Israel

were seeking to secure arms from abroad to prepare for a military showdown. When Egypt appealed to the US for weapons, it became increasingly clear that Britain was no longer the primary international force in the region. In the subsequent negotiations, the US attached conditions to the arms deal. Nasser, fearing that these terms would undermine his influence at home, rejected them and announced that Czechoslovakia would supply the necessary weapons. But this move jeopardized another arrangement with America: a loan to finance the Aswan Dam, which was designed to provide both electricity and irrigation to a massive and previously underdeveloped region of Egypt. When the US reneged on the loan, Britain also withdrew its financial support, and Egypt responded by dismissing British forces from the Suez region, compensating foreign canal shareholders at the current market price and nationalizing the canal.[7] □

McCombe adds to this characterisation of Britain's decline in power by turning to Prime Minister Anthony Eden, who came to power just as Farraday took over Darlington Hall in the spring of 1955. Moreover, Eden shares some similarities with Lord Darlington. As Sutherland pointed out earlier, the two are certainly put in comparable positions, a parallel McCombe develops:

■ In August 1956, Anthony Eden made a ministerial broadcast to the nation, the second ever televised, and his rhetorical appeal was grounded in two principal concerns [...]: the commercial importance of the canal to Britain and the dangers of appeasing 'dictators' such as Nasser. Ishiguro's novel cleverly highlights and juxtaposes two discourses of appeasement, one concerning a genuine threat in post-Weimar Germany and the other serving as a farcical justification for a British military action opposed by much of the world community in the mid-1950s.[8] □

Initially Eden was supported, support illuminated by one of the rural villagers in Tavistock who seeks confirmation from Stevens of the Prime Minister's good character (*RD* 188).[9] In fact, Eden even found support in the opposing Labour Party: Hugh Gaitskell (1906–63; Labour Party Leader 1955–63) 'compared Nasser to Mussolini and Hitler and invited comparisons with the 1936 German occupation of the Rhineland'. The American response, formulated with Dwight D. Eisenhower (1890–1969; US President 1953–61) campaigning for reelection on a platform of peace shortly after the Korean War (1950–3), was not so supportive: 'In *Remains*, at the time when Mr. Farraday departs for several weeks from his new English home – August and September 1956 – the US eschewed gunboat diplomacy and abandoned its longtime ally Britain.'[10] This abandonment led to charges of American self-interest, a response for which McCombe finds an

allusion in the novel's flashback to the conference: 'the American "duplic-
ity" during the Suez affair connects with the "deceitful" thinking of
the American senator, Lewis, whose desire to relax the terms of the
Versailles Treaty is related to the repayment of American war loans',[11]
an accusation made in the novel by the Frenchman Dupont (RD 101).

Finally, McCombe looks at the consequences of the Suez campaign,
calling it 'a military success but a political and economic disaster'.
Another strong connection to the novel is the portrayal of the British
government's decision-making. The government's attempt to deceive
the public, as well as the rest of the world, 'was apparent when British
explanations for the military strike shifted over time. Tory officials
initially claimed to have been merely separating Israel and Egypt and
denied any foreknowledge of the Israeli attack'.[12] McCombe quotes
historian T. O. Lloyd on the consequences:

■ This shows what was really to be condemned about the British
government's attitude toward Suez: it knew that what it was in fact doing –
going back into Egypt to recover control of the canal – could not be
defended in public but nevertheless it went ahead. As nobody outside the
country believed its story, it gained the discredit of being dishonest as well
as imperialist.[13] □

Although McCombe does not note it, this is one of the more menac-
ing parallels to the novel: an elite part of society attempts to make
decisions without going through the proper decision-making process.

Surprisingly, McCombe seems hard-pressed to provide evidence of
the anti-Americanism that he reads permeating the novel.[14] For example, McCombe offers Stevens's reaction to Farraday's desire for banter
as proof of anti-Americanism. He cites Stevens's preference for the
English landscape over that of Africa and America, then suggests it is
evidence of anti-Americanism (but not anti-Africanism). But readers
clearly need to question why incidences of anti-Americanism would
turn up in Stevens's writing. McCombe is asking us to accept that
Stevens, who McCombe describes as 'a walking anachronism',[15] and
who has not heard of the Suez Crisis, has been biased by the resulting
anti-American sentiments even though his journey is in late August
or early September 1956, the period during which those sentiments
based on the Suez Crisis are just being seeded, as McCombe himself
indicates.[16] If anti-Americanism is to show up in Stevens's fictive
present, it is most likely to do so without his conscious awareness. Not
surprisingly then, the only place that McCombe can find real anti-
Americanism is in the delegates' reaction to Mr. Lewis in March 1923,
not 1956. McCombe is more capable of demonstrating the opposite:
that Anthony Eden's successor Harold Macmillan (1894–1986; Prime

Minister 1957–63) understood the need to maintain strong diplomatic ties with the US.[17]

McCombe's essay usefully illuminates this historical background and social upheaval, 'And although Ishiguro might insist that he "wasn't so interested in history per se", those political, economic, and cultural changes are very clearly reflected in *The Remains of the Day*.'[18]

G. Bo Ekelund, 'Complicitous Genres'

G. Bo Ekelund examines the novel's history from a broader perspective. While he acknowledges that the narrative's primary effect is to reveal its characters, his interest is in 'the cultured forms' of the revealing. He questions, that is, the ideological implications of the genres used to convey the narrative, and argues that the failure to perceive the implications that these genres surreptitiously import into the novel constitutes readers' misrecognition of history. Thus, he intends to 'investigate how the novel deals with a complicity that is inherent in the very forms it relies upon for its disclosure of the theme'.[19]

Ekelund begins by pointing out the variety of genres that constitute *Remains*. Although the novel begins like a travelogue, the account is riddled with digressions that Ekelund finds substantive enough to constitute separate genres.[20] Ultimately, he distinguishes five genres: 'travelogue, political memoirs, country house romance (which, as we will see, is related to the detective genre), farce, and an essay on values'.[21] Each of these disparate genres that make up the whole of *Remains*, he contends, is complicit in 'a less visible history'.[22] Generic conventions have both histories and effects, and Ekelund's original contribution to the study of the novel is his teasing out of the ways that these histories and effects operate: for example,

■ The political memoir has not always and in every case sought to cover up crimes of omission or commission [...] but the particular political memoirs that belong to the range of historical references established in *Remains* did use the conventions to gloss over such misdeeds. □

The different genres also reinforce one another, their interrelationships preventing analysis of them from ever being 'given a comprehensive treatment at any one point. Rather, all issues are subject to the "drift" that takes us from one strand to another'. By understanding the novel 'as a literary construct rather than a psychological representation', Ekelund argues, the novel's reliance on what he calls the 'complicity of genres' becomes apparent.[23]

Ekelund is led to two points: first, 'although it is Stevens who introduces the narrative's themes, it is Ishiguro who manipulates the genres, which carry sets of meanings in themselves' (a point that overlooks that it is technically Stevens, not Ishiguro, who provides Stevens's account); second, 'these meanings are not easily controlled or automatically subverted by a strategy of generalized irony'.[24] Ekelund contests the postmodern commonplace 'that the undermining of genre is a structural function of any incorporation of other genres into the novel'.[25] Instead, he suggests that 'What remains unexposed by the irony of the narration [...] is the structural complicity of cultured forms that narrativize and defuse guilt even as they perform the service of exposing it.'[26] Consequently, 'the postmodern irony may even tend to conceal cultural patterns that may legitimately be held to account by a less postmodern sort of critique. The ironic, postmodern staging of history in my view amounts to a misrecognition of history'.[27]

Ekelund works through the different genres explaining how each works, how each carries 'particular burdens of meaning and subversion'. For example, elements of Stevens's narrative that mimic travel writing at the time imports another assumption:

■ that landscape is a key to national or regional values of a less concrete nature. The title of the work Stevens consults, *Mrs. Jane Symons's The Wonder of England,* echoes other titles that hold out to tourists the promise of having a share in the extraordinary properties of a nation or region. The English landscape comes to stand for Englishness.[28] □

As is often pointed out, Stevens's reading of England's greatness, undercut by his lack of political judgement and put up against the historical backdrop of the never-mentioned Suez crisis, is ironic. Although the travel narrative as a cultural form is not invoked ironically, it does expose the ironies of Stevens's story.[29]

The novel's invocation of political memoirs functions similarly in the novel. It reveals the irony of 'the servant of the public servant [...] shut off from the most important deliberations, not least by his own ignorance concerning the policies that are being deliberated'. That irony introduced by the political memoir aspect of the novel keeps readers focused on the irony portrayed and prevents them from investigating 'the way reader expectations are guided by the conventions established by such memoirs: the focus on pivotal moments, the character sketches of famous statesmen, the anecdotes, the post hoc [after the event] explanations for less successful initiatives'. Ekelund illuminates this point further by comparing *The Remains of the Day* to the memoirs of E. F. L. Wood, First Earl of Halifax (1881–1959), *The Fulness of Days* (1957). Not only are the titles similar, both mention numerous similar names, and in general, 'the novel captures a familiarity with the memoir genre'.[30] Ekelund's discussion of how Lord Halifax was viewed reveals generic conventions seen in *Remains*: 'The image of a wrongdoer despite himself, one caught up in a web of deceit of someone else's doing, good intentions paving roads to hell, are certainly part of Ishiguro's picture, and *Remains* actually reproduces this aspect of the political memoir genre.' The political memoir, Ekelund asserts, has a large role in the novel, one that illustrates his principle of genre complicity:

■ [T]he genre exists as a cultured form that, on entering the novel, brings a complicitous history in its baggage. This complicity relates to the historical theme of the novel in a general way, but in the genre predecessors that pertain to that epoch we can see a deeper involvement in the complicity of appeasement and, more importantly, a more profound investment in the formal maneuvers of evasion, distortion, and self-justification that characterize the genre.[31] □

The generic conventions of the political memoir have histories and effects that make it complicit in a history that is often obscured.

Several genres, in fact, are present in the novel – Ekelund also details the presence of farce and the detective story – but they are twisted by the presence of others. So, on the one hand we recognise their conventions, but on the other hand, we ignore their 'ideological premises, much the way Stevens, for the longest time, treats the implications of his history. The complicitous genres are servants of a plot whose effects of mastery absolutely depend on them while its recognition of guilt – private, individual, even sentimentalized – demands that they remain smoothed over by the surface discourse'.[32] Stevens continually returns to 'the essay on values' giving it a predominant position among the other genres. The novel gets either theoretical or practical whenever one of the other genres predominates:

■ On the level of genre orchestration, the discourse on professionalism installs itself whenever the sentimental romance threatens to take precedence. In terms of psychology, Stevens's need to explain the professional background for his actions so as not to be misunderstood by his narratee is also a need to defend himself from properly understanding his interest in the letter. In the complicity of genres, the essay on professional values dominates the other genres by its constant euphemization of other contents, its appropriation of other narrative energies.[33] □

Ekelund sees the novel as a discussion of values, as in Ono's discussion of his career, aesthetics, and politics in *An Artist of the Floating World*,

and the discussion on portering in *The Unconsoled*. The world of servants portrayed in *Remains* serves as a metaphor for the world of artists
and critics:

> ■ Stevens's meditations of the subject of greatness are certainly naïve,
> but at the same time they shrewdly point out the impasses of traditional
> accounts of literary value: the relativity of judgments made even within
> the profession itself, the tautological dead ends of inherent value (dignity
> reduced to its etymological root, worth; good literature proven by its com-
> plete literariness), and the problematic reliance on 'employers' – patrons,
> publishers, the general public. The attachment to progressive ends then
> appears a reasonable solution to Stevens's question. And there lies the
> rub, of course, since the relation of benevolent intention to ends is com-
> plicated by structures – 'unacknowledged conditions and unanticipated
> consequences' [in the terminology of the British sociologist Anthony
> Giddens (born 1938)].[34] □

The labelling of a quality as 'progressive' or 'moral', that is, requires
a lot of assumptions of what is progressive and moral, the sources of
which, Ekelund claims, are obscured.

Ekelund turns in the end to Ishiguro. While acknowledging
the widely held idea that Ishiguro's writing of a 'historiographical
metafiction' absolves him of complicity and that Ishiguro's use 'of
historically contaminated genres' dispels 'their ideological charge',[35]
Ekelund thinks that the question of complicity is not solved by
Ishiguro's subversion of genres. Although *Remains* transforms the
genres that have come before, the difference between Stevens and
the many servants previously depicted who manipulate their mas-
ters (many examples are given) troubles Ekelund. Consequently,
he is dissatisfied with the novel's politics: 'the theme of complicity
extends to the historical complicity of forms incorporated into the
novel, but as a novel it obliterates those concrete mediations of history in favor of the purely literary ironic subversity that is conferred
on postmodern fiction by default, thus keeping its revelations safely
within the profession.'[36]

Ultimately, Ekelund's examination is most valuable for its discussion
of the novel's mix of genres and the associations that the different
genres bring to readings of the novel. Ekelund fails, however, to separate the implied author, Ishiguro, from the narrator, Stevens. And this
failure leads him to see the mix of genres as a product of Ishiguro's
authorship rather than an aspect of Stevens's narration, a misattribution
that causes him to overlook the mix of genres as products of Stevens's
reading and imagination, as noted earlier by Andrew Teverson.

James M. Lang, 'Public Memory, Private History'

James M. Lang recognises the roles played by public and private histories, a preoccupation of Ishiguro's, Lang asserts, in each of Ishiguro's first four novels. It is a reading first proposed by Cynthia Wong ('The Shame of Memory') in her work on *A Pale View of Hills*. The truth these narrators discover,

> ■ is complicated by the self-interest of the narrators. As the narrators seek to reconstruct, through private memories, a public historical context which they have experienced, they do so at least in part in order to excuse their own behavior in that public context. Hence the recapturing of that 'missing version of the truth' must continually be tempered by the reader's awareness of the potential self-interests of the narrator.[37] □

Stevens, for example, attempts to justify and explain his loyalty to Lord Darlington: he 'struggles to reconcile his own private memories of Lord Darlington (and what seemed to Stevens, in historical context, as Darlington's noble and virtuous – though perhaps naive – intentions) with the subsequent public vilification of Darlington after the war'.[38] Lang acknowledges that conflicts between private memories and public understandings are always present in historical fiction, but argues that they are even more important in Ishiguro's work:

> ■ [T]hey explicitly thematize it and interrogate what the differences between public and private memories mean for our understanding of history itself. Most importantly, Ishiguro suggests that public historical accounts carry with them an inevitable tinge of determinism, one which private memories can help to resist.[39] □

Ishiguro foregrounds the small private history, and in doing so, demonstrates how readily it is able to revise the traditional grand narratives.

This foregrounding follows the changing focus of historiography in the twentieth century. Lang discerns a parallel between 'The competing strategies of historicization in *The Remains of the Day* – official, public, diplomatic history in contrast with the private memories of the diplomat's butler' and the change in historiography in the twentieth century, the drift 'away from the grand narratives and grand characters of earlier historiography toward the lives and experiences of the ordinary, the mundane, the marginalized, and the dispossessed'.[40] The new focus is on the everyday as in the method of Michel de Certeau (1925–86): '"metonymic" glimpses of ordinary men and women, snapshots which will illuminate the character of public and private life as narratives of military strategy and court intrigues and international diplomacy never could.' This focus is evident in the historical novels of the late twentieth century, which 'like their historiographical counterparts, reflect an interest in the ordinary and the dispossessed – those traditionally dispossessed by posterity, as well as those dispossessed materially and politically'.[41] Ishiguro's characters, Stevens especially, clearly fit such a description: not only is he dispossessed, he argues 'that individuals like himself are incapable of contributing intelligently to the governance of the country'.[42] Stevens, by virtue of his position, also allows us to see contrasting histories. Through him readers are offered two perspectives on the important political meetings at Darlington Hall:

■ [O]ne sketched by Stevens in his narration, and one laid out for the public record in the form of postwar perceptions of Darlington's role in the war. As readers of the novel, we receive a less full version of the public record, and that only through Stevens's reaction to it, but we see enough to understand how vastly different the two sets of historical accounts – Stevens's version and postwar accounts of Darlington's role – really are.[43] □

The contrast between public and private memories 'produces a feeling of unease in the reader, caught between conflicting sets of impulses: on the one hand, feeling narrative sympathy for Stevens, and the external and internal restraints imposed on his character; on the other, feeling repugnance at the thought of the willing association he and his employer made with the Nazis'.[44]

Most compellingly, Lang introduces into the discussion of *Remains* the concept of 'backshadowing' developed by Michael André Bernstein (born 1947). Bernstein defines 'backshadowing' as 'a kind of retroactive foreshadowing in which the shared knowledge of the outcome of a series of events by narrator and listener is used to judge the participants in those events as though they too should have known what was to come'.[45] Applied to this novel, Lang argues, 'backshadowing would critique Stevens and Darlington for not foreseeing the Holocaust in the 1930s, and consequently for facilitating dialogues with Nazis'.[46] Although historical backshadowing reflects a deterministic view of history, events could, of course, have turned out differently. The most important point here is that *Remains* offers a critique of backshadowing: 'in part by drawing out our sympathy for Stevens, and letting that sense of character identification interfere with our initial, perhaps thoughtless, urge to condemn him for his association with the Nazis'.[47]

The novel's appraisal of backshadowing is also effected in 'its insistent critique of the discourse of, in the novel's phrase, "turning points'". In contrast to the perception of turning points 'as marking a significant development or transformation', Lang proposes that retrospectively interpreted

> ■ Turning points are inseparable from backshadowing, because we can only identify moments of development or transformation in light of the narrative's next or final stages. The discourse of turning points, like the practice of backshadowing, encourages us to see history as a static field, one which we observe, rather than construct.[48] □

Thus we see Stevens attempting to reconcile the gaps, notably that between his perception of Darlington and the public's condemnation of him. Stevens 'focuses upon the admirable qualities of Lord Darlington's character: he is a gentleman, he has noble instincts, he feels compassion for a defeated foe.' This assessment is juxtaposed with 'the backshadowing critiques of Lord Darlington's behavior in this novel – namely, the criticisms of his behavior which stem from the postwar public knowledge of how events surrounding the war unfolded'.[49]

One of the ways that Stevens attempts to forge this reconciliation is in his reporting of Lord Darlington's conversations.[50] Consequently, readers should not be too surprised to read Stevens's depiction of 'Senator Lewis as a crass boor, while Lord Darlington has the grace and aplomb of a gentleman diplomat'. In contrast to Stevens's depiction, however, Cardinal confirms Lewis's description of the need for professional diplomats: 'Both [...] suggest that Lord Darlington is holding on to a lost historical ideal, one in which men of power can settle their international affairs with informal and honest deliberations.'[51] While Lord Darlington is portrayed espousing an idealism whose time has passed, Stevens, by providing the fuller context, enhances sympathy for Lord Darlington.

Stevens's project, however, clearly has its difficulties. The most obvious problem is Stevens's unreliability. As well, Stevens's recontextualisation can neither excuse nor justify Lord Darlington and himself for actions such as the dismissal of the two Jewish maids; 'while Stevens certainly helps us to construct a more accurate historical context for Darlington's decisions, he also is interested in excusing both Darlington and himself through that narrative construction'.[52] Alongside the story of the dismissal of the Jewish maids, Stevens points out how highly perceived Herr Ribbentrop was, and how he visited the very best houses: 'Stevens cleverly and explicitly links this critique of the forgetfulness of public memory, especially as it pertains to Ribbentrop's visits to Darlington manor, with the more sensitive issue of the dismissals of the Jewish girls.' Stevens, however, compromises the value of his history with 'His narrative unreliability and his evident interest in using his critique of backshadowing to justify his and Lord Darlington's actions'.[53]

The same problem complicates Stevens's discussion of 'turning points'. Stevens selects two: his performance at the conference the night his father died (RD 110), and his cancelling of the evening chats with Kenton (RD 175). These turning points, of course, 'are a narrative mechanism for imparting a coherent line of development to a sequence of events'.[54] We can only see turning points after the fact as Stevens himself acknowledges (RD 176). Once Stevens begins to understand how many different moments could serve as turning points, he sees the difficulty of his attempt to reconcile his private memories with the public:

■ While Stevens recognizes some truth in that grand narrative, he also wants to counter it with his personal narrative, one which resists the clumsy, broad brush strokes of collective history. [...] While Stevens's personal redescriptions of Lord Darlington do suggest convincingly that we should be cautious in simply ascribing Darlington his fixed place in the public account, they also give evidence – through the vehicle of the unreliable narrator – that might cause us to doubt the reliability of his own narrative.[55] □

Ishiguro has given the reader reason to question Stevens's memories. Stevens's account is undercut by his unreliability and his desire to exonerate Lord Darlington and himself. While the counterpoint to public memories that Stevens's private memories offer, through the 'countering of backshadowing and the retrospective illusion of fatality', give readers a more complete historical reading, Lang asserts that 'in order to contribute to a fuller understanding of the past, these memories must engage in dialogue with the grand narratives of public memory and history'.[56] The past is not the static field that public narratives would have us believe; consequently, Lang urges for an approach that would offer 'what Ishiguro has called [...] "the texture of memory"'.[57]

POSTCOLONIAL READINGS

Susie O'Brien, 'A New World Order'

Susie O'Brien begins her discussion of the politics of Remains by citing a 1994 GQ article by poet John Ash (born 1948) 'Stick It Up Howard's End' in which he develops a definition of Merchant Ivory Syndrome (MIS): 'a form of cultural necrophilia, a slavering delectation of things we are (or should be) well rid of' and a 'symptom of a lingering colonial mentality'.[58] Ash appears puzzled by the fact that American culture 'founded in opposition to the stodginess of British tradition' should be so infected, but O'Brien counters 'that the Merchant Ivory phenomenon has found a captive American audience not through the denial, but through the amplification of the mythic opposition'; that is, these films are popular because of the 'contrast to the image of a liberated, "postcolonial" America' that they provide.[59] She never supports her supposition about the response of American viewers, and although Farraday is of an earlier time, his fascination for genuine Englishness (*RD* 124) suggests the opposite, as O'Brien herself later notes.[60] Instead, she points out that the novel establishes a contrast between 'the colonial ambience' of British tradition and 'a liberated, "postcolonial" America'. Notably, she employs the language of postcolonial theory, but she is still writing about the contrast in the traditions of the two countries: that *Remains*

■ is thematically constructed around an opposition between what are commonly regarded as Victorian values – formality, repression, and self-effacement, summed up under the general heading of 'dignity' – and those associated with an idea of 'America' that has expanded, literally into a New World – freedom, nature, and individualism.[61] □

Ishiguro's claim that he intended to 'rework a particular myth about a certain kind of mythical England' adds support to O'Brien's argument.[62] O'Brien glosses Ishiguro's statement, connecting it to her position:

■ One significant strand of the myth which Ishiguro attempts to subvert is the notion of benevolent paternalism which was invoked to legitimate the deployment of power by the British ruling class, both at home and abroad. The coercive terms of this myth are exposed ironically through the narration of Stevens, whose failure to find personal fulfilment is directly proportional to his commitment to the ideal of the faithful servant.[63] □

While the novel reveals a society progressing towards new ideals, Stevens, much to his misfortune, remains focused on dignity. O'Brien cites the example of dignity in the story told by Stevens's father about the butler who, while working with his employer in India, calmly shot a tiger, a story she links with the story about Stevens's father serving a man responsible for the death of Stevens's brother, before concluding, 'The suggestion here, and throughout the rest of the novel, is that dignity, like the Empire it served, is predicated on surrendering the dictates of individual conscience and "natural" human feeling to the authority of a rigidly (if arbitrarily) stratified social hierarchy.' It is an opposition, O'Brien continues, based on traditional legitimisations of hierarchies: that is, the ways that one's social position is established as a given. O'Brien perceives this legitimisation of hierarchy as operating similarly in 'the model of filial devotion deployed by empire to mask the enforced servitude of its colonies', as well as in Stevens's devotion to Lord Darlington.[64]

Filial devotion, in turn, leads O'Brien to consider the odd relationship of Stevens and Stevens Sr. It is a devotion that leads Stevens to violate his professionalism when 'he colludes in the old man's attempts to conceal signs of his increasing disability from his employer',[65] an important qualification of Stevens's dedication to Lord Darlington that previous scholars have overlooked. While Stevens does, seemingly unconsciously, collude with his father, he remains reliant 'on an anachronistic social order' as evidenced in his adherence to 'the law of "natural" succession'. The shift of power from father to son is parallel, O'Brien argues, to the larger power shift in the novel, the shift of power from Lord Darlington to the American Senator Lewis who explains the shift in his postprandial speech on amateurs and professionals (*RD* 102). This speech is obviously prophetic in relation to the manipulation of Lord Darlington, but O'Brien sees it as prophesying, as well, the end of British colonialism: 'the decade following the war saw Britain divest itself of most of its colonies, a tangible acknowledgment of its diminished role on the world stage.' While this is true, Lewis does not suggest that British power will wane, so this reading of prophecy is somewhat ambitious. The more important prophetic element in the speech is surely in the yielding of Lord Darlington's 'code of honor [...] to a new professionalist ethic'. This professionalist ethic, O'Brien claims, reduces the value of 'knowing one's place', supplanting it with 'a new emphasis on social and economic freedom'.[66] Although she does not explain the logic of this chain whereby the adoption of a professionalist ethic leads to this emphasis on freedoms, her citing of Farraday's quite different approach to running Darlington Hall serves as a compelling example.

Stevens's steadfast cultivation of dignity gives way to the need to banter. But Stevens has trouble with this switch, seeing it as a duty rather than play and by the end imbuing it with gravity when he suggests it to himself and his readers as 'the key to human warmth' (*RD* 245). Citing the suggestion of Pico Iyer (born 1957), that 'Stevens's great tragedy lies in his inability to speak "the language of the world"',[67] O'Brien reconfigures Iyer's use of 'world' to mean 'the new world order represented by Farraday', a connotation not evident in Iyer's review. Nevertheless, for O'Brien, Farraday's penchant for bantering, now a trait of 'the new world order', becomes 'a liberation from the tyranny of dignity'. From this questionable manipulation of Iyer's quotation, O'Brien argues that in opposition to its playful and liberating qualities, bantering not only has rules but also often conceals power relations: 'almost invisible structures of class and gender privilege'.[68] The observation of this hierarchy clearly contradicts O'Brien's construal of New World values as associated with values such as 'freedom, nature, and individualism', but it is a contradiction of which she is seemingly unaware.[69] Regardless, her observation provides an extremely important and highly original contribution to the discussion of bantering that the novel has inspired.

O'Brien continues her attempt to outline the novel's portrayal of a contrast of values by examining the different conceptions of 'country' supported by Stevens and Farraday (*RD* 4): for Stevens it is a 'sociopolitical construction' composed of the nation's important people, but for Farraday, it refers to nature. However, it is Stevens's meeting with Harry Smith that most clearly establishes an opposition to Stevens's initial value system. Smith outlines dignity in a way diametrically opposed to Stevens's 'model of self-effacement'[70] by describing a 'democratic vision [that] invokes the possibility, indeed the urgency, of speaking for oneself'. Stevens is thereby exposed to the possibility of not living his life based on the narrative of another. As Iyer has pointed out, however, Stevens does not know 'the language of the world' and although Iyer has not precisely described the characteristics of this language, 'Stevens's failure to grasp them is implied through his consistent violation of the "natural" logic of the romance plot of the novel', violations that mark not only his failure, O'Brien claims, but also the failure of his 'social order'.[71] (Stevens's failure to adhere to the conventions of genre was noted in Rushdie's review[72] and later taken up by Teverson.[73]) Additionally, Stevens's failure has a larger sphere, 'for he violates the terms not only of the narrative of romance, but also of the narrative of *history*, whose consummation may be read in the vision of democracy described by Harry Smith' (O'Brien's emphasis).[74]

In the playing out of these contrasts, Stevens's romantic progress is tied to the progression of history in the novel because it is the latter which allows the expansion of individual freedom. His tie to politics, through his serving of Lord Darlington, on the other hand, is presented as a critical obstacle to romance because he is always focused on the important matters taking place in the house. O'Brien notes Stevens's constant deferrals of romance and proposes that their purpose

> ■ is to enhance the reader's desire that these global matters might be quickly dispensed with [...] so that Stevens and Miss Kenton can consummate their relationship. Thus the goals of freedom and individual

fulfilment, invoked as political no less than personal ideals, ultimately converge on a single romantic image against which the political recedes from view. □

Consequently, Farraday's new world is not characterised 'by universal participation in history' as proposed by Smith, but by history's end 'symbolized by the unlimited play (or banter) of human desire', its terms 'subordinated to and concealed within the universalist logic of a love story'.[75]

Molly Westerman, 'Splitting the Subject'

Molly Westerman begins with a provocative interpretation of the novel. She argues that Stevens's 'painful emotional life manifests itself in narrative pecularities – struggles on the page – which form not merely the narrative structure of the story but the story itself'.[76] It is a remarkable thesis that looks back to narratologist Kathleen Wall and to elements of the narrative: 'the novel's frame structure, implied audience(s), temporal structures, repetitions, inconsistencies, gaps, and ambiguities'. Westerman perceives Stevens's identification with Darlington Hall as both home and workplace as the source of his difficulties because with this identification he 'objectifies himself and internalizes a deep divide'. His identification, Westerman proposes, can be read in terms of Homi Bhabha's conception of stereotype so that England is signified 'by its "big houses" and their butlers', thereby stabilising both the social narrative and the narrative of Stevens's life. Consequently, by fixing Englishness in place and assigning butlers as markers for Englishness, Stevens devises a 'single identity category of "butler"' that allows him to understand his world. It is obviously a fragile endeavour buffeted by not only the outside world but also by his own desires, and his 'conspicuous failures pull reader and narrator out of the imaginary sense that all is well'. That 'these attempts and failures occur at the level of the text' is Westerman's starting point. She reiterates her argument: 'The attributes often taken as proof of Stevens's narrative unreliability are actually the very mode by which *The Remains of the Day* inscribes Stevens's ever-conflicted subject position and the processes through which it is created and maintained.'[77]

One of the questions the novel raises but that has not been addressed is the identity of Stevens's audience: to whom is he writing? Westerman begins to answer this question noting the unidentified 'you' to whom Stevens sometimes addresses his account and the incongruity of someone who professes the importance of maintaining the appearance of professionalism at all times 'unless completely alone' writing to a 'you' about 'his feelings, memories, and flaws'.[78]

The novel, she observes, does not explain how Stevens comes to be writing in this mode, one that in some respects recalls the style of a journal or diary, but in other ways, such as the heavy reliance on dialogue, resists this categorization. On the identity, or identities, of his audience, she fares slightly better: from Stevens's assumptions about their knowledge and interests, she deduces an audience 'of servants in big houses, arguably only butlers'.[79] His inclusion of his audience with himself while describing other nationalities, such as Americans, suggest his audience is, like himself, English. Much of his narrative, including his justifications for his actions, 'suggests that the text works at least in part as internal dialogue',[80] but at other moments, he refers to the audience in the plural. Furthermore, his refusal to name particular individuals because his audience might still remember them (*RD* 37) implies 'a close and contemporary audience beyond himself'.[81]

This inability to pin down the audience is in keeping with the other irresolvable aspects of the narrative in which 'Uncertainty, revision, pretending, and lying figure prominently'.[82] It is a claim that has been established in a variety of contexts, and here Westerman supports it by pointing to Stevens's lying to the Taylors and Harry Smith which he labels a 'misunderstanding' (*RD* 193), his inability to track down the source of a comment followed by his construction of a story with Lord Darlington as the source (*RD* 62), his denials of Lord Darlington (*RD* 120, 123) and the subsequent explanations (*RD* 125–6), and his eavesdropping and reporting on the conversation between M. Dupont and Senator Lewis (*RD* 94–6) followed by his strenuous disavowals of any 'subterfuge' on his part (*RD* 94). So prevalent are these anomalies that Westerman proposes they 'constitute the story',[83] and 'Stevens can be a reliable narrator of *that* story only by including contradiction'.[84] It is a point derived from Wall's assertion that unreliability 'saturates both form and content',[85] but Wall, who posits Stevens's inability to reconcile the conflicting values by which he wants to live as the source for his unreliability, does not, in Westerman's estimation, take the issue far enough. Consequently, Westerman pushes Wall's point about unreliability saturating 'form and content' further, arguing that 'What Stevens enacts on the page is a personal utterance. It is an expression of his life within, creating, and created by a symbolic structure – language, texts, mythology, an internalized father'[86] all in the midst of vast societal change.

The text itself is a demonstration of Stevens's working out of the conflicts in his life. It may appear that Stevens, the diligent worker pegged into place by 'his national identity and the service system (which masks and yet is part of the class system)',[87] endures no conflict of values. For example, Renata Salecl, using the terms Marxist philosopher Louis Althusser (1918–90) develops in 'Ideology and Ideological State Apparatuses', (1970) calls Stevens 'the prototype of an "ideological servant": he never questions his role in the machinery, he never opposes his boss even when he makes obvious mistakes, that is, he does not think but obeys'.[88] But Westerman asserts the contrary: 'as the world around him changes (over time and, as he travels, spatially), he begins to suspect the internal tensions and contradictions of his subjecthood. Stevens *does* think: he thinks every word of the text, and these tensions are the content of this novel.'[89] One of these tensions is Stevens's repeated return to the question of English greatness. Notably, he shifts abruptly from his extended description of the English landscape (*RD* 28–9) to the question of what constitutes a great butler (*RD* 29), a move that 'associates butlering (and himself) with Englishness'. Similarly, when Farraday remarks that Stevens has been unable to see the country and Stevens counters by stating that he has seen the country because he has worked in the houses where the greatest people in the land gathered, Stevens is investing butlers with the role of constructing and ordering 'the houses that take on the whole meaning of England'. Stevens's definition of Englishness, however, cannot be held together, and 'begins to split open at the level of the text' because, in his scheme, 'England is its "greatest ladies and gentleman", its ruling class, and at the same time England is butlering, dignity-as-obedience, knowing one's place'.[90] Similarly, Stevens must find a way to cover the disparity between the mythic father he has constructed, one who achieves dignity, in part, by serving a man responsible for the death of Stevens's older brother, and the real father with whom he has a difficult relationship.[91] As the world around him shifts, as portrayed in the fall of Lord Darlington and the purchase of Darlington Hall by a wealthy American, the contradictions cannot be maintained.

Stevens does, however, have patterns of thought that shield him from these contradictions, such as his 'amazing ability to think in binaries when he imagines the public and private spheres'.[92] Similarly, Stevens takes a kind of solace in the rigid structure of his professional life: 'He ignores and denies his emotional life almost out of existence. [...] Instead of telling himself that he fears the intimacy, risk, and change associated with acting on his desire, Stevens produces a mythology for his constraints and congratulates himself for his constancy to them.'[93] The freedom inherent in Stevens's first motoring trip, however, issues a substantial challenge to his mythology of constraint, one that the mythology cannot withstand, and the road to Kenton becomes a path of 'melancholy introspection'. It is an introspection that pierces the shield protecting him from his contradictions, leaving him scrambling for new armour:

■ He seems driven both to understand and to ignore his life's schisms. As changes of time, place, and employer disrupt the systems he has so carefully constructed, it becomes more difficult for Stevens to patch over the cracks as they widen, and he anxiously repeats, revises, and explains in excess.[94] □

This drive 'to understand and to ignore' structures the text that Stevens produces.

At this point, Westerman's essay falters. Having established Stevens's mindset, Westerman introduces Bhabha's concept of 'the stereotype', 'a complex, ambivalent, contradictory mode of representation, as anxious as it is assertive'[95] representing the situation in which 'the subject finds or recognizes itself through an image which is simultaneously alienating and hence potentially confrontational'.[96] Here she finds a connection between Bhabha's theorising on racial stereotype and the white English butler:

■ Stevens stereotypes *himself*, living on inertia, unable to progress toward any other goal. Even as he attempts to plant himself in a golden past and cling to its ethic of loyalty, Stevens almost compulsively paints for us a portrait of Darlington as political and moral failure ([*RD*] 146). He cannot control his language, his story, himself. Stevens attempts to make a manageable object of himself, to narrate himself into stillness, but the meaning of Stevens's image of himself slips constantly away, as in the chain self – Darlington Hall – England, and Stevens faces the image with identification and repulsion.[97] □

It is a reading that adds to the interpretation of the novel only in its final claim, but that claim remains unsupported by textual evidence. Westerman briefly recalls O'Brien's arguments for considering Stevens as colonised but only, in the first instance, to point out the fault in O'Brien's attempt to read the difficult relationship between Stevens Sr and Stevens as a metaphor for the strained relationship between the old power (Britain) and the new (U.S.A.). The metaphor breaks down, Westerman observes, when readers detect Stevens's own decline. Westerman agrees with O'Brien's argument that 'Stevens' first person account [sic][...] ironically comments on the pathology of colonial nostalgia without ever completely disavowing it',[98] but disagrees with how it does so. Rather than in 'a straightforward alignment of Stevens with American values', she perceives the account's comment on 'the pathology of colonial nostalgia' in the ambivalence Stevens expresses. In fact, part of this ambivalence is that Stevens *does* accept some American values, such as those that reject 'traditional British snobbery regarding recently acquired wealth'. Her attempt to demonstrate the opposing view, Stevens's support for the 'traditional British ideas of Empire', is less convincing.[99] It consists of citing Stevens's willingness to work for Mr George Ketteridge (a figure scholars have not identified) who despite his humble beginnings contributed 'to the future well-being of the empire' (*RD* 114), and connecting this use of the term 'empire' to a previous sentence to conclude that Stevens is proposing that 'To contribute to the British Empire is to "further [...] the progress of humanity"'.[100] Stevens, however, says no such thing: Westerman has simply spliced together quotations to make it appear so. In the previous sentence, which Westerman uses as the predicate of her conclusion, Stevens explains how his generation of butlers were ambitious to serve those 'furthering the progress of humanity' (*RD* 114). He offers George Ketteridge as an example of such a person. The quoted passages only prove that Stevens uses the term 'empire' according to its meaning at the time. While it is certainly possible to develop the claim that Stevens supports traditional British ideas about empire, Westerman does not do so here.

Westerman returns to O'Brien's noting of 'colonial nostalgia' to argue that it 'operates within the disorienting temporality of Stevens's unhomeliness'.[101] Again, the concept of 'unhomeliness' adds nothing to her argument: she is simply making the claim that Stevens moves quickly between the past and the present and in doing so uses a large variety, or 'multiplicity', of tenses. Unfortunately, she does not look at any specific instances where 'In less than a page, Stevens [...] narrates events of the five-minutes-ago past, the continuing present, and the decades-ago past', but to carry out such a detailed analysis of Stevens's use of tense would surely lead to interesting results. Instead, Westerman determines that Stevens attempts 'to stabilize his world': that is, to focus on the present and resist the allure of the past. And apparently, Westerman finds that he has been successful because she reads Stevens at the end of the novel as resolving the doubts he expresses about the value of his life's work by turning to bantering (*RD* 243): 'Bantering will fix everything. It will let the world make sense again. Ultimately, Stevens returns to the house and all it means to him, leaving his symbolic structures more or less in place.'[102] To suggest that Stevens's symbolic structure, what Westerman defined earlier as his 'language, texts, mythology, an internalized father' is unchanging is a shockingly erroneous assessment that she has not directly addressed and that has been repeatedly disproved by narratologists such as Deborah Guth, Kathleen Wall, and Westerman herself in the early stages of her paper.[103] Stevens's change is not linear, but he does change. His resolve to improve his bantering is worrying, but we need to note that it was inspired by Stevens's desire for 'human warmth', and that his trip is not yet over when he makes this resolution. Thus, the glaring mistake in Westerman's statement, 'Stevens returns to the house', becomes more than just a failure to attend accurately to the novel's plot: although viewers of the film see Stevens return home, readers of the novel do not, an important point briefly noted by Ryan Trimm[104] and developed by John Su.[105] The novel ends with Stevens on the pier contemplating going home the next day, but we cannot know that he does so, and if he does start the drive home, we cannot know where his thoughts on the drive will lead him. As Westerman previously argued, the trip has caused cracks to appear in his façade. The trip has led him to see aspects of himself that he had not seen before, and readers might take comfort in the hope that he will soon see that it is 'human warmth' rather than 'banter' that is the key. Ultimately, Westerman's response is valuable for the excellent analysis of narration that helps explain Stevens's text, but then, in the attempt to add a layer of postcolonial analysis, it loses its way.

CONCLUSION

The historical readings of *Remains* illuminate the novel's rich background to the point that one might begin to doubt the sincerity of Ishiguro's claim 'of not being so interested in the history per se'.[106] Most importantly, these studies provide an impetus for further study of this aspect of the novel. Specifically, while McCombe's noting of Anglo-American tensions is compelling, more work needs to be done to explicate more carefully the relationship between the two countries, especially as portrayed in the novel. On a related note, leaving aside the work on the Suez Crisis, there is a dearth of scholarship connecting *Remains* to its historical context: what connections exist between the historical settings of the novel, for example, 1956 England, and the novel? For instance, no one has addressed the questions that Mr Spenser puts to Stevens (*RD* 194–6). How prominent at the time were the issues on which he questions Stevens? Knowing whether or not Stevens knew, or could know, the answers to these questions plays a part in discussions of the reliability of the narration and the larger theme of 'having one's say'. Similarly, although Ekelund's work on genre is original and important, especially in his uncovering and analysis of Lord Halifax's memoir, it also suggests the further work required. Notably, Ekelund has overlooked that it is Stevens, not Ishiguro, who narrates this story, and thus it is Stevens's use of these various genres that demands attention. This qualification suggests the need for an investigation of Stevens's reading influences. At the very least, Ekelund has demonstrated the need for a closer look at the historical genres that constitute the novel. Lang's essay, finally, demonstrates the value of applying the methods of contemporary historiographers to the novel's detailed portrayal of history.

The postcolonial approaches to this novel, so far, are frustrating in that while they occasionally highlight useful interpretive angles, the insights that are gained are almost never a result of applying the methods of postcolonial theory but always by-products of the attempt to make the novel *fit* a postcolonial reading, a fit usually achieved by overlooking or manipulating the text. They are almost all readings that are, at their roots, not postcolonial at all but interpretations based on class, psychoanalysis, and narratology.

Against this mass of work that attempts to take Stevens as *like* a colonised subject, and Ishiguro as a postcolonial writer, it has seemingly been challenging for theorists to take the opposing view. While *Remains* does not seem a promising text for postcolonial analysis, if such a study is to be attempted, one possible issue to be addressed is the novel's portrayal of a society at the end of its imperial career. For example, what are the values that the world of Darlington Hall espouses which led to Britain's surrender of its colonies? Similarly, rather than taking Ishiguro as a postcolonial writer, he is surely better read as a British novelist (he has been a British citizen since 1982); however, even this conception of his identity is too simple. Although Ishiguro was never a citizen of a colonised country, he has emerged from a complex, albeit increasingly common, cultural position. He may be *most* firmly entrenched in the Western literary tradition, as evidenced by the clear influence on his work by writers such as Henry James and Anton Chekhov, and his continual play with forms of the Western literary tradition, such as his play here with the work of P.G. Wodehouse (1881–1975); however, his childhood, influenced by the idea of a future return to Japan, and his familiarity with Japanese film (best illuminated by Mason) and literature, as seen in his preface for Yasunari Kawabata's *Snow Country* and *Thousand Cranes*, reveals a complex identity that escapes easy categorisation. The vague label 'International' may well emerge as the most suitable description of Ishiguro as writer. But it is not only his influences that are varied: *Remains* has captured the attention of writers who have found a variety of applications for his work, and these applications, of the work of psychologist Daniel L. Schacter (born 1952), of philosopher John Stuart Mill (1806–73) and of legal theory, are the subject of the next chapter.

CHAPTER FIVE

The Remains of the Day 3: Interdisciplinary Approaches

While several scholars have used responses based on standard interpretive approaches, such as those resting on the narrative and historical elements of *Remains*, to extend readings of the novel in new directions, others have developed responses using interdisciplinary methods. In doing so, they not only add to our knowledge of the novel but also illuminate previously unforeseen sites for discussion. This final chapter on *Remains* traces these varied and compelling responses starting with the role of memory in the novel. Lillian Furst uses the anatomy of memory errors proposed by psychologist Daniel L. Schacter to power a useful investigation into problems in Stevens's narration resulting from his faulty memory. John J. Su, in one of the most penetrating readings of the novel, starts with a look at nostalgia but then investigates the novel's portrayal of a shift in *ethos* embodied in Stevens's journey.

Despite its tightly focused narrative, *Remains* has proven of immense interest to scholars concerned with applying socio-political approaches to the novel. In particular, Stevens's role as a butler has continually attracted notice. His reconciliation of dignity and service serves as a starting point for analyses of the decisions he has made and the principles that he has used to guide his career. Kwame Anthony Appiah finds Stevens's dignity problematic but ultimately uses the novel to make a case for the moral power of individualism. Likewise, David Medalie uses *Remains* to investigate the difficulty of discussions of dignity and to highlight the role that literature can serve in examining ethics. Finally, legal scholar Rob Atkinson compares Stevens's relationship with Lord Darlington to that of a lawyer and client to illustrate the ethical difficulties in serving, a comparison which not only supports the claim for the value of the novel in highlighting ethical issues but also adds valuable insight into Stevens's character and actions. It is an impressive range of response for what is, on its surface, the story of an aging butler reviewing key moments of his career during the course of a short motoring trip.

MEMORY AND NOSTALGIA

L. R. Furst, 'Memory's Fragile Power'

Lillian Furst approaches *Remains* by examining the flaws in Stevens's memory. Citing the work of psychologist Daniel L. Schacter on the imperfections of memory, Furst outlines seven specific problems: transience, absent-mindedness, blocking, misattribution, suggestibility, bias, and persistence.[1] Memory problems are frequently explored in literature, and works that employ a frame narrative pose particular problems: readers have no access to the real evidence, and must, therefore, consider the narrator's susceptibility to the flaws of memory. Although inconsistencies in the narrator's account alert the reader, they still create 'an uncertainty often amounting to unease', an unease that leaves readers 'unsure of the truth quotient of the events as recounted'.[2] The large amount of time between the fictive present of the frame and Stevens's flashbacks provides 'the opportunity for the exercise of memory and the revelation of its quintessential fragility'.[3]

Like all of Ishiguro's novels, *Remains* thematises memory by constantly reminding readers that the narrator is attempting to recall the past:

■ So a kind of chorus frames and punctuates the entire action, as memories are dredged up – vividly, tenuously, or perhaps mistakenly – in accordance with the fluctuations of the mind's fragile powers. Stevens not only constantly resorts to the words 'remember' and 'recall' but even elaborates on such moments [*RD* 73, 83, 96, 150, 151, 152, 165, 173].[4] □

Moreover, Stevens admits to memory problems: 'inadvertently, as it were, Stevens discloses chinks of uncertainty about some of his memories. The appearance of the particle "as" – "as I recall" ([*RD*] 145, 157) – insinuates a small amount of doubt.'[5] Elsewhere, Stevens plainly acknowledges his memory's limitations as when he admits, 'I cannot recall precisely what I said' (*RD* 167; see also 87, 95, 212). Furst acknowledges the ordinariness of an elderly man having trouble recalling events that occurred over thirty years ago before adding, 'these sporadic defects in Stevens's memory do have the effect of casting a shadow over what he claims to recall well. How much credence can be invested in his version of the happenings at Darlington Hall?' In *Remains* memories 'can never be wholly trusted; they may unexpectedly prove to be correct but generally are unmasked as patchy, partial, tainted – in short, shaped by at least some of Schacter's "sins"'.[6]

Furst matches Schacter's list of seven flaws of memory with Stevens's account. She begins with transience:

> ■ The interplay of sharp remembering with phases of fuzziness or forgetfulness reflects the oscillation between transience and persistence. Transience is most forcefully exemplified in the disjointed design [...] constructed as mosaics which the reader has to cobble together. The narration jumps disconcertingly from one period to another, drifting associatively in a discontinuous movement that is the literary correlative of a mental stream of consciousness. The effect is one of fragmentation, as the time-line leaps between the various segments of Stevens's memories.[7] □

Furst notes, however, that Stevens appears to have covered up much of the effect of transience on his memory, which 'may in itself be deceptive, a product of the patina of self-assurance and unremitting control of every situation that is the core of the professional profile he foregrounds'.[8]

Persistence, 'the continued graphic recall of salient experiences', plays a larger role in Stevens's memory, especially with regards to Darlington's important conference in 1923. Stevens continually foregrounds the significance of his position:

> ■ The entire sequence is carnivalesque in its indiscriminate jumbling of the trivial and the consequential, as well as the comic and the tragic. For it is not only time that is scrambled in this set of memories but also levels of significance. Stevens regards the luster of the silver as a matter of the utmost seriousness.[9] □

While Stevens introduces many names of important political figures of the time, he does so seemingly without any knowledge of their rank:

> ■ What persists in Stevens's memory is the importance of polishing the silver to perfection. An even more gross disproportion is evident in his recall of two problems that occur simultaneously on that evening: the blisters on the feet of M. Dupont, the cantankerous French delegate, and the death of [Stevens's] father. □

Furst sums up the effect of Stevens's recollections of the conference: 'persistence is allied to transience to a disturbing, indeed grotesque, extent.'[10]

Having discussed flaws of memory that 'define the incidence of memories', Furst turns to flaws that affect the content of memories. Stevens is particularly susceptible to bias and misattribution, 'perhaps because he has always worked in a group setting where he is likely to be exposed to and influenced by others' opinions'. While other critics have reflected at length on the content of Stevens's disquisitions on greatness, Furst investigates the context of Stevens's discussions, noting that he usually discusses it with his colleagues working at other homes, and proposes that they reveal his 'openness to suggestibility'. Furthermore, Stevens thinks about the great butlers of the time and compares himself to them:

■ He thereby engages in stereotyping and in what Schacter terms 'congruity bias' (*Seven Sins* 156) in his sustained endeavor to conform to the paradigm of the great butler. So his actions, his conduct, his bearing are all geared to his preconceived notion of how a great butler should behave.[11] □

Stevens's ideals, therefore, are based on 'memories of the past',[12] an 'exclusively retrospective posture'[13] that marks Stevens as somewhat of an anachronism, as heard, for example, in his stilted speech. Stevens is entrenched in the previous era, and for this reason, Furst asserts, is disoriented by Farraday's bantering (a rather simplistic explanation of a complex dynamic that includes class issues).[14]

While these examples of suggestibility indicate some of the lesser defects in the formation of the content of Stevens's memories, Furst turns 'to the graver [defect] of misattribution', by investigating Stevens's dismissal of two Jewish maids.[15] Here, 'misattribution takes the form of misinterpretation. His devotion to Lord Darlington is such that he fundamentally misinterprets his secret negotiations with the Germans.'[16] Again, however, Furst's analysis elides the depth of the situation, and one cannot help but wonder if Stevens can be said to do anything as active as 'interpret' in this situation.

Furst is on more solid ground when she considers the use that Stevens makes of blocking. For example, Stevens's memory is playing a trick on him by highlighting Dupont's blisters rather than his father's death, 'foregrounding the trivial as a self-protective means to displace the more grievous loss'.[17] Furst overlooks Stevens's failure to describe his emotional state accurately, a failure indicated by Lord Darlington and Cardinal's repeated questioning of his condition, 'Are you alright?'; but the scene does provide further support for Furst's position. Stevens's need for blocking is intensified by 'his active condoning of a course of action that has proven to be mistaken. His stance illustrates the possibility of our blindness to the fundamental truths of our lives'. There are, however, 'two mitigating factors for Stevens's behavior': ignorance of what's going on in the outside world[18] and total loyalty to Lord Darlington.[19] Despite confronting Darlington's misguided efforts (*RD* 201), Stevens 'has shut his mind, blocking out all that was uncomfortably in conflict with his creed of loyalty'. Eventually, however, readers find evidence of Stevens's denial of Lord Darlington: 'He conceals, even denies, his connection with him. However, in his heart of hearts he continues to try to defend him.'[20] When Stevens does try to defend him his rhetoric becomes 'overblown'. Stevens's memory problems also reveal themselves in his account of his relationship with Kenton. Again, blocking is a problem leading him to convince himself of the exclusively professional nature of their relationship and construe the nightly meetings over cocoa as work:

■ So he recalls her in a highly selective manner that repeatedly empha-sizes her outstanding competence as the housekeeper. […] In his concept of her, as of himself, he follows what Schacter calls a stere-otypical self-schema that privileges certain aspects to the exclusion of others. His perception of Miss Kenton is as biased as his attitude to Lord Darlington; in both instances he projects a unidimensional image. □

What Furst does not fully acknowledge is that if Stevens was blocking, the trip begins to chip away at this block. She does, however, observe that when Stevens rereads Kenton's letter, 'he begins to realize that his interpretation may be an exaggeration, an expression of what he wants to hear – in other words, misattribution, as indeed it turns out to be'.[21] But what Furst is describing here is really the correcting of a misattribution: an important point that complicates the static portrayal of memory that Furst has described.

Stevens also represses feelings for Kenton. After noting that Stevens has what might be called a 'fixation' on having her back to work for him, Furst proposes that

■ he adamantly represses any other way of thinking about her. This is where he repeats the position of victim and victimizer that he enacted toward Lord Darlington; by blocking the possibility of a human relation-ship between them, he shortchanges himself as well as Miss Kenton.[22] □

What is most clear about Stevens's memories is that 'the persistence and vividness of his memories of Miss Kenton more than twenty years after she has left Darlington Hall betray a deeper attachment than he can allow himself to acknowledge'.[23]

It is a useful reading although occasionally Furst's specific suggestions are clumsy or too simple. For example, she exaggerates when she characterises Stevens as *interpreting* Darlington's actions, which misconstrues Stevens's mindset of blind acceptance;[24] on Stevens's problems bantering with Farraday, she overlooks the class dynamic in play (as noted by O'Brien); she sees Stevens's failure to answer Mr Spenser as evidence of his limitations, but that scene is not nearly so straightforward (*RD* 194–6).[25] Her work here, however, is an excellent introduction to the topic. Perhaps most importantly, it provides a starting point for readings of Ishiguro's fiction based on cognitive poetics.

John J. Su, 'Refiguring National Character'

John J. Su's essay picks up several lines of argument previously suggested in an earlier essay by M. Griffith,[26] and subjects them to a more thorough investigation. His thoroughness leads to a powerful reading of nostalgia in *Remains* as essential in the forming of national character, but a national character that is refigured through the novel's dismantling of the *ethos* of expertise and the replacing of it with the interaction of conversation. Contrary to those who would emphasise irony but deny the nostalgia in *Remains*, Su wants to argue for nostalgia as *essential* in reenvisioning 'what constitutes "genuine" Englishness'. Through the contrast of the estate in its time of glory with its time of neglect, Ishiguro establishes 'an "originary" set of national ideals whose betrayal is indicated by the condition of the estate'.[27] In turn, this betrayal 'is specifically a moral failure' because national identity in the novel has been cast in ethical terms. Arguing that 'the diminished condition of the estate is taken to be emblematic of the nation as a whole', Su suggests that, like the estates, the English character 'has been neglected, uncultivated, and left to decay in the postwar period'.[28] The disappointment brought on by decline leads to 'an ethical critique that insists upon a return to the "true" *ethos* or spirit of nation. This *ethos*, however, is constituted in the process of remembering it'. Consequently, Su suggests 'that only in the midst of decline can the purportedly true ideals of Britain be recognized'. Nostalgia, then, is a crucial aspect of the novel's vision: articulating 'a vision of nation couched in terms of restoration through imagery and language resembling that employed by British postwar politicians'. But rather than the essentialist national identity aimed at in the nostalgia of Prime Minister Margaret Thatcher (born 1925; Prime Minister 1979–90), Ishiguro aims ' to redefine key terms associated with national character: dignity and greatness. This refiguration of national character is mapped spatially as the novel ultimately associates British *ethos* with the pier at Weymouth rather than with the estate'.[29]

While Ishiguro revives the estate novel tradition, he also worries about the ways nostalgia is used and rejects an essentialised national identity. In an interview, Ishiguro positions himself contra the 'enormous nostalgia industry' in Britain[30] and notes the ubiquitous use of nostalgia as a political tool, a note from which Su extrapolates Ishiguro's understanding 'that the myth of England was invoked to justify the Falklands Islands conflict [April–June 1982], union busting, and immigration quotas during the years leading up to the [novel's] publication'. Similarly, Thatcher's references to national 'greatness' in her 1979 campaign suggests that her use of 'greatness' 'represented a tacit but widely recognized code for white England' (a reading for which Su, unfortunately, offers no support).[31] By pairing Thatcher and Stevens's interest in the topic of 'greatness', Ishiguro compels readers to consider the speciousness of Thatcher's call by juxtaposing it with Stevens's fumblings with the topic. For example, the characteristics of this greatness, for Stevens, are merely 'the very *lack* of obvious drama or spectacle' in the landscape; consequently, 'In an unconsciously ironic deflation of Thatcherite rhetoric, Stevens defines greatness as a purely negative quality, a "lack".' In this way, Ishiguro allows readers to probe what is assumed in Thatcher's essentialisms, suggesting that they 'depend upon a tacit understanding that race, class, and religion define a set of unchanging characteristics'.[32] In *Remains*, for example, greatness reproduces and reinforces hierarchies based on class structures: 'virtue comes from serving the virtuous.' On the estate, however, all of the values are dependant on the ethical judgment 'of the "great gentlemen", creating a social hierarchy of experts and nonexperts, where the latter are understood to be dependent upon the former for ethical insight'.[33]

This idea, that on the estate, the top of the hierarchy has special expertise, is 'at the heart of the British estate novel'.[34] Lord Darlington, in fact, 'claims to speak on behalf of the nation, "We English"' (*RD* 87), and as Griffith points out, Darlington has definite antidemocratic leanings.[35] Furthermore, Darlington ties his perceived expertise to ethics by suggesting that those lacking it 'hinder ethics'. As Su observes, 'ethics becomes the final ground from which the privileged lay claim to their "entitlement" and assert their right to govern the nation'.[36] Clearly, *Remains* challenges these claims to ethical expertise. Most obviously, Darlington's expertise is cancelled by his blindness to events in Germany. Along with Senator Lewis's bungling of his mission with the French delegate, the novel presents a number of more mundane failures of expertise: the letdown of Stevens Sr who fails to live up to his reputation; the failure of the Hayes Society to provide a clear definition of 'greatness', rather than vague principles (to which one might add its failure to maintain its membership); and the disappointment of Stevens's guidebook, which in the pursuit of finding the beautiful and the moving, is always outdone by locals. The experts shun the opinions of the populace, but they fail, failures that connect the novel to its larger historical background, for during Stevens's trip, Prime Minister Eden with consultation of neither the public nor the majority of the parliament is pushing the country into the Suez Crisis.[37] The point is not that *Stevens's* journey parallels

Eden's; the point is that the story that Stevens tells about *Darlington*, the story of an expert perceiving himself above democracy and being led by that perception to betray the nation, parallels Eden's story. As Stevens gets closer to the Pier, he gets further from believing in Lord Darlington's expertise. The novel's rejection of expertise is embodied in the spatial shift of its action, and this move from estate to pier 'suggests an attempt on Ishiguro's part to relocate the *ethos* of England and to challenge the primacy of the estate as its representation'. Similarly, 'The revision of *ethos* depends upon the narration of personal disappointment [...] for the betrayal of trust drives Stevens to question ethical identity and thereby national identity.'[38] In this questioning, Stevens Sr's narrative, in which he tries 'to convey desired virtues', becomes crucial, for it is the role of his story that indicates the need to shift from a model based on expertise to one based on debate and discussion:

■ The absence of an essentialized ethical foundation or national character denies the basis of expertise – principles, such as national character, are *constituted* not given. Hence a story such as the one that Stevens's father tells acts as a proposition regarding the defining terms of moral and national character, a proposition that is subject to scrutiny, debate, and revision. In this sense, storytelling opens up the conversation on Englishness. □

With this change from relying on expertise to relying on storytelling and the discussion it initiates, the significance of the novel's key terms shift: 'greatness' and 'dignity' 'become thick ethical concepts that provide a common vocabulary for debating and envisioning ethical action. They remain crucial to a conception of *ethos* because they provide a basic vocabulary for conversations about ethics'. And as Stevens revises his terms, he revises 'his vision of ethical duties'. Retelling his father's story, he realises that his father was telling the story of the person that his father wanted to become: 'The nostalgia for ideal butlers felt by both Stevens and his father represents neither an unguarded praise of the past nor an unqualified sense of present decline; it seeks to project into the past particular characteristics that are longed for in the present'. What existed in the past could exist in an improved form in the future. Rather than relying blindly on 'expertise', Stevens is able to assess what was desirable in his father's generation and redefine 'the role inhabited by his father and himself'.[39] Notably, Su does not attempt to distinguish when Stevens enacts this shift. It appears that the shift is a part of the slow churning through the past that occupies Stevens over the course of his trip. Significantly, this conversation that challenges the assumptions of the estate can only come from outside of it. The hierarchy of the estate does not permit challenges: 'Within Darlington Hall, we see all manner of requests, demands, and inquiries made, but little conversation'. Su asserts that on the estate

■ conversation itself is structured and delimited so that it challenges neither the authority of nor the terms associated with *ethos*. It is only when Stevens steps outside of the estate space that his foundational premises are questioned and his own actions made to appear suspect.[40] □

One of the key conversations inspiring this questioning is Steven's discussion with Harry Smith. As has often been pointed out, Smith's ideas about dignity and freedom do 'not extend to those living in the colonies',[41] a limit that sets up an intriguing conundrum. On the one hand, Smith, in contrast to Stevens, serves as a figure of political advancement who attempts to draw more voices into the conversation. On the other hand, Smith espouses a retrograde opinion on the colonies and even looks to Stevens for his perceived expertise to counter Dr Carlisle's opinion on the matter. The seeming contradiction in Smith's politics surely suggests that the conversation Su has described has no scripted end; national character is not decided by an expert; but through 'ongoing conversation. And despite his unwillingness to heed the voices of working-class people, Stevens finds that his conversations with them alter his experience and understanding'.[42] With nostalgia as the impetus, conversations lead Stevens to reinterpret the past: 'Nostalgia guides Stevens to redefine his ethical concepts, for the act of concretely representing these concepts through stories begins a communicative circuit with an imagined audience that resists foreclosure by the teller.'[43] At the same time, however, the role of conversations in reproducing hierarchies of power must also be acknowledged, a caveat Susie O'Brien explains when she accurately determines the power relations concealed in bantering.[44] As well, the centrality of dignity 'to a British *ethos* is never disputed'. Smith demands 'a notion of Englishness that accommodates a wider class spectrum' but 'remains blind to his own racism toward colonized subjects'.[45] This blindness is crucial, because its diagnosis and remedy is in conversation, and it is the pier that the novel presents as 'the space most associated with the open interactions necessary for genuine conversation'. That the novel ends with Stevens on the pier, therefore, is a recognition of 'the need for, and inevitably of a shift in, representative national spaces'.[46]

Arguing for the close relationship of ethics and morals in the concept of the nation, Su asserts nationalism's need for collective imagination: 'Nationalisms depend upon the ability to merge nation and *ethos* in the collective imaginations of their putative communities.'

Although Ishiguro appeals to national character, it is a different national character than the one defined by Empire:

■ The image of the people collected together on the pier waiting for the lights to come on represents an imagined national community that preserves the incompatibilities and conflicts that are effaced or willfully forgotten in nationalistic narratives. This Britain might accommodate those who, like Ishiguro, sense themselves outside history. □

It is a reconfiguration expressed by the spatial terms the novel develops: 'the final pages concern not the English estate but the pier.'[47] England's future, in Su's reading, is not in the 'elitist isolation' of the estate: the future requires embracing what is met 'on the pier'. It is a vision that Su suggests 'lacks grandeur', but one that 'offers some future for a nation preoccupied with its own recent decline and concerned for what might constitute its own "remains of the day"'.[48]

THE DIGNITY OF SERVICE AND ITS ETHICAL DIMENSIONS

The novel's portrayal of service, one of its most prominent plot elements, has attracted a number of commentators working from a variety of angles. In particular, they have found Stevens's representation of professionalism and his attempts to define dignity particularly fruitful areas for discussion.

Kwame Anthony Appiah, 'The Moral Good of the Individual'

An analysis of the complexity of dignity in *Remains* appears in the middle of Kwame Anthony Appiah's 'Liberalism, Individuality, and Identity', an excellent essay that uses Stevens as an example in Appiah's attempt to understand the importance of individualism in liberalism. While reading Mill's *On Liberty* (1859), Appiah arrives at a distinction about the value of self-creation for the individual, proposing that 'reading Mill can lead you to think that sometimes something matters because someone has chosen to make a life in which it matters and that it would not matter if they had not chosen to make such a life'.[49] Citing Ishiguro's Stevens as an example, he offers a fuller understanding of Stevens's individuality and motivations.

Appiah first reveals the flaw in Stevens's attempt to find dignity. Stevens had found meaning in serving Lord Darlington because of the latter's public role, and now, under the employ of Farraday, Stevens finds meaning in improving his bantering skills. While readers might not see Stevens's desire to improve his bantering skills as valuable, it is a valuable pursuit for Stevens and fulfils his concern for dignity. Despite this value, however, Appiah perceives Stevens an example of a failed life because of his acceptance of servility, not the servility of a servant, but the servility of a slave: 'Servility isn't just happily earning your living by working for another; it's acting as an unfree person, a person whose will is somehow subjected to another's.' Appiah's distinction reveals one of the novel's difficulties because 'Ishiguro's depiction of Stevens obscures the relationship between dignity and individuality by conflating servant and slave; he prevents us from seeing that it is servility, not service, that is undignified.'[50]

Still, Appiah believes Stevens helps demonstrate his argument for the moral power of individualism. In fact, Stevens 'exemplifies it even though he doesn't himself believe in liberty, equality, and fraternity. Even someone as illiberal as Stevens, that is, demonstrates the power of individuality as an ideal'.[51] Individuality has value because it allows individuals the freedom 'to make the best of themselves, to cultivate their higher natures, and attain their full moral and aesthetic stature'.[52] Only by allowing individuals the freedom to follow their own plans do we get the best results from people. Consequently, when individuals, such as Stevens, choose a particular course for their lives, the key aspects of their course acquire value simply because those aspects represent part of a course the individuals have chosen to take. Appiah notes that this equation 'applies to Mr. Stevens even though he has chosen a life that makes sense only if dignity is not (as he wrongly believes) something everyone shares equally'.[53]

There are, Appiah acknowledges, two problems with this recommendation of individualism: the problems of the arbitrariness of basic choices and the unsociability of individualism. The first problem is that it is difficult to accept someone's individual choices if they have not thought out their path (as Mill would have expected). The important choices that constitute one's individuality should not be made arbitrarily. The second problem is that Mill's work here can lead to unattractive individualism: a life in which one's individualism overshadows family, friends, and public service, aspects of life that Mill would include in a plan of life, suggesting that 'self-cultivation and sociability are competing values, though each has its place'. Given the importance of these problems, Appiah sets out 'to reframe Mill's understanding' using Stevens as an example of how 'unsociability and arbitrariness need not be involved in self-creation'. Stevens has chosen to be a butler, a social role as Stevens asserts throughout the novel, and a role with an established tradition required by a particular element of society. It was not an arbitrary decision.[54]

Given the importance in this argument of Mill's idea about a 'plan of life', Appiah aims to define it more closely. It is not like an architect's blueprint. Instead he describes it as 'a set of distinctive organizing aims,

aims within which you can fit your daily choices and your long-term vision'.[55] This distinction leads Appiah to a crucial observation about Stevens: 'what structures his sense of his life is less like a blueprint and more like what we nowadays call an *identity*' (Appiah's emphasis).[56] Stevens's plan for his life is to inhabit fully his role as a butler. It is, Appiah asserts, his identity.

Individuality, Appiah concludes, is a requirement for a dignified human life: it 'gives us our dignity, our distinctive human worth'. It is a conclusion that provides readers with a better understanding of Stevens whose slave-like qualities can be disturbing. His failure of individualism exemplifies why we so value it, for 'his servility reflects false beliefs and leaves him unable (or dissuades him from trying) to understand Lord Darlington's attempts to reconcile the English government to Hitler'.[57]

David Medalie, Defining Dignity

In his investigation of representations of dignity in *Remains*, David Medalie attempts to trace the political and philosophical lineage of dignity breaking it into two categories: 'qualities which the personality reveals in and of itself' and the 'relationship between individuals with the obligations imposed by the recognition that other people have a right to dignity'.[58] Stevens provides an excellent example for exploring such complexities, for in *Remains* dignity 'is presented [...] neither as an uncomplicated virtue nor as an absolute good. Instead, it becomes a problem, a crisis and a site of contestation, implicated in and inseparable from awkward questions of power, race and class'.[59] Medalie quotes Aurel Kolnai's summary of the characteristics of Stevens's dignified character: 'composure, calmness, restraint, reserve, and emotions or passions subdued and securely controlled without being negated or dissolved',[60] but cites the further complication in the novel: the attempt to reconcile dignity with service and professional conduct. Stevens looks to the Hayes Society and their criteria for professionalism, the most important of which is that 'the applicant be possessed of a dignity in keeping with his position' (*RD* 33). For Stevens, the Society's depiction, with dignity as the mark distinguishing the great from the competent, is the defining description.

The Hayes Society's phrase 'in keeping with his position' is a particularly important part of Medalie's argument because it implies that

■ where servitude is concerned, there cannot be an intrinsic dignity, but only one that is maintained in the context of one's position and the conditions of service. From this perspective, dignity is neither inherent nor the mark of an evolved self; it emerges instead from the nexus of social relations, class and economics.[61] □

Dignity is not defined here for the free-acting individual. It can only be distinguished based on one's situation. Stevens reinforces this view when he asks and answers his question 'of what is "dignity" comprised?' (*RD* 33) His analysis reveals that he does not see dignity as innate, like a woman's beauty, but as something towards which one can strive. He contradicts himself, however, by arguing that only the English can summon up the necessary emotional restraint, an argument that depends on innateness. Medalie takes this one contradiction as proof 'that as a character [Stevens] is a site of contradiction'. Because he is inconsistent on this matter, 'by extension, it will not be possible to regard the kind of dignity he represents as free of contradiction'. Although the logic here is weak (one mistaken view does not prove that all of one's views are mistaken), Medalie's larger point illuminates the difficulty of discussing the role of dignity in the novel:

> ■ The butler holds within himself the problem of dignity, not its solution. The reason for this is that the 'egalitarian' ideal of dignity will of necessity always be compromised if the context in which dignity is obliged to express itself is not 'egalitarian' – and there is nothing remotely 'egalitarian' about Darlington Hall.[62] □

An important distinction here, however, is that Stevens does not narrate from Darlington Hall, and outside its walls Stevens encounters a new context.

In an earlier essay Michael Meyer has proposed that Stevens has dignity 'in accord with the complex social hierarchy of his day' and that Stevens fully inhabits his role.[63] Medalie, however, argues that Meyer does not grasp the complexity of the situation. Stevens's trip to the West Country, for example, renders Stevens out of place, and as a consequence, 'The novel shows what a great struggle it is for Stevens to remain within his own set of self-definitions, arising out of and in keeping with his position.'[64] Similarly, society has changed:

> ■ The changes in society which [Darlington Hall] represents make Stevens seem an anachronistic figure, and his conception of dignity begins to seem similarly anachronistic: this is because his definitions of self and service have not been flexible enough to adapt to 'the complex social hierarchy of his day.[65] □

And as the Harry Smith scene demonstrates, 'a complete identification of the man with the role that he plays requires the suppression of the critical faculty.'[66] Although Stevens initially believes that one cannot provide good service while questioning one's employer, he too eventually finds it impossible to suppress his critical faculty and believe that Lord Darlington did not make mistakes. By the end of the novel, he realises that at least Lord Darlington made his own mistakes, unlike himself. He has realised that dignity is comprised of something more. This outlining of the complications of dignity leads Medalie to conclude that dignity's status and meaning, continually influenced by ever-changing socio-political relations, is constantly changing. This change, moreover, is visible in the novel's presentation of 'two diametrically opposed conceptions'. On the one hand, the Hayes Society prescribes a dignity correlated to one's position (*RD* 33), and consequently, one's position in the social hierarchy. Directly opposed to this view is Harry Smith, urging political activism and social change, insisting that dignity is not the exclusive property of gentleman, but something for all (*RD* 186), and advocating dignity as 'an instrument in the quest for a free society'.[67] Smith's conception of dignity, however, is prescriptive rather than descriptive, and equality, Medalie observes, is not so easily achieved. Dignity, he concludes, is a concept available to 'disparate ideologies – one determined to keep things as they are, the other to change them for the better'. It is a protean concept, 'conservative or radical as the case may be, in the service of vastly discrepant moral and political imperatives'.[68] Medalie ends by suggesting that Stevens's response to Dr Carlisle – that dignity involves not taking off one's clothes in public (*RD* 210) – defines the concept so generally that it would meet with almost universal acceptance. However, once beyond such a simple conception of the term, consensus evaporates.[69]

Rob Atkinson, Stevens as Lawyer

Like Appiah and Medalie, Atkinson, writing for the *Yale Law Journal,* also uses *Remains*, but he uses it as an analogy rather than an example. In an early review, Gurewich notes that while the firing of the two Jewish maids is Lord Darlington's decision, 'it is Stevens who has to do the firing, and thus cross the line between the loyalty that is the essence of his professionalism and the blind obedience of "just following orders"'.[70] Atkinson picks up on this inequity. Having noted Stevens's attempts at professionalism, he evaluates the responses of Stevens and Kenton to Lord Darlington's command in order to explore their different moral stances through the lens of legal theory and, like Medalie, to cite the value of narrative in understanding ethical behaviour.

Lord Darlington's command to dismiss the Jewish housemaids leads to two responses: Stevens's compliance and Kenton's outrage (*RD* 24–5). Atkinson outlines the legal application: if Darlington had consulted his solicitor, the professional might have determined the dismissal to be legal but still repulsive, a situation which leads to an interesting ethical question: 'Should a professional always do all that the law allows, or should the professional recognize other constraints, particularly concerns for the welfare of third parties?' There are two broad schools of thought among legal scholars: one, exemplified by Stevens, that argues that anything within the limits of the law is permissible; and in contrast, a school, exemplified by Kenton, that argues that there are constraints, such as morality, other than what the law deems permissible that limit one's actions.[71] Both approaches lead to moral difficulty, and to further moral analysis.[72]

Atkinson evaluates the reactions of Stevens and Kenton by applying two contemporary theories of lawyer professionalism: Stevens's 'neutral partisanship' and Kenton's 'moral activism'. The former Atkinson defines as 'advancing client ends through all legal means, and with a maximum of personal determination, as long as the ends are within the letter of the law'. Because the theory is based on neutrality, the professional can keep personal opinions and morals separate from the client's case: even if the professional finds the client's proposed course distasteful, the professional need not feel morally accountable for fulfilling the duties of a professional.[73] This definition aptly describes Stevens's response to Lord Darlington's command (RD 146–7).

Although this approach might seem to introduce the notion of moral scepticism – the position that no one has moral knowledge, or more extremely, that moral knowledge is impossible – Stevens is not exactly a moral sceptic. His reaction is based on his understanding of his role in the house and his belief that Lord Darlington knows best: he believes that people in his position are not capable of understanding the subtleties of such matters, a belief that he expresses to Kenton in what she clearly takes as a defence of Darlington (RD 149), and one that he illustrates in his failure to answer Mr Spencer (RD 194–6). Stevens focuses his attention on his clearly defined duties. Here Atkinson is again able to chart a similarity between Stevens and the legal profession because adherents of the neutral partisanship theory argue that lawyers need to allow their clients to be able to pursue their own ends: the lawyer advises the client and helps untangle the law's complexities. Not to explain the client's full range of legal options would be to assume the role of judge and jury.[74]

In contrast to Stevens's 'neutral partisanship' is Kenton's 'moral activism'. Atkinson provides a thorough description of the tenor of her response to the dismissal of the Jewish housemaids: 'She recoils from the technocratic, antiseptic attitude of Stevens.' While Stevens distances himself from the girls with the terms 'contracts' and 'employees', Kenton uses their first names and describes her personal relationship with the girls. Rather than avoid her values or dismiss them as 'foibles and sentiments', she indicates her outrage and the obvious immorality of the dismissals (RD 149). What Atkinson finds most significant is that she does not hide behind her position but assumes moral responsibility for her part in the situation. Unlike Stevens, she cannot support an immoral action by adopting a professional neutrality when she herself opposes that action. Kenton acts in agreement with critics of neutral partisanship who believe that 'lawyers should not merely decline to assist in such acts; they should also act affirmatively to promote justice in their representation of private clients'.[75]

Moral activists find support in societal and professional norms. Most basically, they support their position by looking to ordinary morality: for example, Kenton's assertion that the dismissal would be simply wrong. Knowing that society has moral norms, such as 'our common obligation not to harm the innocent', professionals incorporate this morality into their professional *ethos*. Kenton can also draw on norms of her profession, which Atkinson discerns in her defence of the girls. They have demonstrated what Kenton sees as the important attributes required for the position: they are loyal, honest, and skilled.[76] Consequently, dismissing them would violate the norms of the profession.

There is, Atkinson proposes, an alternative to this rather bleak binary: they could raise their moral concerns with the client in an effort to persuade him to follow the moral path.[77] Neither Stevens nor Kenton has done so; in fact, not only do they fail to talk to Lord Darlington, they also fail to talk to each other, an example of moral isolationism, the view that we ought not to be morally concerned with people outside our immediate group. Had they been able to overcome their moral isolationism, Stevens may have been able to lead Darlington to a much better outcome. Furthermore, it could be seen as one of the professional's duties to raise concerns, a particularly intriguing point since Darlington later realised his error in ordering the dismissal. In fact, Stevens may be guilty of an oversight here, for had he remarked on his concerns, perhaps Lord Darlington would have seen his error earlier.[78]

Atkinson proposes that two dialogues are missing from this situation: the dialogue between professionals and principals, such as Stevens and Lord Darlington, and the dialogue between professionals and their friends, such as Stevens and Kenton. To understand better what such dialogues might reveal and the ethical imperative of having such discussions, Atkinson takes the highly unusual critical step of providing hypothetical dialogues. He suggests that Stevens might respond to Lord Darlington by indicating Stevens's duty to dismissed employees to provide feedback so that they might better themselves and his duty to his employer to ensure that others do not think his employer has acted improperly. Even further, Stevens could suggest that the dismissals seem contrary to the English sense of fair play.[79] Atkinson sees the possibility of success in his hypothetical dialogue, in part, because it rests upon the importance of fair play, a lesson that Darlington himself cites in his criticism of the treatment of Germany following World War One. Furthermore, it was possible for servants to voice opinion as seen in the story of Stevens's father who refused 'to chauffeur a carload of his employer's rowdy house guests after their drunken insults blundered onto the character of their host'.[80]

Turning to the dialogue that might have occurred between Stevens and Kenton, Atkinson notes that Kenton was trying to develop a deeper dialogue with Stevens, and had Stevens been open to her, she might have helped him develop a proper response to Lord Darlington. A discussion between Kenton and Stevens may also have helped develop solidarity between the two. Consequently, in conjunction with keeping Stevens and Darlington from moral error, it may have lightened the moral burdens each had to carry: 'it might have helped [Stevens] bear a potentially greater burden: not the burden of choosing the lesser evil with open eyes, but that of making a serious moral misjudgment about the right thing to do.'[81]

Stevens fails to have such a dialogue with Lord Darlington, Atkinson proposes, because of his flawed notion of dignity. Stevens's dignity, he suggests, has two aspects: the substantive – whom and what one serves – and the procedural – how one performs. The substantive aspect of his dignity fails Stevens because he conceives dignity to mean that he must defer to his employer's wishes, a conception described by the neutral partisanship model of legal theory. Atkinson qualifies this point by discerning that neutral partisanship does not prohibit 'bringing moral qualms to the employer's attention'.[82] It is the procedural aspect of his notion of dignity that is the real problem: 'Stevens tends to conflate expressing outrage with being outrageous.' He takes pride in his success at concealing his reaction and in his concise discussion of the incident with Kenton although he does not seem to comprehend what the concealment and concision will cost the three of them.[83] Furthermore, the dialogue that Atkinson proposes would not have meant acting without dignity.

Kenton fails to establish a dialogue with Stevens because Stevens resists a life outside of his work: he appears to believe that a fuller personal life has nothing to offer him. Stevens's keen desire for professionalism leads him to limit discussions of professional values to high levels of generality, to resist Kenton's attempts to shift their talks from the professional to the personal, and to leave his trip towards self-discovery until late in life.[84] Stevens acts, Atkinson proposes, based on the model offered by his father. Theirs is a relationship exemplified by the episode in which Stevens has to reduce his father's household duties (RD 64–6), a terse exchange that seems to exclude human emotion and in which the son observes the father as professional rather than person.[85] For Atkinson, this scene answers Kenton's pleading question, 'Why, Mr. Stevens, why, why, why do you always have to *pretend*?' (*RD* 154: Ishiguro's emphasis). Stevens follows the paternal example despite its flawed insistence on the denial of a person inside the professional. His belief in 'the suit' of professionalism denies him the life and conversations of a person, dialogues that might save both his personal and professional lives.[86]

In contrast to the general theorising of his generation, Stevens notes the stories of professional excellence that his father's generation told. But, Atkinson argues, Stevens's story demonstrates the need for both types of discussion. Atkinson concludes, therefore, by arguing for the importance of stories in the study of virtue. Stories, as this analysis of the novel suggests, give their readers and listeners an opportunity to work through these difficult ethical issues. Moreover, 'Stevens's signal lapse was his failure to interpret adequately the stories from which he derived his fundamental values, to apply those values in the moral dilemma he faced, and to see how they fit into a coherent whole, a viable whole – in a word, a life'.[87] Atkinson sees the importance of our stories in figuring out how to live.

CONCLUSION

The varied and thorough response to *Remains* instigates a rewarding questioning of the novel on several fronts. Furst's work on memory recommends itself not only by contributing to the understanding of the novel's narration, but also by suggesting an original interpretive path. Her essay illustrates the value of sifting through Stevens's cognitive processes to understand better his decision-making patterns and motivations. John J. Su also provides a starting point for further research. His argument that the novel illustrates a switch from an expert-based *ethos* to one based on conversation is provocative and recommends, among other lines of inquiry, the value of close textual analysis of the role, context, and substance of the novel's dialogue. Responses to the novel's portrayal of service have also been suggestive. While Appiah and Medalie provide crucial groundwork studies on the portrayal of dignity in *Remains* and Atkinson demonstrates the value of literature in understanding legal theory, all three readings suggest that research still needs to be done in narrative ethics. Although the readings discussed in this chapter use varied interpretive lenses, they can be seen to coalesce in the larger issue, the dominant issue of Ishiguro's *oeuvre*, of how we live our lives. They investigate the institutions and social structures that govern our lives, and the mental constructs we employ in our ongoing attempts to negotiate life's hardships. In his next novel, *The Unconsoled*, Ishiguro's concern with how we live our lives remains, but his investigation of how to represent our mental constructs takes a fascinating leap.

CHAPTER SIX

Who Are *The Unconsoled* (1995) and Where Do They Live?

In his fourth novel, *The Unconsoled* (1995), Ishiguro attempts a work that at first glance differs from his earlier novels in almost every conceivable respect. Ostensibly, it recounts the visit of an internationally acclaimed concert pianist named Ryder (as with Stevens in *The Remains of the Day*, his first name is never given) who is visiting a city (that is not named but seems to be somewhere in the middle of Europe) to perform at a concert aimed at resolving a cultural crisis in the city (although the specifics of that crisis are never made clear). The specific details that so carefully located earlier novels in time and place are gone, but Ishiguro's precise prose and keen ability to capture details are not. The switch in style was a deliberate artistic choice. Frustrated by critics who attempted to categorise him as a realist and who continually sought to ground his novels in their historical context, he introduced a radically new structure that has had a sharply polarising effect on readers: some find the novel baffling and boring while others have recognised its unique contribution to the representation of consciousness. Almost as long as his three previous novels combined and much more challenging to read, *The Unconsoled* encountered readers unable or unwilling to follow Ishiguro's new path. Many tried simply to link the novel's style to Franz Kafka (1883–1924) or Samuel Beckett (1906–89). Other critics have discussed the novel's dream-like qualities and its playful representation of space and place. This chapter reviews the novel's critical reception before moving on to describe the structural components that critics have discerned, to investigate Ishiguro's experimental form, and to try to answer the question on the minds of most readers at the end of the novel: who are the unconsoled?

THE INITIAL RESPONSE

Critics who expected a novel similar to Ishiguro's three previous novels were often disappointed by *The Unconsoled.* Brian Shaffer, in the middle of an excellent summary of the response to the novel suggests, 'A probable reason for this cooler critical reception is that the book follows in the tradition of the "baggy monster" school of novel-writing while the earlier three books are far shorter, far less "messy" novels.'[1] Ishiguro, in 1989, describes wanting to move from Chekhov to Fyodor Dostoevsky,[2] while philosopher Richard Rorty (1931–2007) reads the novel as representing a change from James to Kafka.[3] Despite Ishiguro's reference to Dostoevsky, there has been no published work that considers this influence; instead, it is the comparison to Kafka that reviewers and scholars have seized upon.

Many critics were quick to indicate the challenges they found. Pico Iyer describes it as 'a book that passes on the bewilderment it seeks to portray';[4] Alan Wall calls the novel 'a phantasmagoria of frustration, irritation, and presumption';[5] and Rorty sees that Ishiguro is 'trying to do something nobody has ever done before'[6] but does not appear to know what *has* been attempted or achieved. Interestingly, the reviews started to become a subject of other reviews and very soon the mixed response to the novel became a standard part of any new review or critical article. Just six weeks after the first reviews appeared, Booker Prize-winning novelist Anita Brookner (born 1928) summed up the response finding in it a demonstration of 'The short attention span of readers and critics in the electronic age' suffused with 'impatience and bafflement, as if the task of reading the novel were too onerous, too "boring"'.[7] Unexpressed but readily apparent in Brookner's comment is that it is a difficult novel to read, a point on which there is considerable agreement. Richard Eder writes that 'It is a book that is not given but has to be earned.'[8] 'Frustration' is another word that appears repeatedly throughout the reviews. Lucy Hughes-Hallet captures just a faint sense of the emotional stir when she writes, 'The form, a story of a man repeatedly failing to do what he sets out to do, is as frustrating for the reader as it is for the fictional character.'[9] Other readers would surely agree with Charlotte Innes's diagnosis: that the novel 'feels like a nervous breakdown waiting to happen'.[10]

Confronted with such difficulty, many reviewers did not even try to understand the new style that this novel offers. Negative reviews of the novel often reveal a critic who has not understood the radical newness of Ishiguro's project. Wall appears to believe that the novel must either subscribe to the tenets of realism or Kafka or Beckett: he refuses to see that Ishiguro is attempting a representation of consciousness different from fiction written before.[11] Many seem simply to want the Ishiguro they had grown to know, and perhaps appreciate, in the first three novels. Few reviewers reveal this atavism as thoroughly as novelist Amit Chaudhuri (born 1962). Chaudhuri focuses primarily on Ishiguro's three earlier novels, which he obviously appreciated, but finds *The Unconsoled* lacking, at least in part because it is 'ahistorical': 'it is a novel without any discernible cultural social or historical determinants (surely fatal to any novel).' Similarly, he finds an absence of 'compelling women characters'. He is content to point to some 'echoes of Kafka' but fails to acknowledge the technical challenge that Ishiguro has set for himself.[12] Chaudhuri obviously wants a particular kind of novel and, consequently, cannot accept this novel for what it is. Film critic Stanley Kauffmann (born 1916) begins his review by explaining why he so highly values Ishiguro's first three works before noting some of *The Unconsoled*'s techniques, some of its images, and its apparent debt to Kafka. Kauffmann, however, laments the new technique Ishiguro has used to portray his characters, dismissing it as lacking in character development, leaving readers with only 'charade figures'.[13] In his perceptive review, cultural historian Louis Menand (born 1952), proposes that 'If no one had ever heard of Kazuo Ishiguro, if he had never published a word before, it would have been much easier to see how singular the vision behind *The Unconsoled* really is.'[14]

One of the most strident of the early critics is literary critic and novelist James Wood (born 1965) who opens his review, 'Kazuo Ishiguro's new novel has the virtue of being unlike anything else; it invents its own category of badness' and goes on to call the novel 'ponderous, empty, and generally unaffecting'.[15] His criticisms, however, reveal his refusal to read the novel on its own terms, as this novel and not some other. Like Chaudhuri and Wall, Wood complains that though the book has Kafkaesque elements, Ryder, the protagonist of *The Unconsoled* who is known only by his family name, behaves differently than Kafka's Joseph K. Wood seems to ignore the possibility that the novel might have similarities to Kafka but still be attempting a different project. He expresses how difficult he found the novel to read, although he did not, evidently, read too carefully: he notes that Brodsky uses an ironing board as a baton, but this is not so. (He uses it as a crutch).[16] It may seem like a small slip, but if we observe that Brodsky's ordeal with the ironing board, necessitated by a recent amputation, is an episode that spans three pages and a range of emotions, Wood's careless misreading begins to look like a plain refusal to adjust his reading to fit the novel.

These reviews point to one of several places in the novel where the novel seems to comment on itself. Innes remarks that 'people cannot handle complexity',[17] an observation based on the novel's reception but a judgement that can be matched with Christoff's remark on the townspeople of the unidentified city in which the novel is located: 'The people here, they were out of their depth, they were breaking down. People were afraid, they felt they were slipping out of control' (*Unc* 190), a remark that reads rather like a comment on some readers. Many, however, did see the challenge that Ishiguro was taking on and attempted to understand the project for the original venture that it is. Writer Brooke Allen (born 1956) writes that 'Its melding of conscious and subconscious is effective, and the novel is entirely fresh, with no old-fashioned surrealism or Freudian cliché.'[18] Similarly, novelist Rachel Cusk (born 1967) describes knowing that Ishiguro has undertaken something interesting, which 'achieves coherence only at such great length that the novel's remarkably sustained and complex inner order and direction remain opaque for an inordinate amount of the time required to read it'. While praising its originality, 'the scope of its intentions', and its precision, Cusk also sees that 'it is above all a book devoted to the human heart'.[19]

THE WORLD OF *THE UNCONSOLED*

Some reviewers proclaim the originality of the difficult form that Ishiguro has created, what Shaffer calls Ishiguro's stretching of the conventions of prose fiction.[20] Their reviews also reveal some of the 'quirky' spatial world[21] or what Menand describes as the strange 'spatiotemporal medium' of this novel.[22] Vince Passano, in one of the most insightful reviews, perhaps sums up the novel's world best when he writes, with some exaggeration, there is 'no basis in anything resembling real time, real behaviour, or real manner'.[23] Passano's observation is based on the novel's obsessive play with space and time. Ishiguro sends Ryder out of the city and through the countryside and allows him to come back through a door that inevitably leads to the next place he needs to go, the atrium of the hotel, or the back of the café where Boris, who may or may not be his son, is waiting for him. Lewis attempts to read the novel's playing with space through psychoanalysis and art, reading the play as a displacement of space and seeing in the town's geography 'a painting by Giorgio di Chirico [1888–1978] and the impossible geography of a print by M.C. Escher [1898–1972]'.[24] Wong turns to science to describe this world, writing that Ishiguro manipulates 'reality by altering a physics of space'.[25] Conceptions of space are further complicated when Ryder is able to see and hear things outside his range. He is able to put himself in the minds and spaces of others. For example, as several reviewers have noted, Ryder occasionally knows more than a first-person narrator should,[26] or as Wong writes, he can 'read minds',[27] a point reiterated by Pierre François.[28]

He sees things outside his perceptual range. Similarly, 'sometimes Ryder becomes privy to what other people are saying about him.'[29] Lewis too notes Ryder's unusual extrasensory perceptions and offers the example of Ryder accompanying Stephan Hoffman to the home of Miss Collins: Ryder waits inside the car but is still able to hear the conversation that takes place inside the home and evaluate the thoughts and feelings of the participants (*Unc* 56–61).[30]

Michael Wood has identified three features of this 'strange territory' that Ishiguro has created.[31] Wood points out the tendency of characters to appear at the moment that Ryder thinks of them or that they are mentioned and uses the appearance of Miss Stratmann in the elevator to support his claim (*Unc* 9). Second, Wood notes that everyone Ryder meets begins their encounter with a retelling of his or her life. At the very opening of the book, for example, the porter, Gustav, takes several pages to tell Ryder his story (*Unc* 3–9). Wood complicates this second characteristic by noting how parts of Ryder's past are transposed to the town that he initially seemed to be visiting.[32] Finally, Wood proposes that every scene is inconsequential.[33] No matter what has transpired previously, Ryder continues on almost obliviously. This is an element that is most important to note at the novel's ending, which Wood uses as his example: although Sophie has taken Boris away from Ryder, apparently breaking off their relationship forever, Ryder sits on the tram taking comfort in the improbable buffet located at the end of the car (*Unc* 533–35).

Manipulations of time complicate the novel further, a point that Iyer picks up when he notes that 'Time and space is weirdly exploded'.[34] Pointing out how time is dislocated, Lewis describes Ryder's elevator ride early in the novel, a ride of only a couple of floors which takes over four pages to narrate.[35] Shaffer adds that readers are not able to get a 'concrete grasp of time':[36] there are no clocks or watches. Wong writes that the novel lacks 'clear referential reality'[37] while Rorty points out that the background is not of real history and that Ryder demonstrates almost no long-term memory.[38] Francis Wyndham (born 1924), however, makes the distinction that although the town's buildings and parks are minimally described, they are no less real: 'in their conformity to symbolic fundamentals they are subliminally recognizable.'[39]

The terrain is recognizable enough that most reviewers have determined that the novel is set somewhere in Europe. Ishiguro, however, has been careful to strip his setting of any marker that would allow critics to comment on the socio-historical context of the novel. Iyer has observed that there are no points of reference except North Road, South Road, and Old Town.[40] However, in one of the stronger critical responses to *The Unconsoled*, Richard Robinson argues, first, that 'an idea of a particular space can be recovered from an ostensibly anti-realist novel', and second, that the novel's 'Central European shadings' should not be ignored.[41] Robinson, while aware of Ishiguro's assertion that the novel could be set anywhere, demonstrates how Ishiguro has eliminated much of Europe by indicating where the novel is not set: for example, if Gustav's family went to Switzerland on holiday (*Unc* 5), the novel cannot be set there. Using this logic Robinson eliminates France and England (*Unc* 379), Germany (*Unc* 65), Scandinavia (*Unc* 165, 199), Hungary, and Italy (*Unc* 321).[42]

Robinson then divides critical responses of the novel into three categories based on their response to the unnamed city: first, those who did not attempt to place it; second, those who wanted the place named (a category that coincides with those who thought the novel was not Kafkaesque enough); and third, those that felt the Central Europeanness was critical for understanding the novel. It is those last two groups that Robinson investigates. He cobbles together what the novel does offer as a place and makes the important distinction that 'the city setting of *The Unconsoled* is only depicted insofar as it might release its metaphorical potential'.[43] Ishiguro, he acknowledges, has avoided a realistic representation but has left readers some recognizable details: 'trams, hotels, high-sided streets, monuments, housing estates, an Old Town, a Hungarian café' and suggests that these details come from a variety of places although that variety is 'circumscribed in an area which signifies "Central Europe"'.[44] These slight references help readers place the novel, vaguely, but Robinson argues, 'It is inevitable that in a text that avoids "out-and-out fabulism", the mists clear, and some sense of historical and cultural target comes into focus'.[45]

After sketching out the political scene in Central Europe and its difficulties and connecting Ishiguro to other writers who have used 'nowhere' – Alfred Jarry (1873–1907), Robert Musil (1880–1942), Hermann Bahr (1863–1934), and Jan Morris (born 1926) (but not Beckett) – Robinson argues

■ that many of the characteristics familiar to cultural historians of Central Europe, its teeming microcosms, its spectral borderlands including the confusion, facelessness and indifference of which Foucault speaks – suggest an allusive historical space in *The Unconsoled*, a potential territory where *atopia* can be imagined.[46] □

This atopia, however, is part of the larger history of twentieth-century Central and Eastern Europe, and it is Robinson's position that this history helps us understand the novel not by matching the details of Middle Europe to the novel but by acknowledging the historical inferences:

■ The reader may profitably think of one allegorical potentiality – the Central European anxieties of the novel – while at the same time placing them, in Derridean terms, 'under erasure'. This single historical locus does not *explain* the hyper-sensitivity of the citizens to their identity – how to memorialize or forget their pasts, to decide between them, and how to present a new face to the world; nor does it account for the strange mixture of Old European custom (the Porters' Dance) and New European modernism (the post-Schonberg music programme, the huge housing estates) – which converge in the passive-aggressiveness of some of the characters, like Hoffman. But it cannot help but act – *pace* Chaudhuri – as a historical paradigm which at least the European reader, coming to the novel at the end of the twentieth century laden down with that continent's 'culture and horror' (Kauffmann), may validly bring to the novel.[47] □

Once readers have discerned that the novel's setting is Central Europe, they will start to make associations based on Central European history. Readers will bring their responses.

Having identified this latent content, Robinson sets out to trace the effect it might have on our reading. He begins this part of his argument by connecting the fantastic to the real. In an earlier review, Rubin Merle alludes to the labyrinth elements of *The Unconsoled*, suggesting that the novel's claustrophobic atmosphere is reinforced by the 'physical layout of the city'.[48] Robinson has also noticed the city's tangled layout and traces the labyrinthine city back to myths and fantasies, such as the labyrinth of Theseus, before carrying the idea of the labyrinth forward to 'more recent configurations of European political space: the materialisation of geopolitical stalemates which have led to surreal but nightmarishly concrete urban topographies'.[49] The wall that Ryder encounters on his way to the concert hall (*Unc* 388) enhances the connection to the nightmare aspects of the novel because it reminds us of how communities have been divided by larger political forces; consequently, 'We bring to our reading of *The Unconsoled* the knowledge that the twentieth-century sequestering of political territory has contributed to the "nightmarish quality" of absurdly divided cityscapes in Central Europe.'[50] Similarly, Robinson connects the novel's oneiric qualities to Central European history: 'When the space-time of dreams is given a hybrid European, Germanic backdrop [...] an old literary-cultural inheritance emerges – that of Central European modernism.'[51] Ultimately, Robinson argues that Ishiguro's placing *The Unconsoled* nowhere, 'into the pure realm of the metaphorical', establishes the novel even more strongly as Central European. That is, rather than representing one city in Europe, the unnamed city of *The Unconsoled* takes on the attributes of the whole region.

Although Robinson has developed a useful and compelling interpretation based on the novel's setting, readers need to be careful about trying to read specific characterisations of place into *The Unconsoled*. Ishiguro seems to be writing to prevent comments such as Kauffmann's:

> ■ Previously, he dealt with the psychological and spiritual aftermath of WWII in Japan, then with English confusions and self-betrayals in that war. Now he moves to the continent, to the involuted psyche and spirit that was the root of much of that war, that bred most of our culture and also of our honour.[52] □

Although Kauffmann's nod to the individual appears appropriate, the more dominant leaning of this reading is unhelpful and creates a tinted vision of the text. That is, when all the shifts this novel depends on start to get fastened into place, the cognitive freedom readers need to follow this ride, or odyssey, that is, to accept its logic, starts to get bogged down.

An example of one such misreading is Shao-Pin Luo's '"Living the Wrong Life": Kazuo Ishiguro's Unconsoled Orphans' (2003) which provides several careful compilations of some of the novel's image clusters while trying, unfortunately, to read *The Unconsoled* to agree with a reading of *Orientalism* by literary theorist and cultural critic Edward Said (1935–2003). Luo argues that Ryder, like Banks in *When We Were Orphans*, encounters disillusionment when he realises 'that the "wound" of the loss of parents and home will never really heal'.[53] She begins by unpacking the evidence of Ryder's unhappy childhood: Ryder's recognition of his childhood bedroom at the beginning of the novel and the sounds of his parents fighting that accompany that memory (*Unc* 16); Ryder's need for 'training sessions' to deal with the intense emotional strain to which his parents subject him (*Unc* 171–2); and Ryder's desperate response to the remains of the old family car (*Unc* 260–4). Like Stephan Hoffman, Ryder is consumed with the desire to win approval from his parents. Luo presents two contrasting scenes that describe the arrival of Ryder's parents and notes his despair when he realises they will not be coming.

Luo's analysis does help readers understand Ryder. She begins her discussion of space in *The Unconsoled* by proposing that 'there is only profound disappointment, disillusion, and desolation in the bleak landscape of *The Unconsoled*'. Although her constant references to Ryder as 'an exile' overlook the novel's complex approach to space and time, Luo provides useful catalogues of the novel's imagery, as when she supports her claim that 'Ryder is essentially a solitary traveler':

> ■ The novel is full of descriptions of rainy, dark, deserted streets (64–5, 88–9, 289–90) and solitary lamps (51, 119, 389, 413) that exist as if only to accentuate the complete darkness that surrounds them. He is forever

'walking around in slow circles' (125), 'wandering aimlessly around' (133), or 'walk[ing] in circles indefinitely' (212), and losing himself 'in the network of narrow little alleys' (389). Thus he repeatedly gets lost in the labyrinthian streets of the city, misses appointments and breaks promises, literally runs into walls and goes in circles on a tram, and eventually leaves for Helsinki, 'just another cold, lonely city' (107). □

Like Lewis before her, Luo connects the novel's landscape to the paintings of de Chirico but does not develop the connection further.[54] She dedicates more space to a connection she perceives with French philosopher Gaston Bachelard (1884–1962) and uses his analysis in 'The Significance of the Hut' (1957) to make a superficial connection to the importance of the house in *The Unconsoled*. Again though, Luo provides a useful catalogue of motifs which demonstrates how Christoff (*Unc* 188), Brodsky (*Unc* 309), and Ryder and Sophie (*Unc* 34, 224) are all in search of homes. Ryder may be in search of a house, but he is also determined to keep travelling, 'in search of not only fame and recognition, but also a meaningful role and standing in society'.[55] For the travelling Ryder, the home not found has distinct costs:

■ The house, a symbol for settled life, familial affiliation, community connection, is never found. Feeling betrayed, disappointed, and even destroyed, all women characters abandon their search for house/chalet/farmhouse: thus Sophie leaves Ryder, Rosa leaves Christoff, Christine leaves Hoffman, Miss Collins leaves Brodsky. In the end, there is neither reconciliation nor consolation.[56] □

Luo has provided some important analysis of the novel's space, but her attempt to make the novel into something it is not – about foreignness – again betrays her: 'most importantly, [the novel] is about a foreigner's traumas and anxieties associated with dislocation and disorientation.'[57] Labelling Ryder a foreigner fails to recognise the shifting territory Ishiguro has created. Luo ventures further away from the novel when she writes that it 'particularly addresses the loss of the orphan and connects this loss to the pain of the exile as a never-healing "wound"'.[58] But Ryder is neither orphan nor exile. His parents may treat him badly, but he does seem to have parents, unlike the protagonist of *When We Were Orphans*, Christopher Banks, the character Luo wants to connect to Ryder. Moreover, a term like 'exile' in connection with a city that cannot be located is obviously problematic. Moreover, since Ryder seems to be a resident of the city, referring to him as an exile seems similarly misguided. Luo's craving to tie the novel down to this theme of foreignness means establishing boundaries of place, between domestic and foreign, that the novel rejects.

Finally, Luo connects *The Unconsoled* to *Alice in Wonderland* (1865) by Lewis Carroll (1832–98) and with the help of Bachelard proposes that Ishiguro has created an alternative world:

■ Ishiguro has constructed in *The Unconsoled*, as in *Alice in Wonderland*, an alternative world, with its numerous mirrors and doorways, with alternative rules and random possibilities. This is a world where the landscape takes on a dreamy quality. As if to remind the reader that all is not what it seems, each section of the novel is framed with a scene in which Ryder invariably wakes up in panic or is roused from sleep by an insistently ringing telephone (18, 117, 155, 293, 413).[59] □

To support this claim she adds references to instances when Ryder dozes off (*Unc* 38, 44, 79, 147, 191, 209, 263, 357) and points out the novel's imaginative elements:

■ The fairy tale qualities of the novel, with its imaginary castles, horse and carriage, Boris's and the young Ryder's imaginary games and battles, magnificent sunsets and pastoral grassy fields, are juxtaposed with scenes of urban traffic and carparks, identical apartments and artificial lakes, as well as deserted city squares and night streets. Unhappy memories of the past, the weariness and anxieties of traveling, the pressures and demands of society are also in contrast with enticing fantasies of rest, comfort, tranquillity. □

Ultimately, Luo attempts to demonstrate that 'by providing a "fantasy" world, Ishiguro shows that the "real" world is forever shadowed by the possibility of alternative worlds and alternative lives'.[60] It is in this imaginative conclusion that Luo's analysis is most useful in understanding the method and themes of the novel, a usefulness more readily observed by attending to the novel's oneiric characteristics.

MORE THAN DREAMS

Discussions of the novel, faced with this shifting and disputed geography, often respond with language such as 'dreams' and 'nightmares'. Perhaps most dismissively, Richard Eder, failing to read much of the novel's complexity, sees the novel only as a 'long nightmare'.[61] Similarly, Paul Gray, who starts his review with an appreciative look back to *The Remains of the Day*, fails to adjust his reading strategy for this novel and calls this work 'the literary equivalent of an endless bad dream'.[62] Allen points out several events in Ryder's account that seem like events from nightmares:

■ He addresses a formal gathering with his genitalia exposed; trying to identify himself, he is unable to articulate his own name and can only strain and grunt; an unbreachable brick wall separates him, just before curtain time, from the concert hall; he is borne away on a tram by bossy journalists, having left a small child alone in a café.[63] □

Like Allen, Lewis describes the many dreamlike features in the late-night reception to which Hoffman takes Ryder (after waking him up):

■ There are the outlandish, illogical events, such as the visit to a reception in the middle of the night, and the exaggerated grief about the dog. Then there is Ryder's fear of public exposure, signalled by the wearing of the dressing-gown, which is undercut by the neglect he receives at the function. And there is a noticeable degree of wish-fulfilment in the success of Ryder's eight-word speech.[64] □

Michael Wood is often quoted as pointing out that at the beginning of all three sections after the first, Ryder wakes up after a nap (for example, *Unc* 18). However, Wood is not proposing that the novel is the record of a dream:

■ It's more like a long metaphor for deferred and displaced anxiety, and the point about anxiety is that it doesn't occur only in dreams. [...] the novel takes the opportunity that fiction so often resists and pursues the darker logic of a world governed by our needs and worries rather than the law of physics.[65] □

Passano too points out that 'dreamlike' is insufficient as a description of the novel's events because the term does not evoke the anxiety and fascination that the novel stirs in us.[66]

Several critics have, in fact, noted the novel's firm grounding in details. Brookner observes that while 'Delay is the stuff of nightmare', the 'agonising flow is punctuated with surreal detail',[67] an observation supported by Kauffmann[68] and Menand.[69] Lewis, however, adds that 'buildings and landscape keep melting into something else in a Daliesque way'.[70] 'Melting' is not an apt description, and the Cubism of Pablo Picasso (1881–1973) might be a more helpful reference than Salvador Dali (1904–89), especially Synthetic Cubism which saw Picasso attaching wallpaper and newspapers to works, but Lewis has captured the transitory nature of Ishiguro's landscape. François, who finds a 'blend of objective reality and subjective wish fulfilment' expands on this idea, noting how the novel alternates between the mundane and the 'recognizably alien and mystifyingly familiar, depending on the degree of magic or mimesis prevalent at any given stage of the novel'. It is a delicate balance for Ishiguro because while he continually reminds the reader of how time and space are being manipulated, he does so without ever 'alienating the reader sufficiently from sensory data to suggest that he has been allowed into another dimension'.[71] In an interview with Sylvia Steinberg, Ishiguro recounts 'working out the rules that might apply in the alternative landscape he was creating',[72] and writing a series of short episodes 'in which time is distorted in the manner of a dream where events occur in slow motion or with dizzying swiftness'.[73] These shorts were not written for publication but as 'tryouts'. Lewis notes three examples: when Ryder demands a practice room and is shown first to a toilet stall and then to a small hut; when Ryder and Brodsky encounter a funeral and Ryder becomes the centre of attention; and the scene which takes place in the aftermath of a car accident that leaves Brodsky badly hurt.[74] Ishiguro wanted, he recalls, 'to have a go at creating a dreamlike landscape'.[75]

This idea of a 'dreamlike landscape' is an important one for understanding the novel. Writing on *A Pale View of Hills*, Michael Wood points out that Nagasaki comes to mean not the politics or morality 'but *the landscape of feeling* created by the bomb' (emphasis added).[76] Wong, meanwhile, points out that Ishiguro's interest in *The Unconsoled* is 'in the unfamiliar world evoked by what the author calls "the language of dreams"'.[77] 'The landscape of feeling' Wood finds in *A Pale View of Hills* helps readers understand the unfamiliar world of *The Unconsoled* created through Ishiguro's 'language of dreams'. François describes this landscape as a 'near magic beyond telepathic eavesdropping, uncanny blending of events past and present, expansion of temporal sequences and distortion of spatial referents'.[78] These characteristics give Ishiguro 'a certain episodic freedom – to open the book up and allow himself to experiment – but also to render a certain condition of consciousness'.[79] Cusk, for one, has understood the immense potential of this openness: 'once accustomed to his strange landscape, with its tricks and reversals, its sudden transparencies, its possibilities and humiliations, it soon becomes clear that one is in a place one knows better, and more intimately, than any other.'[80] Readers, then, must learn to respond to this condition of consciousness, to what Kauffmann has perceived as 'a kind of interior cubism'.[81] Allen, in her review, sees that Ishiguro is after a more challenging expression of experience: 'Imagine an alternate world in which life is not a dream but in which the dream is your life – in other words, where you must live your life by the inexplicable logic and ever-changing rules imposed by the dream itself.'[82] The novel requires the reader to accept a different kind of logic, a different kind of realism.

RYDER'S APPROPRIATIONS

One of the most important concepts required for understanding the
logic of this novel is its use of appropriations, or extensions. Shaffer
provides the earliest explanation of this idea:

> ■ Of the major characters, three clusters of three people each are most
> germane to an understanding of Ryder's situation. These characters,
> while 'real', are mainly to be understood as extensions, versions, or varia-
> tions of Ryder himself – individuals, like Sachiko for Etsuko in *A Pale View
> of Hills,* through whom he projects his own story. While these characters
> should not be regarded as mere fabrications of the protagonist's [*sic*],
> then, they should be understood as conduits for Ryder to remember and
> forget, judge and censor his own past.[83] □

To his first cluster, or triangle, he assigns Brodsky, Miss Collins,
and Brodsky's dog Bruno; in the second, Hoffman, Christine, and
Stephan; and in the third triangle, Gustav, Sophie, and Boris (although
he later substitutes Ryder for Gustav in this triangle). Having set up
these triangles Shaffer then works through each cluster pointing out
the similarities and connections among the various characters.

Carlos Villar Flor adds two family triangles to this scheme: one of
Ryder, Sophie, and Boris, and another of Ryder and his parents. He
does so to support his argument that one of the novel's major themes is
'the neglect of family relationships, with special emphasis on the plight
of children deprived of the love of one or both parents, and the aftermath in adult life of such emotional injuries'.[84] To summarise briefly,
Villar Flor proposes that the Hoffmans' neglect of Stephan creates a
young artist who is desperate for his parents' approval and who believes
that by giving a superlative performance at the concert he might actually earn their love. Boris is a victim of the lack of communication
between his mother and his grandfather. Understanding these relationships and taking note of Ryder's allusions to his childhood and his
parents allows readers to see that Ryder 'like Stephan, or Boris, must
have been severely hurt in his childhood by being a witness of constant
parental fighting and by suffering a subsequent neglect'.[85] Ishiguro
claims that he had such a scheme in mind: 'I wanted to have someone
just turn up in some landscape where he would meet people who are
not literally parts of himself but are echoes of his past, harbingers of his
future and projections of his fears about what he might become.'[86]

Citing this interview, Gary Adelman argues that 'Psychological
complexity is built up through the use of doubles'. Adelman does not
explain how his theory differs from Shaffer's earlier work (he does not
even cite Shaffer) but proposes a similar scheme:

■ Primary characters, including Ryder himself in different relationships, represent Ryder's original family situation at different times of his life. Increasingly, Ryder plays his own father, re-creating his family of origin in his relationship to his wife Sophie and to his nine-year-old son Boris. The relationship of Stephan Hoffman to his parents reenacts Ryder's life until his mid-twenties, when his career takes off.[87] □

Adelman continues on through some of the subordinate characters attempting to establish a one-for-one relationship: Stephan *is* Ryder at a younger age. Adelman, however, later suggests that 'Every encounter is Ryder encountering ego projections of himself',[88] a slight shift from his earlier position. In effect, he suggests a simplified form of Shaffer's theory, one that does not account for Ryder's manipulations of the narrative.

Lewis uses the Freudian concept of displacement to understand some of these relationships. (Freudian displacement, briefly put, is the substitution of an insignificant element for the significant. Lewis cites Freud's example of the single person who transfers his or her emotions to a hobby or the care of animals.) After pointing out dream-like aspects of the novel, Lewis proposes that 'Each of the musicians of the town – Stephan, Hoffman, Christoff, and Brodsky – represents displaced versions of Ryder as he has been in the past or as he may be in the future.'[89] Hoffman, who is not a musician but the organiser of Ryder's concert, does not appear to fit into this category, nor does Lewis indicate how he represents Ryder. It is certainly likely, however, that the Hoffmans' unhappy marriage and poor treatment of Stephan parallels the poor treatment a younger Ryder received from his parents. Brodsky, a conductor who has assumed the role of town drunk and who is consequently separated from his great love Miss Collins, is possibly 'an image of what Ryder might become in later years – a Ghost-of-Ryder-Future'.[90] Lewis proposes that 'Brodsky's relationship with Miss Collins and his music is a displacement of Ryder's own marriage and commitment to art'.[91] In fact, Ryder's troubles with alcohol do surface in the novel. When Ryder returns to the family's old apartment, the neighbour's reference to the previous tenants, who argued in part because the father drank heavily, could be a reference to Ryder: 'The musician's shame at his own behaviour is displaced, dreamily, on to someone else.'[92]

Lewis expands his theory of displacements to account for other characters as well. The weight of the favours constantly requested of Ryder is displaced onto Gustav who at the very beginning of the novel gives Ryder a long talk about luggage and later performs the bizarre ending to the Porter's dance. Gustav's death leads Lewis to a discussion of absent fathers in Ishiguro's work, a motif found throughout Ishiguro's oeuvre.[93] The relationship between Ryder and Boris is not good: the two do not often speak and Ryder often ignores Boris, most crushingly in Chapter 18 when Sophie has promised Boris and planned a special family evening. Boris's fantasy of fighting off a gang of thugs suggests the extent of the unhappiness in the family home: it is the thugs, in Boris's fantasy, who have been causing Sophie to be irritable and Ryder to be away for long periods (*Unc* 220–1). Lewis connects Boris's unhappy situation to Ryder by proposing that Boris functions as 'a Ghost-of-Ryder-Past'. Ryder too experienced an unhappy childhood as is revealed in the flashbacks to his friendship with Fiona Roberts where he describes his 'training sessions' (*Unc* 171–2).[94]

While Adelman assumes that Ryder faithfully represents his reality, Lewis reads Ryder as displaced onto the other musicians so that they represent him as past and future versions of himself. Ryder, however, is not as easy to read as Adelman suggests and takes more of a conscious role than the term 'displacement' implies. To some degree this is a novel about manipulating reality, a point that is illustrated by three important moments that have received little discussion. First, near the very opening of the novel Ryder explains how he used to manipulate the truth when, as a child confronted with an irritating tear on a mat that he used for his toy soldiers, he devised the solution of using the tear as a type of rough terrain:

■ This discovery – that the blemish that had always threatened to undermine my imaginary world could in fact be incorporated into it – had been one of some excitement for me, and that 'bush' was to become a key factor in many of the battles I subsequently orchestrated (*Unc* 16–17). □

Ryder changes the circumstances with which he is confronted to make them better fit his needs and to help himself. Notably, he makes this discovery while his parents are in the midst of a ferocious argument, thereby linking his manipulation of reality with the pain of the outside world. Later, he explains his 'training sessions' (*Unc* 171–3): He trains himself to want to be alone, to resist the unpleasant reality that exists in his home. Third, the DIY manual (*Unc* 92) which explains how to tile and wallpaper is critical to understanding the novel; as Boris asserts, 'It shows you how to do everything' (*Unc* 287). Indeed it does, because it shows Ryder how to tile over and wallpaper over the painful moments of his past. Confronted by difficulty, Ryder selects an episode and wallpapers over it.

In her difficult but useful essay, Cynthia Wong connects this method with the novel's meaning. She begins by framing the novel as postmodern, which leads her to note Ryder's difficulty understanding his own identity, and his inability to 'effect any meaningful connection to what readers might determine as significant other people in his life'. It is also a difficulty, she notes, that connects Ryder to previous characters in Ishiguro's fiction. Wong begins, then, by grounding Ryder's difficulties at the level of the individual: he cannot connect. She finds here the themes of this novel, 'confusion and ostracism' and helpfully locates them in Ishiguro's earlier work.[95] Unlike Etsuko, Ono, and Stevens who look back and distort elements of their pasts to make their lives manageable, Ryder appears unaware of the need to look back. Ryder, consequently, is not offered the chance for atonement given the earlier narrators: Ishiguro has created for him, 'a murkier life; Ryder's existence is grounded in a profound insistence that reason is fallible, speculation unnecessary, and chronological unfolding with clearly established causes and effects a plausible premise'.[96] Ishiguro has created a hazier, more difficult world for Ryder to negotiate, and Ryder's response is simply to ride out the difficult journey he is on.

The contemporary world, Wong asserts, relying on her framing of the novel as postmodern, is a more complex one, with people more obligated to matters outside their personal sphere, and in turn, more nomadic.[97] Ryder's difficulties, ordinary as they are, are greater than those faced by Ishiguro's earlier narrators. He is not forced to respond to the devastation of a nuclear bomb or the lesions left by fascism; 'Ryder's conflicts also seem to lack transcendence of meaning, which makes the narrator's purpose more puzzling: how can contemporary readers celebrate the ordinary and usual?'[98] Wong answers this question by making an important connection to the method Ishiguro employs in this novel:

■ [M]ethod of discourse, not description of situation, becomes the important metaphor for understanding myriad existence. In other words, not *what* Ryder struggles against, but rather, *how* he goes about it will reveal the meaning of Ryder's character and the implications of that character.[99] □

As with the test to which the tragic hero is subjected, readers must look beyond the subject matter to the method. The appropriations are not just a layer of difficulty that Ishiguro has impressed on the reader's experience but an expression of Ryder's experience.

Wong recognises Ryder's use of what Shaffer has called the 'appropriations' strategy. Although she does not cite it as such, she describes Ryder's strategy in similar terms, such as 'Using Stephan's presumed past to access aspects of his own,' and sees the strategy in previous Ishiguro protagonists who look back to address the state of their lives. Specifically, she proposes, 'by remembering events of other people's lives, they begin to assess the meaning of their own. This approach both reflects and deflects their own pained pasts onto the present narrative'. Not only are these fabrications made by the narrators one of Ishiguro's master themes, Wong asserts that it is Ishiguro who developed the technique of having a character remember 'one's own painful past in context of another person's'.[100] More to the point, she also sees how the strategy helps transform *The Unconsoled* into a deep psychological investigation. Noting Ryder's manipulations of space and time, she suggests Ryder's constant encounters with his murky past, 'cast in intentionally absurd situations or conditions [,] further strengthen Ishiguro's view that one's dreams and imagination have great potency'.[101] Ryder's solitary perambulations through the unnamed city give readers an insight into postmodern existence: 'deep loneliness and isolation are at the heart of the flurry of social activity for us contemporary nomads. What comprehension we might seize of life's meaning is as fleeting and disconnected as it is unfulfilling.'[102] This novel, like Ishiguro's earlier fiction, demonstrates Ishiguro's concern for 'how people console themselves through necessary emotional manipulation',[103] a conclusion that must lead readers to ask who the unconsoled are and for what wound they need consolation.

WHO ARE THE UNCONSOLED?

Ishiguro's use of appropriations marks a new method for representing consciousness, and one important benefit of this method is that Ryder's wound can be examined through its reflection in Boris, Stephan, Hoffman, and Brodsky. But these characters are not the only ones who remain unconsoled. The category of the unconsoled can be expanded to include the wider public. Cusk makes this connection in her early appraisal of the community in which she sees 'the specters of human unhappiness, a community of woes whose attempt to form a secure collective consciousness is continually sabotaged by personal failure'.[104] Lewis too concludes his discussion by suggesting that

■ virtually every character in the novel is looking to be consoled, either by loved ones, through the satisfaction of a demand or in the pursuit of a valued activity. Yet it is the fate of the citizens of this nameless town to remain unconsoled, unsatisfied, and unceasingly chasing goals they cannot reach.[105] □

Pierre François perhaps dedicates the most attention to this element of the novel. He reads it as revealing 'the crisis of culture in our postmodern times from, paradoxically, a modernist vantage point'. He argues that Ryder's condition represents a larger

■ collective crisis, for the artist as potential 'saviour' turns out to be the carrier of a bug that has arguably undermined western societies for more than a century. In this deeply disturbing vision of a civilization turning infantile, depths have gone and have been replaced by *persona*, time has become the alienating factor *per se*, and the sense of community has made way for scapegoating.[106] □

This crisis is embodied in Brodsky and his conducting: his 'leg/thigh wound is a metaphor for the city's sterility, and [...] the old man would parodically be hailed as the city's "saviour" if his performance as a conductor were to re-instil vigour and strength into the cultural wasteland'.[107] But Brodsky is an egoist who cannot step outside his personal desires. As he does with Ryder, François labels his longing to return to prominence and win back Miss Collins's love 'infantile. He is the old man fixated on his youth, hankering for the phallic pleni-tude that ageing has deprived him of and fleeing the real in alcoholic addiction'.[108] For Miss Collins, this egocentrism is abhorrent: she is dedicated to service and social well-being, but Ryder and others lean, like Brodsky, towards less desirable qualities.

Ryder, François points out, blames others for his problems. Although he has come to heal some unnamed problem of the city, he indulges in scapegoating. He too is an egotist, only able to communicate with those around him in his dream-like versions of public transportation.[109] François picks out two 'scenes of community' on public transport, the bus ride that Ryder and Boris take on their way to the artificial lake (*Unc* 206–9) and the tram at the end the novel (*Unc* 528–35), because of the ideal representations of social life they provide. Unlike the representa-tions of social life throughout the novel, both of these cases present posi-tive portrayals of life in the community. The people on public transport are kind and say the right things to console Ryder. The tram at the nov-el's end even offers a buffet breakfast: 'All this is parodic and exemplifies Ishiguro's use of "oneiric realism", which, in this instance, transmutes scapegoating into its dialectical opposite through the swaying magic of public transportation.' François parses these scenes to support his claim that Ryder has paired scapegoating with wish fulfilment. The private counterpart to public transport is the old family car (*Unc* 262) which Ryder finds outside of the Karwinski Gallery and which Ryder acknowl-edges served him as a 'sanctuary' during his childhood: 'The tram, the bus and the old car are childish substitutes for the womb, shelters in which Ryder as a child and Ryder as an adult sought/seeks asylum in the face of parental/social enmity.'[110] He stretches this point, connecting it to the work of psychologist Carl Gustav Jung (1875–1961), to suggest that Ryder's success comes at the expense of a normal maturing personality:

■ The novel can be read as a novel of masks in which the first-person narrator prances around in bright sunlight, but his *persona* gradually fizzles under social pressure and an inner chasm opens 'down' to glooms that have become even murkier since early childhood.[111] □

For François, Ryder's wound is, in part, a 'father complex', a term that he borrows from Jung but does not define beyond pointing out that complexes are constellations of unconscious associations or strong impulses. Specifically, François appears to argue that Ryder is uncomfortable as a father figure: consequently, he panics whenever he is expected to act as a father (*Unc* 90, 176, 258),[112] childishly retains his passion for football which he shares with son, and turns the DIY manual, a symbol of what fathers are supposed to do in homes, over to Boris. Although it seems certain that Ryder's childhood was traumatic, François' diagnosis of a Jungian father complex is weak and an unconvincing element of his reading. It lacks the critical robustness of the appropriations strategy and overlooks François' own arguments on infantilism and the specifics of Ryder's childhood that the novel provides, specifics supplemented by the experiences of Stephan and Boris. Ishiguro is not writing about Ryder's relationship with his father here; he is writing about the relationships between parents and children. Ryder's wound is a product of the flaws of the unhappy childhood that others, such as Luo, have described: his need for 'training sessions' (*Unc* 171–2), Stephan's need for parental approval (for example, *Unc* 520–1), and Boris's need for his fantasy of overcoming the street thugs that have beset the family (*Unc* 218–22). These are the symptoms of the wounds that demand consolation.

François finds the larger significance of the wound suffered by the entire community in the Sattler episode, which François suggests as 'an alternative for the individual and collective retreat from profundity'.[113] Sattler's project, local councillor Karl Pedersen explains to Ryder, was to invigorate the city by transforming it into a major centre: consequently, Sattler has become an almost mythic figure because he signifies the rejection of '"timidity", for the social-cum-psychic ailment fictionalised in *The Unconsoled*'. And it is this 'timidity' which François perceives as 'the cultural crisis in the western world round the end of the twentieth century'. The novel's final three chapters are particularly important in François' reading for they 'show that our civilization is experiencing the end of depths on the psychic plane and the end of community on the social plane, and blames either woe on cultural infantilism'. In contrast to the introspective modernist artist's attempt at 'a new mental order on the shambles of cultural apocalypse', Ishiguro presents Ryder who, with his artistic powers at their peak, can only long for a lost childhood that was never his. Ryder does not investigate 'what "made him"' or, like Sattler, try to devise a bright new future. Instead, he is consumed by the dream that some day his

mother and father will acknowledge him.[114] While acknowledging
Ishiguro's wariness of having his novels stand in for socio-political
commentary, François expands the significance of the story: "'his"
city and "his" visiting pianist are respectively "our" world and "our"
psyche, albeit at some removes from mimesis.'[115]

Some early reviewers did pick up on this theme. Hughes–Hallett
and Cusk both perceive Ryder's anguish over his inability to reconcile
his private and public lives. Hughes–Hallett describes the problem as
a lack in one's own personal space: that Ryder, like many of us who
spend years 'responding unthinkingly' to multifarious demands 'come
to ourselves, in the middle of our lives, in a dark wood, with only the
haziest understanding of how we arrived there or what is next to be
done'.[116] Similarly, Cusk sees the conflict as between inner and outer
human relationships, between, that is, the families and friends that are
so important in the development of an individual and the society in
which that life takes place. The private failures of his characters leave
them with the outer society as the destination for 'their desires for
control, success, admiration and normality; in short, for consolation'.[117]

CONCLUSION

The Unconsoled reveals Ishiguro working in a style extremely different
from his three earlier works, but as noted by critics such as Shaffer[118]
and Wyndham, the novel also bears similarities to his three previous
novels. Shaffer notes one of the most important similarities: its use of
first-person narration by a narrator who, seemingly unintentionally,
reveals his past life. Wyndham describes the novel as a 'variation on
the themes of bewilderment, shame and regret which [Ishiguro] has
previously and more gently presented as dominant strands throughout
human existence'.[119] In the differences, however, lie one of the most
exciting aspects of this novel: its attempts, through Ishiguro's use of
appropriations, to create a different 'representation of consciousness'.[120]
This different representation of consciousness, however, does not lend
itself to easy reading. *The Unconsoled* is a challenge; moreover, Ishiguro's
decision to not provide a name for the city in which it is set seems to
have been taken as a puzzle to be solved, and many critics who have
written on the novel have felt compelled to locate the unnamed city.
The technical aspects of Ishiguro's work here have received very little
attention. It is a technique replete with risks, which Wyndham outlines
in one of the best reviews of the novel. He describes how the design
and atmosphere of the novel require repetition to create effect,[121] and
the risks of characters giving long speeches.[122] Kauffmann has pointed
out Ishiguro's use of disproportion, by which he appears to mean

inappropriateness: the instances when, for example, Ryder is asked to perform some small favour or embarks on some minor undertaking even though he is required for some much larger duty.[123] Misreading Ishiguro for Ryder, Hughes–Hallett adds that 'Ishiguro has chosen to express himself in stilted, non-colloquial prose'.[124] If 'Ishiguro has mapped out an aesthetic territory that is all his own,'[125] more analysis of that territory is needed. There is certainly much more work to be done on this novel, particularly in the study of its cognitive poetics. Given that the novel provides a new representation of consciousness, the efficacy of that portrayal needs to be questioned.

Ultimately, however, the critical response to *The Unconsoled* demonstrates that Ishiguro's work is about people. In an interview Ishiguro outlines his intention in this novel:

> ■ I wanted to show that sort of hopeless, slightly pathetic kind of optimism, which in the end is something that we all have to resort to in order to keep going. [...] In a sense all my books end on that same note – after the character discovers how empty life is. Here Ryder is trying to gain something profound from what normally would be a superficial contact with other human beings. He's looking for some kind of *consolation*. □

Fortunately for his readers, 'Though Ishiguro fills his fictional world with self-deceiving people trying to surmount failed lives, in the end he grants them the dignity to endure their sorrow.'[126] In *The Unconsoled*, as elsewhere, Ishiguro writes about the difficulties we all have getting along in life, the broken tools we have to address those difficulties, and the dignity that we must cobble together to respond to life's challenges. His next protagonist, the famous detective Christopher Banks, appears more than ready to take on these challenges and uncover the truth in a case that takes him around the world.

CHAPTER SEVEN

Detecting the Past: *When We Were Orphans* (2000)

For many readers, Ishiguro's fourth novel, *The Unconsoled,* had failed to communicate. Aware of this failure, Ishiguro set out to try again,[1] an attempt that produced *When We Were Orphans*, the notebooks of purportedly celebrated detective, Christopher Banks, born and raised in Shanghai until being sent to England following the mysterious disappearances of, first, his father and, then, his mother. Of all Ishiguro's novels, *Orphans* has instigated the most puzzling response. While most reviewers responded positively, citing, for example, the novel's originality,[2] power,[3] and 'surpassing intelligence and taste',[4] there has been considerable dissent, a situation most easily recognised in the vastly differing opinions of the two reviewers from *The New York Times*. While Michael Gorra, in a thoughtful review, describes the novel as Ishiguro's 'fullest achievement yet',[5] Michiko Kakutani begins by calling the novel 'disappointing'.[6] In her useful review, novelist Alice McDermott (born 1953) captures this bipolar response all on its own, referring to the novel as 'by turns, brilliant and dull, absorbing and unfathomable, fascinating and a bit of a mess'.[7] The scholarly response to the novel has been equally enigmatic, but in this regard, the most surprising aspect is simply the dearth of scholarship on such a complex novel. Highlighting the novel's key critical issues, this chapter unpacks these varied responses and offers possible directions for further critical readings.

SIMILARITIES TO EARLIER NOVELS

Despite the disagreements on other issues, readers have agreed that *Orphans* shares several similarities with previous works in Ishiguro's *oeuvre*. Gillian Harding-Russell finds a similarity based on the search for truth in the third and fourth novels (although her comments seem to apply to the first two novels as well):

■ The wonder of these tales is that the reader does not finally uncover the whole truth [...] as a sort of holy grail to be pursued and then known completely. And the narrative of this truth is never a straight line, nor even a serpentine one, but is found piecemeal, among the unstable memories of everyone concerned.[8] □

There are also several technical similarities with the earlier works. As with earlier narrators, 'Christopher's memories are unreliable; he unwittingly reveals his self-delusion as he represses painful memories or lies to himself to make them more palatable'.[9] Shaffer connects the ending to all of Ishiguro's previous work:

■ Banks, now fifty-three years old and rheumatic, is settling into late middle age and attempts to sum up his life. All of Ishiguro's novels end in this poignantly understated way, leaving the reader to grapple with the question of whether the protagonist's life has been as successful or complete as he or she would have us believe.[10] □

Perhaps most important, however, is the novel's reworking of 'the innovative technique of *The Unconsoled* – dubbed "appropriation" by the author – where, as in a dream, other characters feature as projections of the narrator's fears and desires, people from his past or himself at different stages of life'.[11] The bipolar response to this novel can, in fact, be largely attributed to readers' varying abilities to negotiate this technique.

By working in a mode closer to realism in *Orphans*, Ishiguro removed the appropriation technique from the novel's foreground. That is, while Banks's story appropriates Sir Cecil Medhurst's just as Ryder's story appropriates Brodsky's, because *Orphans* is so much more closely aligned with realist modes, it does not so forcefully compel readers to perceive the connection. In Ishiguro's shifting of the appropriation technique out of the foreground, however, some readers fail to see its use. This failure often appears in responses that attempt to split the novel's mode into two, as when novelist Benjamin Anastas (born 1971) finds 'profoundly mixed' results in Ishiguro's reconciliation of 'the cloistered technique of his early works with the liberties of *The Unconsoled*',[12] or when Kakutani describes the novel as 'an uneasy composite of his last two novels' that 'lacks the experimental ambitions of *The Unconsoled*'.[13] Novelist Joyce Carol Oates (born 1938), however, suggests that '*The Unconsoled* would seem to be a groping precursor of the much superior *When We Were Orphans*', a judgement she supports by noting that in *Orphans* 'the Kafkaesque compulsion to question, to puzzle over, to analyse is given a dramatic urgency that makes psychological sense, for Christopher Banks is an orphan who as a schoolboy is fascinated by the "connectedness" that is taken for granted by his non-orphan classmates'.[14] The development of this theme of 'connectedness', embodied in the appropriation technique, suggests the further work required to understand Ishiguro's fiction more fully.

NARRATIVE AND PROSE

Critics were also largely in agreement lauding Ishiguro's 'stunning exhibition of narrative skill',[15] especially in regards to Banks's recollection of 'his charmed boyhood in China'.[16] Similarly, Ishiguro's prose is described as 'at once rich and taut',[17] 'gorgeous, perhaps matchless',[18] and 'extraordinarily seductive [...]: precise, controlled, cautious'.[19] Novelist and biographer Andrew Barrow (born 1945), more specifically, adds an insightful observation on Ishiguro's 'narrative tricks': 'New characters are slipped into the story by sleight of hand and readers are enticed into new sections with rambling remarks'.[20] Likewise, Brian Bouldrey finds Ishiguro's use of omission rewarding: 'Somehow, Ishiguro has achieved a disturbing balance between omission and intense, immediate action as seen through the wrong end of a telescope, where details, however complete, are misunderstood.'[21]

Novelist and journalist Philip Hensher (born 1965) provides a unique dissension. Agreeing with those who detect Ishiguro's narrative skilfulness, he contends that Ishiguro's 'virtues are all architectural ones. His timing and orchestration of events is practically unrivalled'. But despite Hensher's admiration for the novel's structure, he judges Ishiguro's prose lacking, particularly in what he perceives as its failure to provide 'the particular concrete detail which pins down a scene to a locality and a time'. Picking up on the novel's allusion to Dickens's *Great Expectations* (1860–1) (noted by Henry Carrington Cunningham, III[22]), Hensher claims that 'a less Dickensian novelist can hardly be imagined', for while Dickens revels in details, for Ishiguro details are 'impeding and irrelevant'.[23] Tova Reich's description of Ishiguro's use of details, however, establishes an opposing view: she acknowledges the novel's failure to describe 'what the main character looks like or of what he eats', and acknowledges that 'some of the scenes, such as the quest through the warren, are as dark and dreamlike as a descent into the underworld', but finds 'the total effect is concrete and vivid'.[24] Hensher finds another problem with Ishiguro's prose in his 'avoidance of phrasal verbs [...] it gives his narrator a circumlocutious, cautious air which isn't really very helpful. More than that, it gives him a particular tone of voice which is not that of his social setting'. The problem here for Hensher is Ishiguro's choice of 'depart' over the phrasal verb 'set off', but Hensher has failed to separate Ishiguro's authorial voice from Banks's narrating of his story.

Once readers distinguish that the notebooks, the text of the novel, are not Ishiguro's, but Banks's, Hensher's criticism can be understood to point to one of the themes of the novel, the difficulty of being English. His simplification that 'Phrasal verbs are, in a way, at the heart of English',[25] should be connected to Banks's trouble being English, first in Shanghai and later in England:

■ Englishness – in fact, human interaction of all kinds – will remain for him a form of learned behaviour, in which he compounds the simulacrum of a character from both the gestures of the people around him and his reading in *The Wind in the Willows* [1908] or Sherlock Holmes.[26] □

Thus, an explanation for Banks's language emerges: 'Ishiguro has been not deaf but bold in his gaucheish use of the RP of the time. The reason he screwed it quite so tight is that Christopher is putting himself under the most deadly control'.[27] James Wood develops an even stronger case for the appropriateness of Banks's language based on Banks's need to conform to English society.[28] Consequently, Banks

■ speaks to us – and thus the novel is written – in a style of English that seems, more even than in Ishiguro's previous work, almost a spoof, something between a pastiche of Conan Doyle [1859–1930] and a parody of the kind of gossipy, metropolitan, highly 'English' prose written by Anthony Powell [1905–2000]. □

Wood provides a short passage from both *Orphans* and Powell to illuminate his point before concluding, 'Most of *When We Were Orphans* is set in the 1930s, and Christopher seems to be using the artificiality of upper-class language to upholster his own artificiality.'[29] Alongside the superlatives, then, Ishiguro's prose in *Orphans* binds together his narrator's estrangement and motivations.

BANKS'S CHARACTER

Although Banks is a complex character under immense pressure, his character has not generated much response. Aside from Harding-Russell's conclusion that 'this is a psychologically subtle novel, and it presents Banks as a character at once sympathetic and flawed',[30] most discussions of Banks have focused exclusively on the question of his reliability. Like others, Gorra understands the significance of the early reference to the narrator as 'rather an "odd bird"', a point from which Ishiguro 'begins to orchestrate an ever-growing dissonance between the detective's own judgements and those the book presents as "normal"'.[31] Shaffer describes the unreliability of Banks's account of his childhood:

■ It slowly emerges [...] that Banks's golden childhood in Shanghai before the Japanese bombing campaign and before the mysterious disappearance of his parents was far less happy or stable than he would like (and like us) to believe. This is hinted at not only in the hesitantly revealed facts about his parents' less-than-ideal relationship but also in the details of the other marriages depicted in the novel, all of which are failures, and all of which, we come to understand, mirror that of Christopher's parents.[32] □

Banks blusters on, but his 'veneer of self-confidence is paper-thin. Though Christopher never allows it to crack, Ishiguro's hand lies confidently behind the text, showing us far more than our narrator thinks he has been shown'.[33] Shortly after he gets to Shanghai, readers are compelled to consider if 'his inflated sense of his own importance in the worldwide fight against evil suggests that he is also suffering from severe delusions'.[34]

In contrast to readings focused on Banks's unreliability, Wood's reading focuses on the difficulties that Banks experiences. He begins, however, by noting the artificiality that marks Banks:

■ Christopher's world seems to have been borrowed from an English novel, and this is surely Ishiguro's intended effect. Christopher is producing a masquerade of a style that is already something of a masquerade; he is not entirely real – not to himself, not to those who encounter him, and not to Ishiguro's readers. □

The intent here, Wood suggests, is not simply

■ to suggest that this kind of 'Englishness' does not exist, though the stability of the entity is certainly a casualty of his novel. It is more, I think, that he wants us to see Christopher as a man deformed by the effort of conformity – deformed into genre, into unreality, and, if necessary, into falsehood.[35] □

Wood's reading, then, allows readers to see behind the role Banks has assumed to the man who was once an orphan. Other reviewers provide further support for this reading: 'Like other Ishiguro heroes, Banks is crippled by politeness, cursed by the fear of doing something "inappropriate" or "unworthy". On a superficial level, he admits to being "quite fatigued" and "somewhat overwrought" while underneath he remains confused and angry.'[36] Similarly, Maya Jaggi connects Banks's drive for conformity with his motivations: 'Christopher and Sarah are orphan outsiders striving to belong – the man through a brilliant career, the woman vicariously, through men – in a viciously exclusive society, where being well-connected bestows the crucial leg-up in life.'[37] Here, however, Jaggi seems to have misread Banks. Banks's fixation on 'connections' does not seem motivated by the thought of a 'leg-up' so much as it does by his need to connect, no longer to be an orphan.

It is perhaps the difficulty involved in understanding Banks's character that has put the efficacy of the second half of the novel into doubt. Readers who fail to perceive how the appropriation technique connects what might be read as the realist mode of *Remains* in the first half to the hallucinatory nightmare mode of *Unconsoled* perceive an awkward switch, a difficulty most clearly expressed by Anastas:

■ It's one thing to create a fictional world with a skewed sense of logic, and quite another to change a novel's guiding force midstream. Banks is just-about-human one moment and shadow the next; his investigation is emptied of significance and becomes a novelist's lark.[38] □

While many readers have responded positively to Banks's description of his journey through the warrens, what novelist Candia McWilliam (born 1955) describes as 'the tightest and neatest description I have ever read of swarming hell',[39] Oates calls 'This protracted, dogged sequence [...] the weakest part of the novel'.[40] The strongest defence of this sequence is to see the connection of landscape and psychological state, that the sequence 'dramatises Christopher's inner battle between perceived duty and the love he has momentarily allowed to lift a "massive weight" from him'.[41]

The novel's ending has also instigated criticism. McDermott finds that despite the seriousness of the ideas Ishiguro incorporates into his novel, he undermines his intent in 'The novel's denouement, a parody of the detective story's summarizing finale, [that] features a full confession by an all-but-moustache-twirling evildoer'.[42] James Francken laments that 'Banks's mistakes [...] aren't shown to have had any consequences',[43] but the more interesting criticism is outlined by writer and physician Phil Whitaker (born 1966) who finds that 'Having taken us on a voyage into a mind unhinged by loss' the novel's return 'to a rational perspective' is its one misstep. Like McDermott, Whitaker sees the possibility here of 'a pastiche of the detective genre' or 'an attempt to illustrate the "calm" that flows from seeing "through our missions to the end"', but suggests that 'while some readers may find it satisfying, the sudden reversion of tone and the neatness of the resolutions leave the ending rather flat and prosaic'.[44] Although

Whitaker's dislike of Banks's 'sudden reversion' merits notice, Oates provides another interpretation: 'Christopher Banks is a public figure whose celebrity seems to be increasing, until at the novel's end, he is awakened from his deluded sense of mission. We last see him in old age, retired to private life, accepting his "ordinary" status.' It is a retreat, but one closely tied to the struggles the novel portrays, a retreat 'with dignity, after having heroically struggled. If [Ishiguro's protagonists] don't succeed in solving the mysteries that confront them, they solve other, lesser mysteries'.[45] The ending, then, is perhaps the right one for this detective.

DETECTIVE STORY

Readers have been keen to scrutinise the novel's reference to detective fiction, especially the novel's play with the rules of detective fiction. Gorra reads the novel's first sentence as belonging 'to the world of John Buchan [1875–1940], to the guilty pleasures of such thrillers as *The Thirty-Nine Steps* [1915]', but qualifies his first impression: 'This isn't a detective novel, it only looks like one.'[46] *Orphans* establishes generic conventions and thwarts them. Barrow labels the theme of detection and Banks's 'bizarre belief in the 'very best' detectives [...] a typical Ishiguro tease' and notes the novel's refusal to conform to the detective genre: 'The final chapters may contain some unexpected twists but there are no clues to ponder over and no descriptions of the great detective at work. As in all Ishiguro's novels, many events happen off-stage or between the lines.'[47] Not surprisingly then, appropriately categorizing the genre of this novel has provided grounds for some discussion, with some referring to it vaguely as 'a new kind of detective story',[48] or, more commonly, finding it a generic hybrid: 'a curious amalgam of detective mystery, period romance, and fictional memoir.'[49]

One obvious difference marking this novel's resistance to the conventions of detective fiction is Banks's narration of his work. Although 'The story is structured like the notebooks of a detective',[50] as Boyd Tonkin, among others, observes, 'What Christopher never does, in any detail, is close a case. Mostly, this detective simply doesn't detect.' (Notably, Tonkin reports that in an earlier draft of the novel he did: 'Ishiguro devised a Golden-Age story-within-a-story to show the sleuth in cracking form. Then he "threw away about 110 finished pages".')[51] Particularly important in this discussion is Banks's failure, sometimes ascribed to Ishiguro, to provide the details of his work:

■ [O]ur hero modestly alludes to such triumphs as the 'Mannering case' or the 'Trevor Richardson affair', allusions that, in proper Holmesian fashion, remain unencumbered by details. We never see him follow a case to what I am sure he would call its denouement.[52] □

Oates reads this omission as evidence 'that the detective is an allegorical savour-figure, whose true mission is to "combat evil" at its source'.[53] For others, the novel's failure to satisfy genre conventions has led them to read it as 'a parody of a British detective novel in which Banks imagines himself the hero',[54] a reading that Gorra argues against:

■ Ishiguro stops just short of parody, and though he won't let his readers surrender to the genre, he doesn't condescend to it either. For by placing its clichés in Banks's mind, Ishiguro makes their slight pomposity an essential part of the man's character, a mark of both his limitations and of the psychic necessity that moves him.[55] □

The novel's failure to maintain the conventions of the detective novel, particularly Banks's failure to detect, has an obvious parallel in the detective's personal failures. Readers have noted Banks's lack of insight,[56] noting in particular that 'Banks remembers that detectives were called in to investigate when his father went missing, but he makes no conscious connection between that event and his own choice of a career, stating that "my intention was to combat evil"'.[57] Similarly, Bouldrey notes that while 'Banks' descriptions and immediate reflections on very important occurrences [are] faithfully and accurately rendered, [they are] never fully digested by an otherwise brilliant man'. Consequently, while Banks is a detective who 'can find subtle patterns and piece together the conflicts that tear apart other lives, he is astonishingly clueless about some very obvious aspects of his own life'.[58] This lack of insight into his own life is one of the novel's key ironies:

■ [T]he very skills that make him such a successful detective – his extraordinary attention to detail, his unwillingness to distinguish between the incidental and the momentous, his childlike single-mindedness – lead him astray as he struggles to understand the tragedy that disrupted his childhood and the currents of his mind.[59] □

It is a theme that Ishiguro has portrayed before. Gorra's comment that 'Ishiguro's real concern is with his main character's unerring ability to miss the call of freedom, in the blindness that his sense of obligation imposes upon him'[60] reads just as accurately as a statement about Stevens as it does about Banks. The difference is that in *Orphans* Ishiguro more prominently foregrounds the novel's irony by portraying a detective who does not realise that 'the real case is himself, and its resolution involves self-knowledge'.[61]

The novel's foregrounding of a detective in a novel that frustrates the generic conventions of detective fiction leads readers into the novel's primary subversion. Ishiguro demonstrates the hopelessness involved in the reliance on a single hero charged with setting everything right again: 'The hand-me-down conventions of detective fiction are shown to be too neat: brilliant feats of detection don't work in a wider, messier world.'[62] It is a theme that originated in Ishiguro's reading of detective fiction from the 1930s that he did in preparing the novel. In contrast to 'the American hard-boiled tradition of an urban purgatory', Ishiguro found English detective fiction presented a more innocent world: for example, 'In a sleepy little Dorset village, the vicar has poisoned someone. And all that is required is for the detective to come along, go click, and everything is beautiful again. Everyone is happy, all the subplots are resolved.' Ishiguro finds poignancy in this ease of resolution by connecting its affect to the era of these readings, the period directly after World War I: 'The people who read those books in such great numbers had experienced darkness and evil in all its modern form. They knew better than we do the uncontainable aspect of evil.'[63] These readings, from 'the "Golden Age" investigative school of Agatha Christie [1890–1976] or Dorothy L. Sayers [1893–1957]', are the foundation of Christopher's beliefs 'in the evil-genius theory of crime and disorder. Nail the culprit, and peace reigns again'.[64] Ishiguro's structural use of detection, at first, signals the possibility of such resolution:

■ Just as the detective story genre offers readers the consolations of an orderly narrative in which reason and logic will triumph, so detective work offers Christopher the illusion that he is using his acumen to restore order to the world around him.[65] □

However, as the novel progresses, it reveals the falsity of this order. The detective's task, to find 'potentially revelatory', meaning everywhere, is beyond one person:

■ [T]he burden of that kind of vision is a weight of responsibility no man could endure. The disconnection between Banks's careful narration and his increasingly skewed interpretation of events creates a harrowing sense of tragedy that only the most extraordinary author could carry off.[66] □

Like *Remains*, then, *Orphans* presents 'a man who thinks he has touched on the centre of important events, only to discover that the real sources of power lay elsewhere'. In *Remains* and *Orphans*, William Sutcliffe proposes, Ishiguro demonstrates the falsity in believing that one individual can change history.[67]

In contrast to Banks's attempt to carry out the role of the detective who single-handedly solves the case and restores order is the passivity of the international community in Shanghai which places its ill-founded optimism in Banks's ability to resolve their situation. Not only does Banks portray their failure to respond to the Japanese shelling of the Chinese sector of the city, he also does so in terms that prompt readers to see them as part of the problem, a problem already introduced into the novel through Banks's mother's description of the complicity of Morganbrook and Byatt, the employer of Banks's father, in the importation of opium into Shanghai (*WWWO* 62). Jaggi connects this complicity to postcolonial concerns by linking Banks's guilt to the guilt of England, 'which fuelled opium addiction as a matter of policy and abandoned the Chinese to Japanese invasion in their abject 'warren' dwellings'. She finds the proof of this link in Banks's disgust with the international community in Shanghai, 'its European elite clutching cocktails during the Japanese bombardment of the Chinese quarter as though watching a cricket match'. Notably, to accept this argument readers are required to accept this unreliable narrator as reliable, a complication that has not yet been addressed in the response to the novel. (Similarly, we should believe that he really is a celebrated detective.) The novel does, however, appear to sanction this reading with its weaving of 'a deft parable of colonial immoral earnings, through a life built on tawdry spoils. "You see how the world really is – what made possible your comfortable life in England?" Christopher is asked'.[68] Surprisingly, postcolonial critics have not investigated this argument.

Alexander M. Bain provides the one essay to inquire into Ishiguro's portrayal of the failure of the international community. After noting that the novel was written during the same period that Western countries failed or chose not to intervene in the Balkan, Somalian, and Rwandan crises, Bain reads the novel as exploring 'the consciousness of an "international community" haunted by its recent failure to protect and by the prospect of a future in which unlimited obligations to intervene prompt endless self-examination about "values" and "interests"'.[69] Bain's reading, although marred by its failure to acknowledge the elusiveness of Banks's narration, provides a useful start to comprehending this element of the novel. It asks us to consider how our memories of the past interrogate our present.

ON MEMORY

In all of his novels, Ishiguro foregrounds the role and processes of memory. Shaffer perhaps summarises memory's role best: 'Ishiguro's novels are psychological mystery-voyages into the protagonist's problematic or compromised past',[70] but in portraying these voyages, Ishiguro also demonstrates memory's 'stratagems, its selectivity, its obsessional quality, its refinements, its expedience and use'.[71] As in his first three novels, *Orphans* foregrounds memory through the method of narration and the narrator's admissions of uncertainty in the veracity of his recall. The events of the novel 'are told in retrospect – sometimes from the distance of only hours, sometimes from a great many years'.[72] Additionally, the structuring of Banks's account in notebook format, established in part by the detailed dates and places provided at the beginning of every chapter, is continuously overrun by the narrator's memories: 'despite this superficial fixing of time in his work, the narrative frequently spins wildly through different eras. The dates Ishiguro likes to fix are merely the dates of recall'.[73] Memory is foregrounded as well by the narrator's trouble with them: 'Banks makes it clear again and again that he is well aware of the fragility of recollection.'[74] Ishiguro's focus, in fact, appears to be the struggle that memories impose on the individual, the insistence of the past in a character's present: 'His narrators, all of whom have suffered a deep psychological rupture in their lives, are often fighting a long-standing battle to relate their past to a present with which it does not seem to fit.'[75]

Additionally, as John J. Su has argued in relation to *Remains*, Ishiguro uses memory to trigger nostalgia, an emotion he then uses to reconfigure the present.[76] He refers to nostalgia as 'a much-maligned emotion' and suggests that the English undervalue it 'because it harks back to empire days and to guilt about the empire'. Ishiguro argues, however, that 'nostalgia is the emotional equivalent of idealism. You use memory to go back to a place better than the one you find yourself in.'[77] This harkening back to a previous time is not unproblematic, a point that the novel emphasises most clearly in its portrayal of Shanghai's International Settlement but also in Banks's failure of memory: 'Banks's growing amnesia, which arouses panic in him, is symptomatic of a generalised cultural amnesia regarding British and European exploitation of China.'[78] Rather than forget, the novel proposes, better to incorporate the positive qualities of the past into our lives in the present. The nostalgic desire, then, can lead 'us imaginatively to create a better world'.[79]

ON CHILDREN

Memory's role is most prominent in the novel's portrayal of children. The novel's title points readers to this connection: the 'When we were', indicating a reference in the present to a time in the past, and 'orphans', taken literally, indicating children. It is also this intersection of memory and childhood that most touches readers' emotions: for Wood, 'The novel's highest achievement is the gentle way it offers Christopher's tale as a surreal allegory of the ways in which we are the prisoners of our childhoods, the criminals of our pasts, always guilty with memory'.[80] Shaffer, similarly, reads the novel as exploring 'the awful burden of guilt that such children take on to correct or undo their orphaned states' and sees this guilt in characters' 'need to "rescue" their parents and others [...] all, apparently, to no avail. In instance after instance, such attempts at rescue are "betrayed"'.[81] Banks's pursuit of memories back to his childhood 'is only an echo of a more universal "chasing of the shadows of vanished parents", in which we all, in one way or another, engage'.[82] He looks to his childhood past trying to solve its difficulties, but here Ishiguro has equipped him with a different set of tools: 'Relying on the detective's tools of deduction and rationality, Banks tries to heal the wounds of his childhood.'[83]

The nature of these wounds has not been well articulated. Notably, Wood, while trying to reason out the title, provides a provocative attempt to locate them in one of the novel's largest omissions. Having noted that the 'we' in the title suggests the presence of another orphan alongside Banks that the novel does not provide, Wood points to a further problem that a literal reading of the title enjoins:

■ Nor does the novel, in defiance of its title, really describe any moment when Christopher *was* an orphan: we see him as a happy child, and then as a successful adult. The time when he was an 'orphan' (at St. Dunstan's) is precisely the book's and presumably Christopher's painful lacuna.[84] □

The novel provides some support for this reading. While the most obvious source of proof, the few scenes that Banks recounts from this period, provide some clues, most obviously, his desire for 'connections', further evidence might be deduced from the possible foreshadowing provided by Akira's unhappy time at school in Japan and the possible backshadowing provided by Jennifer's time at St. Margaret's and her later unhappiness, and as well, the larger theme of the difficulty of being English (for example, *WWWO* 76, 79–80). Ishiguro provides a more general origin for the wound while discussing the origin of the novel in 'the metaphor of orphans'. It is a metaphor that marks a crucial moment in life, as Ishiguro puts it, 'that moment in our lives when we come out of the sheltered bubble of childhood and discover that the world is not the cosy place that we had previously been taught to believe'. Moreover, not only is it a universal experience, Ishiguro suggests that 'Even when we become adults, something of this disappointment, I think, remains.'[85]

As in *The Unconsoled*, one of the novel's key images instructing readers how to understand the narration appears near the novel's beginning. In Ishiguro's previous novel, it was the tear in the carpet documenting Ryder's manipulations of reality (*Unc* 16–17); here the novel's use of the detective genre, its reliance on memory, and its investigation of childhood are joined in the image of the magnifying glass for which 'a second magnifying glass is needed to read the inscription saying that it was made in Zurich in 1887' (*WWWO* 9).[86] The magnifying glass does not appear again until near the novel's conclusion when it provides the 'surreal mismatch between the society sleuth's myopic mind and the oceanic misery around him – "using a magnifying glass to look at corpses in a war-zone", as [Ishiguro] says'. As Tonkin suggests, this myopia 'effectively stops the hero from achieving much of an adult inner life until the book's final pages'.[87] Reich, too, picks up on the absurdity of Banks looking through his magnifying glass at the large wounds of the little Chinese girl's dead mother, and proposes that for Banks the glass's limiting of details 'makes the unbearable, at least for a moment, bearable. For the reader, viewing the accretion of detail that constitutes and transcends memory through the prism of Ishiguro's ordered larger vision reveals the truth'.[88] But the earlier appearance of the magnifying glass, in which the instrument built for detecting requires another to detect itself, provides readers with a model for reading Banks's narrative, in particular his need for another to detect himself. This model is most valuable for interpreting his final meeting with his mother, for 'From her brief dislocated words, Banks discovers that his mother never expected him to rescue her, and that her love for him remains unconditional.'[89] Banks, the great detective, has been unable to solve the case of himself, but his mother, looking through a lens that magnifies her memories, reads the word 'Puffin' on the detective and provides him the information that allows for the case's resolution.

CONCLUSION

While it exhibits themes and elements featured in Ishiguro's earlier work, *Orphans* remains a complex and original novel. The response to the novel provides a particularly fascinating perspective on reader subjectivity and interpretive instability, and the paucity of scholarly response to the novel offers several opportunities. One of the tasks awaiting scholars is to elucidate the various moments of critical contention. Further examination of Ishiguro's innovative appropriation technique might better illuminate how it functions in the novel and how its functioning aids our understanding of the novel. An examination of Banks's narration might also improve our understanding of his character. As well, theorists working from a postcolonial perspective have been largely silent on this novel despite the power imbalances it portrays and despite its thorough questioning of identity, both personal and national. Finally, but far from conclusively, the novel's play on our expectations of mystery and its resolution and its probing of truth and knowledge suggest the work awaiting in studies based on genre analysis and cognitive poetics. Ultimately, however, the novel's power lies in our recognition of and response to its meditations on identity, loss, and childhood. In doing so we can understand the novel's value in its continuing of Ishiguro's investigation into how we create and deny meaning in our lives. His next novel, *Never Let Me Go*, returns to issues of identity, loss, and childhood, but adds a range of new concerns, including medical research and individuality. He does so through a voice entirely new to Ishiguro's work, the voice of a young woman named Kathy, a carer.

CHAPTER EIGHT

Questioning the Possibles: *Never Let Me Go* (2005)

While the response to *When We Were Orphans* was often puzzling, Ishiguro's sixth novel, *Never Let Me Go*, met with almost unanimous critical approval and immediate scholarly interest. Critics have praised every aspect of the novel: it is 'A masterpiece of craftsmanship that offers an unparalleled emotional experience'.[1] Set in a parallel Britain, in a parallel 1990s, the novel, like all of his previous novels, uses a first-person narrator, Kathy H., who combs through memories of her past. Readers eventually realise that Kathy H. is a clone living in a boarding school with other clones who will all graduate to become 'carers', then 'donors', and after four 'donations', at the most, they will die. Amidst her recollections of childhood and adolescence, Ishiguro layers a story that demands a questioning of our values and ethics, and what we take for granted as truth.

THE INITIAL RESPONSE

Readers begin the book unaware that the narrator is a clone but, repeatedly confronted with perplexing details and language, are led by 'the shadows of things not said, glimpsed out of the corner of one's eye' to deduce Kathy's situation.[2] Consequently, as James Wood points out, 'Reviews of this singular novel have tended to stress the first-stage detection involved in reading it; whereas Ishiguro, as ever, is interested in far foggier hermeneutics.' Wood acknowledges Ishiguro's pacing, but makes the distinction that Ishiguro's 'real interest is not in what we discover but in what his characters discover, and how it will affect them. He wants us to inhabit their ignorance, not ours'.[3]

We inhabit their ignorance through Ishiguro's fidelity to a narrating voice that shuns the literary. Rather than the enriched vocabularies of some first-person narrators, Kathy tends to cliché: "'I know for a fact"; "it means a lot to me"; "a complete waste of space". She begins sentences with "actually" and "anyway". She does not exactly have an impoverished lexicon: she readily uses words like "languorous", "ambivalent" and "trammelled."[4] Frank Kermode (born 1919) recognises that her 'familiar, chatty style' suits the character, but adds, 'Whatever the virtues of this authorial decision, the texture of the writing becomes altogether less interesting.'[5] Sarah Kerr, however, goes beyond Kermode's standard, based on 'interest', to contend Ishiguro's matching of Kathy's voice to her experience 'is a feat of imaginative sympathy and technique. He works out intricate ways of showing her naïvete, her liabilities as an interpreter of what she sees, but also her deductive smarts, her sensitivity to pain and her need for affection'.[6]

Despite this heroism and Ishiguro's fantastic, almost sci-fi, premise, the novel's power is in its connection to the everyday and the human. Rather than 'a panoramic dystopia', Ishiguro 'remains fixed on intimate things – on the small social groupings within a school, on the nuances of personal relationships'.[7] His creation of 'horror [...] in the mundane',[8] is made more chilling as readers are led to focus on questions of human existence: 'Ishiguro's dark answer is that the modern desperation regarding death, combined with technological advances and the natural human capacity for self-serving fictions and evasions [...] could easily give rise to new varieties of socially approved atrocities.'[9] Wood finds the novel's power in 'its picture of ordinary human life as in fact a culture of death. That is to say, Ishiguro's book is at its best when, by asking us to consider the futility of cloned lives, it forces us to consider the futility of our own'.[10] Wood's emphasis on futility was also recognised by reviewers who detected Beckett's influence on Ishiguro:

■ As in Beckett, Ishiguro's characters, in their detached world, show us a version of our own minute preoccupations and piddling distractions, and raise life's largest questions for us all. Is this all there is? Must it end so soon? Why strive? Why persist? What is it all for?[11] □

Alongside such questioning, the novel's portrayal of clones used as organ donors until death guarantees responses invoking ethical debates. Novelist Margaret Atwood (born 1939) describes the moral context:

■ The outer world wants these children to exist because it's greedy for the benefits they can confer, but it doesn't wish to look head-on at what is happening. We assume – though it's never stated – that whatever objections might have been raised to such a scheme have already been overcome: By now the rules are in place and the situation is taken for granted – as slavery was once – by beneficiaries and victims alike.[12] □

Questions of ethics and morality permeate the novel: novelist Joseph O'Neill (born 1964) likens these to the issues raised by the German philosopher Friedrich Nietzsche (1844–1900): 'one of the many Nietzschean insights of the novel is that successful crimes produce mutations in morality.'[13] Ishiguro acknowledges the value of his clones to establish such discussions, discussions that suggest some of literature's most persistent questions: 'which in recent years have become a little awkward to raise in fiction. "What does it mean to be human?" "What is the soul?" "What is the purpose for which we've been created, and should we try to fulfil it?" '[14]

Reviewers have also realised the novel's connection to contemporary debates. Gary Rosen describes the novel's intersection with debates on medical research:

■ What's upsetting about Kathy isn't her existence as a clone but rather the fate that has been assigned to her: to die young, used up for the medical benefits of others. She is at once a literary protest against research cloning and, by virtue of her strength as a character, a quiet suggestion that reproductive cloning may not be so troubling after all.[15] □

Daniel Vorhaus also focuses on the novel's contribution to ethical discussions of cloning: 'Whatever our other concerns about the inevitable emergence of reproductive cloning, to continue to imagine the clone as a soulless non-human entity is the mark of a scared and close-minded society.'[16] As M. John Harrison points out, however, 'there's no science here'. The novel's primary concern, he proposes, is not cloning but what keeps us from exploding, 'why we don't just wake up one day and go sobbing and crying down the street, kicking everything to pieces out of the raw, infuriating, completely personal sense of our lives never having been what they could have been'.[17]

Not surprisingly, then, reviewers have called the novel 'an existential fable'[18] and 'a parable about mortality'[19] and noted the immensity of its themes: 'Inescapable death, loss, the destruction or dissipation of what once was valued, love and life reduced over time to detritus cast on the wind.'[20] While Tim Adams describes it as 'Ishiguro's most profound statement of the endurance of human relationships',[21] Atwood calls it 'a thoughtful, crafty, and finally very disquieting look at the effects of dehumanization on any group that's subject to it'.[22] Peter Kemp, similarly, picks up on the novel's theme of exploitation, noting that it 'never hardens into anything as clear-cut as allegory but it resonates with disquieting suggestiveness. Slowly uncovering an appalling system, Ishiguro uses it to stir emotions – shock, compassion, shame, guilt – that exposés of brutally callous social or global injustices might evoke'.[23]

Finally, Ishiguro's reliance on the everyday and foregrounding of questions of human existence allows him to return to the portrayal of childhood. His naming of the children's school, Hailsham, 'As in "sham"; as in Charles Dickens' Miss Havisham [in *Great Expectations*], exploiter of uncomprehending children', immediately suggests the difficulties the children face.[24] Ishiguro describes the boarding school as a metaphor for childhood: 'as a physical manifestation of the way all children are separated off from the adult world, and are drip-fed little pieces of information about the world that awaits them, often with generous doses of deception – kindly meant or otherwise.'[25] It is an idea to which critics repeatedly return: '[the children's] hesitant progression into knowledge of their plight is an extreme and heart-breaking version of the exodus of all children from the innocence in which the benevolent but fraudulent adult world conspires to place them.'[26] Similarly, Theo Tait describes the novel's reflections on 'the uncertainties of adolescence: a time, after all, when we all feel outsiders yet try to blend in [...] and when we all struggle with questions about the purpose of our existence.'[27]

THE SCHOLARLY RESPONSE

In addition to the numerous reviews, two critical readings address some of these issues and extend the understanding of this novel. Rebecca Walkowitz, within a larger argument, reads the novel as a critique of individuality, one that offers a provocative view on unoriginality. Bruce Robbins uses what some critics have referred to as the 'banality' of Ishiguro's themes to introduce a new paradigm for reading Ishiguro.

Rebecca L. Walkowitz, a New Reading of Originality

Walkowitz's discussion of *Never Let Me Go* is situated within an excellent article that responds to arguments suggesting translation leads to cultural and political homogenisation. Questioning the assumption of homogenisation's undesirability, she argues that new world literature's many variables compel 'us to consider not only the global production and circulation of texts but also our ways of thinking about cultural and political uniqueness'.[28] Ishiguro's work provides a compelling example because his entire oeuvre implies 'that it is inadequate, and even unethical, to treat uniqueness as the defining quality of art, culture, and human life'. Instead, she reads his fiction as using comparison to create a different sort of uniqueness: 'the uniqueness of a translation, the uniqueness of a cassette tape'.[29]

Never Let Me Go, she argues, 'is a book about the value of unoriginal expression', replete with 'bad copies and eccentric interpretations', a characterisation she supports with a useful catalogue of examples that reveals the pervasiveness of this theme:

■ there is a cassette tape that plays a monotonous pop song called 'Never Let Me Go' whose lyrics the narrator adapts to her own story (70, 271–2); there is a mediocre television program whose sitcom relationships the adolescent characters take as role models for adult behavior (121); there is a magazine insert whose glossy image and cheerful rhetoric ('Are you the dynamic, go-ahead type?') the narrator's friend appropriates for her ideal future (144); there are the drawings of metallic animals, which are said to look 'laboured, almost like they'd been copied' (241); and there is of course the narrator and her friends, all of whom are human clones brought up to be organ donors for – what shall we call them? – non-cloned, original humans. □

Walkowitz provides both further evidence for this reading and a riposte to the criticisms of Kathy's narrating voice by discerning that it 'seems to be a carrier of the unoriginal expression that Ishiguro wants us to value'.[30]

A critique of individuality also appears in the novel's 'critique of anthropocentrism'. Tommy's drawings, in particular, 'suggest that strategies of abstraction allow us to see some bodies as mechanisms and others as individuals'.[31] This distinction of individuality allows the donation system to function because while the humans value individuality above all and are able to distinguish individuality in themselves, they perceive the clones as *lacking* that highly valued individuality. The clones, moreover, 'lack interiority, which is measured, according to all of the characters, by the capacity for genuine love, authentic expressivity, and artistic originality'.[32] Throughout the novel, then, 'copied' things are portrayed negatively, an economy made clear early in the novel when Kathy explains that when students like the poem of another student, they want the original, not just a copy (*NLMG* 17). The contrast to the copy is provided, for example, by Miss Emily's belief that the clones' production of original art work will demonstrate their sensitivity and intelligence (*NLMG* 261). It is this privileging of individuality, a value to which every character in the novel, human or clone, appears to have been indoctrinated, that the novel critiques:

■ Seeing clones as humans is not the point. Instead, we are urged to see humans as clones. That is, we are urged to see that even humans produced through biological reproduction are in some ways copies; and that human culture, full of cassette tapes and television programs and rumors and paperbacks of *Daniel Deronda* [(1876) by George Eliot (1819–80)], is also unoriginal. It is by seeing the likeness between human originality and the novel's unoriginal objects – Kathy H., the cassette, the song, the television program, the narration – that we recognize the large networks of approximation and comparison in which individuality functions.[33] □

The primacy of uniqueness in demonstrating individuality is reduced and supplanted by a reconceptualisation of the idea of 'unoriginal' that sees the object in its various relationships and contexts.

Interpretations are, likewise, portrayed as flawed. Most obviously, the eponymous song, 'Never Let Me Go', is interpreted twice in the novel, once by Kathy and later by Madame (*NLMG* 70, 272). Walkowitz connects these faulty interpretations with her model of the network: 'For Ishiguro, the point is not simply that art can mean anything – that it is what you say or see – but rather that the content of art will be transformed by expansive circulation and by the local interpretations that readers impose.' Given the significance of these two interpretations, Walkowitz suggests that the novel's title refers not just to the name of a song or the characters' interpretation of the song, but to the cassette-tape recording itself, 'one of the novel's pre-eminent "copies" '.[34] The two copies of this one recording play an important role in the novel, revealing two models for considering uniqueness: one for people and art work, another for objects. In the first, 'individuals have an ontological existence that defines what they are and what they will be; copies simply inherit that existence. The second model attributes uniqueness not to a prior existence but to social embeddedness and the capacity for new contextualization'.[35] Walkowitz offers the example of Kathy's four similarly designed, but differently coloured desk lamps (*NLMG* 208):

■ Kathy doesn't value the desk lamps for what each one normally does (shed light). Instead, she values them because they constitute a group, because they allow her to contemplate similarities and differences, and because they provide an occasion for new comparisons. Kathy's desk lamps are part of a group, but that group is incomplete, and each desk lamp has the potential to join other groups – those defined by, say, color rather than by design.[36] □

Similarly, the Norfolk version of Kathy's cassette tape connects her not only to memories of Norfolk, and the afternoon when she and Tommy found it, but also to her childhood memories of Hailsham when she had the first copy of the tape. In both cases, Walkowitz contends, the tapes take on value through 'social experience – we might say the network – forged by the tapes' circulation'.[37]

The novel's privileging of the second model of uniqueness, Walkowitz proposes, is better seen by considering the cover of the Japanese version of the novel. Unlike the covers of almost every other edition, the Japanese edition does not feature a young woman, in whole or part, or children playing, but an image of a cassette tape the same size as the book. Considering this foregrounding of the image of a tape rather than a person, Walkowitz interprets the novel's conceptualisation of art:

> ■ In Ishiguro's novel, the work of art has no 'deep down': its meanings are collaborative and comparative, and thus affirm, instead of a soul, various social networks of production and consumption. Ishiguro suggests that a song or a novel or a person can be a singular object as well as a multiple-type object. In so doing, he proposes that uniqueness depends not on an absolute quality or a predetermined future but on the potential for comparison and likeness: all art is a cassette tape, for better or for worse. Only by appreciating the unoriginality of art, Ishiguro suggests, can we change the idea of culture itself.[38] □

With this emphasis on comparison, collaboration, and networks, Walkowitz provides a new paradigm for reading Ishiguro. It is a model that looks past the old descriptions based on nation, culture, and Englishness to read his work amidst the complexities of globalisation. In doing so, she not only demonstrates the frailty of many of the attempts to categorise him, but also offers a new method for understanding his fiction. Finally, it is a model that allows readers to see the extent to which Ishiguro writes about the attempts we all make to construct meaning in our lives.

Bruce Robbins, 'Cruelty is Bad'

Having found moments of cruelty throughout Ishiguro's fiction and interested in what he perceives, simultaneously, as their power and the difficulty critics have had in articulating that power, Bruce Robbins unpacks the complicated context of two moments of cruelty in *Never Let Me Go*. Doing so, he addresses the tendency of critics, confronted with the difficulty of these moments, to downplay and challenge the usefulness of Ishiguro's ethical vision. It is a complex but thoughtful reading in which Robbins suggests that Ishiguro offers a context for cruelty that may not explain the cruelty but reveals its necessity.

The language of the novel's opening, in which Kathy introduces herself, provides starting points for two important trajectories that the novel follows. In her very first sentence, she notes that she is a 'carer', one who cares for others. Readers returning to this passage, knowing the fate of carers, recognise that Kathy's offhand remark that she will soon become a donor omits the more relevant point that she will soon be dead. As Robbins notes though, Kathy's language does not foreground this information; instead, she focuses on her job performance with language that suggests her belief in the ideology of upward mobility, a belief that the novel complicates further by setting her 'professional ambitions [...] within a bureaucracy that resembles the welfare state both in its rationale and in its total penetration of the private lives of those in its care'.[39] For the cloned children, however, the idea of upward mobility is a sham. The path of their lives, as Miss Lucy tells them, is fixed: care, donate, die (*NLMG* 81).

The genre, however, is not fixed. Its modification, from the 'bland, squeaky-clean idiom of the middle-class boarding school novel, with its beguilingly motivational assumption that the world is just and that effort will eventually be rewarded', to 'dark, late twentieth-century punk or slacker vision of "no future" ',[40] demonstrates the conflict of individual and collective. The narrative choices are similar to those found in earlier Ishiguro works: 'we look at the world through the eyes of a character of limited consciousness, immersed in concerns and anxieties that one cannot confidently call trivial, who prefers not to contemplate the Big Picture.' Such narration leads, Robbins proposes, to feelings of sympathy for Kathy, Stevens, and Ryder and questions how our own happiness depends 'on a blinkering of awareness' we might at other times find 'outrageous and repulsive'. It provokes this questioning by examining 'the partly existential desire that sustains the upward mobility story'. In our identification with the uncloned, 'the absolute peremptoriness of the practical', our desire and need to assert our individuality, overrides collective justice. Collective justice only reappears when we are driven to contemplate ourselves, 'coldly and impersonally', as part of the mass of individuals, and here the novel equates our focus on individuality as 'literally trying to get away with murder', to live using the organs of those who died providing them.[41] The alternative is to identify with the carers and donors and be murdered. Here Robbins finds a possible argument for arousing social aspiration, if that aspiration leads to changing the system. Alternatively, Ishiguro might be demonstrating that we need to see ourselves, not as individuals, but as units of a mass: 'This is the demand for an impersonal coldness that, by the usual standards of proximity-first, could only register as ethical deficiency, even as cruelty.'[42] It is, then, in the emotionless shifting of the perception of the individual from sovereign to member of a collective that Robbins finds a type of cruelty.

While Miss Lucy's speech exposes the hopelessness of the clones' situation (*NLMG* 81), it does not change their outlook. They break the rules only in the myth they create about deferrals; otherwise, their hope for recognition and rewards, evident in Kathy's opening self-introduction, distracts them from their horrible futures. Reading Ishiguro as concerned with what makes action unthinkable, Robbins ascribes the clones' inaction to 'the ideology of the welfare state, which gives a grateful semblance of meaning and legitimacy to the stopgap efforts of every day'.[43] Only late in the novel does Tommy question the importance of Kathy's work, an exchange in which Robbins detects the collusion of the welfare state with upward mobility. While Kathy excuses her devotion to her work through her belief that its social good justifies it, the social good involved allows her, Robbins suggests, the credit or advantage valued in the ideology of upward mobility. In fact, Robbins proposes that Ishiguro's 'characteristic effects' can be seen as a questioning of the welfare-state vision, 'a vision centered on that bittersweet compromise between social justice and the injustice enforced by capitalist competition'.[44] For example, Kathy's remark on the small size of the recovery rooms is immediately qualified by her acknowledgement of the quality of their design and comfort, a response that quickly obscures the point that the recovery rooms are only necessary because of the required donations and that they signal 'a suffering that is beyond any possible compensation'. Citing Kathy's claim to prevent 'agitation' in her donors, Robbins concludes, 'Blank and bureaucratic, cravenly accepting of monstrously limited expectations, dedicated to suppressing all "agitation" at the deep injustice that underlies the system as a whole: this is the voice of the welfare state much as its severest critics understand it.'[45]

One response to the welfare state is anger, as Tommy demonstrates. However, when Miss Lucy, visibly angry, tells Tommy not to worry about his artistic difficulties and that they are not his fault, his agitation lessens. Consistent with the critical view of the welfare state that permeates the novel, his change reveals how bribery with small compensations aims to occlude the larger causes for anger. Miss Lucy curtails his anger and artistic aspiration, but since aspiration is only meant to distract the Hailsham students, effacing anger by effacing aspiration leaves only his truth, and Tommy's truth should make him angry. Consequently, effacing anger by effacing merit leads back to anger. Since Tommy is again angry, years later when told deferrals are a myth, it is possible that Miss Lucy does not eliminate his anger, but suspends it. Perhaps Tommy somehow understood the inequity of his situation, 'knowledge of a general social injustice to which anger was an entirely appropriate response'.[46]

Miss Lucy's advice on striving is equally complicated. She can only advise Tommy by contradicting herself: she wants him to aspire, but aspiration is only reasonable in a system that rewards it. Before leaving the school, then, she reverses her position, a shift 'from reassurance to what might appear to be another of those moments of gratuitous emotional violence'.[47] She tells Tommy his art is 'rubbish' and she is, in part, at fault (*NLMG* 108). Her criticism, Robbins contends, is an act of cruelty, explained, however, as an attempt to protect him: with no way out of his situation, perhaps self-delusion betters hopelessness. With her admission of fault, Miss Lucy, a representative of the system, reveals a fault in the system. With her demonstration of anger, she presents the possibility of 'angry aspiration, a goal that would require maintaining rather than eliminating the anger that seems to block the passage upward'.[48] Robbins, consequently, posits the possibility of a system able to see merit in those who seek to change it.

Kathy too tells Tommy his art is 'rubbish'. It is her cruelty Robbins reads as 'the paradigmatic [...] scene of inexplicable cruelty between people who love each other'.[49] Ruth, ridiculing Tommy, lies and tells him that, like her, Kathy also finds his artwork ridiculous. Kathy, knowing that she has to tell Tommy that Ruth is lying, does not: 'an act of omission forces us to ask how a character can be so cruel to the one person she has always loved.'[50] While Kathy accounts for her silence thinking, 'let him think the absolute worst' (*NLMG* 195), Robbins wonders if this means the 'worst about her, or the worst about himself?' The latter meaning would duplicate Miss Lucy's final statement to him, but Robbins (making a claim not particularly well supported) suggests she is pronouncing 'a larger judgment about things in general: let him think the absolute worst about his own situation, about what awaits them all, about the system to which they belong'. Either interpretation suggests 'cruelty is indistinguishable from caring', for only with cruelty can she 'lovingly hold open the possibility (however theoretical) of an aspiration that he would be allowed to enjoy'.[51]

Kathy's response is to a particular situation. She has the ability to understand the emotions of those around her, and she is reliable. In fact, Robbins suggests, she is so reliable that Ishiguro might be suggesting readers question her, question whether her reliability does not depend on her ignoring the desperateness of their futures, question whether her calmness does not signal her acceptance of the validity of the system. But if her 'inexplicable cruelty toward Tommy is a sign of anger against the system [...] then the cruelty would of course no longer be inexplicable. Nor would it be simply what it seems: cruelty. It would also be, like Miss Lucy's, an oblique expression of ethical generosity'. Robbins emphasises this point because some have read Ishiguro as 'making only the most banal and uncontroversial ethical statements'. But as Robbins has demonstrated, cruelty here is 'part of a more expansive and counter-intuitive political vision', which requires us 'to consider caring here as possibly conflicting with caring there, that allows us to consider the welfare state as a distanced, anger-bearing project in which the anger is a necessary part of a genuine concern for people's welfare'. It is a vision requiring a look beyond the welfare of those right around us, even if that is cruel, a vision that sends us back to Ishiguro's fiction to consider 'whether what seems to be an ethical platitude [...] might turn out to be a loud warning against ethical platitudes, and in particular against the easy ethical comfort with which Ishiguro is so often associated'.[52]

CONCLUSION

Like the clones who might first be considered copies but quickly reveal their complexity and humanity, the simplicity of *Never Let Me Go* masks a complex novel that questions our ethics and existence. Responses to the novel have risen to the challenge of this complexity and provided numerous starting points to initiate its discussion. In particular, Walkowitz's reading distinguishes a new frame for unoriginality. With her emphasis on comparison and networks, it is a reading that might also lead to a better understanding of the issue of 'connectedness' that suffuses Ishiguro's work, a suggestion made much plainer by recalling Christopher Banks, the narrator of *When We Were Orphans*, and his desire for connections, and Ishiguro's development of the innovative appropriation technique which allowed him to write novels, such as *The Unconsoled* and *Orphans*, that embody connections. Robbins develops a careful reading of Ishiguro's vision that compels a return to the earlier novels for possible reassessment. More importantly, he reminds us of the primary complexity of Ishiguro's fiction: the difficulty of negotiating our lives with ourselves and others.

Conclusion

This guide has aimed to include the most important readings in English of Kazuo Ishiguro's novels, a goal constantly challenged by the continuing and theoretically diverse scholarship on his work. Recently, several more analyses of Ishiguro's work have appeared demonstrating this sustained critical interest. Three such recent essays that merit further study are by Natalie Reitano, Leona Toker and Daniel Chertoff, and Lisa Fluet. Reitano provides a useful reading of *The Unconsoled*, arguing that it 'fitfully interrogates the idea of a founding traumatic rupture by rethinking the relation between the memory and promise that structure any present'.[1] Toker and Chertoff, while attempting to explain the effect of the narration of *Never Let Me Go* on readers, discuss the features that align it with other dystopian fictions.[2] Perhaps most intriguingly, Fluet examines the narrators of Ishiguro's four most recent novels to conclude that they 'give us access to feelings – often ugly, if not always strong – that convey not a comfortably agreed-upon idea of humanity, but rather what it might feel like to lose one's individual sense of "me" in an impersonal, collective "we"'.[3] These are promising efforts which respond to questions established in earlier responses with original arguments that extend the discussion of Ishiguro's fiction.

It is not within the scope of this Guide to cover criticism related to Ishiguro's ever-developing career as a screenwriter. However, his work on the adaptation of *The Remains of the Day*, and his two original screenplays, The *White Countess* (2005), produced with Ismail Merchant (1936–2005) and James Ivory (born 1928), and *The Saddest Music in the World* (2003), produced by experimental filmmaker Guy Maddin (born 1956), certainly merit attention, as does the adaptation of his sixth novel, *Never Let Me Go*. Earl G. Ingersoll has written an informative essay on the differences between *Remains* as novel and film[4] while Edward T. Jones has written an equally entertaining essay comparing the screenplay produced by Merchant and Ivory's long-time collaborator Ruth Prawer Jhabvala (born 1927) with the unpublished screenplay produced by Nobel-prize winning dramatist Harold Pinter.[5] Since the release of *The Saddest Music in the World* and *The White Countess*, both films have received numerous positive reviews: A. O. Scott lauded the former as, 'a strangely joyful spectacle of lamentation and misery';[6] Mick LaSalle described the latter as 'Measured and meticulous, with [...] rich performances.'[7] *The White Countess*, however, was generally reviewed less enthusiastically. Peter Bradshaw's review captures the tone of others calling it, 'interminably long, ploddingly paced'.[8] Despite such criticisms and the lack of any scholarly criticism published on either film, each presents compelling possibilities for understanding Ishiguro's work. Most obviously, by setting *The White Countess* in Shanghai at the start of the Sino-Japanese War (1937–45), Ishiguro invites a direct comparison to *When We Were Orphans*. Despite this similarity, however, the film and novel bear little resemblance to each another. More importantly, the film's wounded protagonists faced with the challenges of their daily lives remind readers of Ishiguro's earlier statement about his choice of settings for his first three novels: 'I tend to be attracted to pre-war and post-war settings because I'm interested in this business of values and ideals being tested, and people having to face up to the notion that their ideals weren't quite what they thought they were before the test came.'[9] It is hard to imagine a film as different from *The White Countess* as *The Saddest Music in the World*, yet this movie, too, has clear connections to Ishiguro's fiction, although its most obvious connection is to Ishiguro's fourth novel, *The Unconsoled*. While at first glance, the film and novel appear to bear few similarities in plot and setting, both foreground the purported healing power of music in the midst of surreal settings. An original and provocative filmmaker, Maddin shot the film 'in a deliberately anachronist[ic] style – tinted black-and-white with color inserts, gauzy glamour, halated backlighting',[10] and this style provides possibly the only filmic portrayal conceivable of the strange peregrinations of Ryder, the narrator and protagonist of *The Unconsoled*. The many connections linking the film and the novel, such as the portrayal in both of a car crash leading to a mistaken amputation, offer scholars of Ishiguro's works interesting comparisons and new paths along which to investigate his art.

Despite the numerous responses to Ishiguro's fiction described in this book, much more remains to be done. Most recently, Ishiguro has published a collection of linked short stories, *Nocturnes: Five Stories of Music and Nightfall* (2009), that requires a response. It is important to reiterate that *When We Were Orphans*, in particular, has not received the scholarly attention it demands: it is a complex novel using an innovative narrative technique that embodies the meaning of the text. Although many gaps in the scholarship have been noted while discussing the novels, these gaps, for the most part, can be grouped into three categories. First, although Ishiguro is continually referred to as a master prose stylist, there has been no major stylistic analysis of his writing. Discussions of his style have been limited to brief episodic analyses, or comparisons to other writers, in the service of some other purpose. It is a glaring omission in the collective response to the work of a writer so adept in conveying nuance and detail. Second, while Toker and Chertoff's recent essay provides a start to cognitive readings of Ishiguro's work, further readings based on cognitive studies of poetics and narrative hold the promise of providing valuable instruction on the psychology of Ishiguro's work. This promise can be understood, in part, by reviewing the propensity of earlier critics to rely on Freudian readings; however, such readings almost always attempt to explain some aspect of a character's motivation (while the most horrendous attempt to read the novels as documents of Ishiguro's motivations). Cognitive readings would, most certainly, provide revisions to those earlier readings, but also offer a better understanding of how the novels connect with their readers. Lastly, the ethical dimension of Ishiguro's novels, particularly *The Remains of the Day*, has received some attention, but given the weight that Ishiguro's fiction places on the missteps of his characters, their often problematic responses to these missteps, and the settings within which these missteps occur, more analysis of the ethics of these stories, not only ethics-based analysis of the depicted events but also the ethics of their narration, is required. The addressing of these omissions and the further development of the engaged scholarship that has characterised much of the response to Ishiguro's novels promises to provide much more fascinating reading and illumination of Ishiguro's fiction.

Following the publication of each of Ishiguro's first three novels, it was easy to find critics who wrote about Ishiguro as though he were Japanese or only writing about Japanese topics. This trend has, thankfully, abated, and Ishiguro's work is now greeted, for the most part, with more involved, critically sound analyses that focus less on his biography and more on the novels that he writes. Although some scholars do still attempt to read Ishiguro as a postcolonial writer, Chu-chueh Cheng's thoughtful overview of Ishiguro's oeuvre might put an end to such simplifications. After contrasting Ishiguro's fiction with the terms postcolonial, ethnic, and immigrant and finding each of these terms inaccurate for describing his work, Cheng observes, 'in addition to his Japanese heritage, Western literary traditions, monumental events, and personal innovation have collaboratively informed his distinctive authorship.' Moreover, such terms elide 'other equally formative factors and subsequently displace the novelist to an imaginary margin without an actual center. Although demographically a Japanese minority in Britain, the novelist has never been a minor figure in the contemporary literary scene'. In agreement with Malcolm Bradbury, Nobel Prize winner Kenzaburo Oe (born 1935), Cynthia Wong, and novelist A.S. Byatt (born 1936) (a list to which she might add Rebecca Walkowitz and many others), Cheng proposes 'that Ishiguro ought to be categorized as an international novelist writing in English'.[11]

The readings of Ishiguro's novels discussed here provide a critical introduction to his status as an international writer. Notably, Ishiguro has said that 'international books are rooted in a very small place',[12] a statement that explains much of his fiction. He is not an international writer because his works have been set in Japan, the United Kingdom, Europe, and China, but because of his ability to peer into the very small spaces of the characters that inhabit those settings. He investigates what it means to be human. While Ishiguro's novels are set during momentous historical times, his concern is for the people of his fictions and what they discover about themselves:

■ What I'm interested in is not the actual fact that my characters have done things they later regret [...] I'm interested in how they come to terms with it. On the one hand there is a need for honesty, on the other hand a need to deceive themselves – to preserve a sense of dignity, some sort of self-respect. What I want to suggest is that some sort of dignity and self-respect does come from that sort of honesty.[13] □

His characters compel his readers to question what it means to plod our way through lives replete with challenges and failures, standing like Kathy at the end of *Never Let Me Go,* 'thinking about the rubbish, the flapping plastic in the branches, the shore-line of odd stuff caught along the fencing', imagining 'this was the spot where everything I'd ever lost since my childhood had washed up', (263) lacking the second magnifying glass Banks uses to uncover the origin of the magnifying glass that establishes his identity (WWWO 9), training ourselves, like *The Unconsoled's* young Ryder, to endure the hurts that confront us (171–2), tiling and wallpapering over the difficult bits, and watching the edge of the wallpaper start to peel, seeing a tile start to crack. He is an international writer because these investigations peer into the experiences of so many of us in so many places.

Notes

INTRODUCTION

1. Allan Vorda and Kim Herzinger, 'An Interview with Kazuo Ishiguro', *Mississippi Review* 20 (1991), pp. 134–5.
2. Barry Lewis, *Kazuo Ishiguro* (Manchester: Manchester University Press, 2000), p. 20.
3. Dylan Krider, 'Rooted in a Small Space: An Interview with Kazuo Ishiguro', *Kenyon Review* 20 (1998), p. 149.
4. Gregory Mason, 'An Interview with Kazuo Ishiguro', *Contemporary Literature* 30 (1989), p. 336.
5. Rocio Davis, 'Imaginary Homelands in the Novels of Kazuo Ishiguro', *Miscelánea* 15 (1994), pp. 139–54.
6. Mark Wormald, 'Kazuo Ishiguro and the Work of Art', in Richard J. Lane, Rod Mengham and Philip Tew (eds) *Contemporary British Fiction* (Cambridge: Polity, 2002), p. 231.
7. Vorda and Herzinger (1991), p. 135.
8. Vorda and Herzinger (1991), p. 136.
9. Kazuo Ishiguro, Introduction to Yasunari Kawabata, *Snow Country* and *Thousand Cranes*, trans. Edward G. Seidensticker (Harmondsworth: Penguin, 1986), p. 2.
10. Lewis (2000), p. 19.

CHAPTER ONE

1. Penelope Lively, 'Backwards and Forwards: Recent Fiction', *Encounter* (June–July 1982), p. 90.
2. Edith Milton, 'In a Japan Like Limbo', *New York Times Book Review* (9 May 1982), pp. 12–13.
3. Michael Wood, 'Sleepless Nights', *New York Review of Books* (21 December 1995), p. 18.
4. Allan Vorda and Kim Herzinger, 'An Interview with Kazuo Ishiguro', *Mississippi Review* 20 (1991), p. 134.
5. Anthony Thwaite, 'Ghosts in the Mirror', *Observer* (14 February 1982), p. 33.
6. Francis King, 'Shimmering', *Spectator* (27 February 1982), p. 25.
7. Jonathan Spence, 'Two Worlds Japan Has Lost Since the Meiji', *New Society* (13 May 1982), p. 266.
8. Spence (1982), p. 267.
9. Dylan Krider, 'Rooted in a Small Space: An Interview with Kazuo Ishiguro', *Kenyon Review* 20 (1998), p. 149.
10. Barry Lewis, *Kazuo Ishiguro* (Manchester: Manchester University Press, 2000), p. 20.
11. Kazuo Ishiguro, introduction to Yasunari Kawabata, *Snow Country* and *Thousand Cranes*, trans. Edward G. Seidensticker (Harmondsworth: Penguin, 1986), pp. 1–3.
12. Lewis (2000), p. 20.
13. Gregory Mason, 'An Interview with Kazuo Ishiguro', *Contemporary Literature* 30 (1989), p. 336.
14. Basil Wright qtd in Gregory Mason, 'Inspiring Images: The Influence of the Japanese Cinema on the Writings of Kazuo Ishiguro', *East West Film Journal* 3 (1989), p. 42.
15. Mason, 'Inspiring Images' (1989), p. 44.
16. Mason, 'Inspiring Images' (1989), p. 44.
17. Mason, 'Inspiring Images' (1989), p. 45.
18. Mason, 'Inspiring Images' (1989), p. 46.
19. Mason, 'Inspiring Images' (1989), p. 48.
20. Mason, 'Inspiring Images' (1989), p. 50.
21. Krider (1998), p. 150.
22. James Campbell, 'Kitchen Window', *New Statesman* (19 February 1982), p. 25.

23. King (1982), p. 24.
24. Spence (1982), p. 267.
25. Fumio Yoshioka, 'Beyond the Division of East and West: Kazuo Ishiguro's *A Pale View of Hills'*, *Studies in English Literature* (1988), p. 81.
26. Peter Wain, 'The Historical-Political Aspect of the Novels of Kazuo Ishiguro', *Language and Culture* (Japan) 23 (1992), p. 180.
27. Cynthia Wong 'The Shame of Memory: Blanchot's Self-Dispossession in Ishiguro's *A Pale View of Hills'*, *CLIO: A Journal of Literature, History, and the Philosophy of History* 24 (1995), p. 139.
28. Wong (1995), p. 140.
29. Milton (1982), p. 12.
30. Paul Bailey 'Private Desolations', *Times Literary Supplement* (19 February 1982), p. 179.
31. Thwaite (1982), p. 33.
32. Nicholas de Jongh, 'Life After the Bomb', *Guardian* (22 February 1982), p. 11.
33. Krider (1998), p. 150.
34. Mason, 'Interview' (1989), p. 338.
35. Lewis (2000), p. 22.
36. Lewis (2000), p. 23.
37. Brian W. Shaffer, *Understanding Kazuo Ishiguro* (Columbia, SC: University of South Carolina Press, 1998), p. 19.
38. Lewis (2000), p. 23.
39. Campbell (1982), p. 25.
40. Milton (1982), p. 12.
41. De Jongh (1982), p. 11.
42. Lewis (2000), pp. 37–8: citing *PVH* pp. 11 and 137–8.
43. Lewis (2000), p. 39.
44. Yoshioka (1988), p. 72.
45. Michael Wood, 'Sleepless Nights', *New York Review of Books* (21 December 1995), p. 18.
46. Lewis (2000), p. 43.
47. Wong (1995), p. 141; qtd in Shaffer (1998), p. 36.
48. Milton (1982), p. 12; qtd in Shaffer (1998), p. 36.
49. Shaffer (1998), pp. 36–7.
50. Lively (1982), p. 90.
51. Bailey (1982), p. 179.
52. Wain (1992), p. 186.
53. Norman Page, 'Speech, Culture, and History in the Novels of Kazuo Ishiguro', in Mimi Chan and Roy Harris (eds), *Asian Voices in English* (Hong Kong: Hong Kong University Press, 1991), p. 168.
54. Wong (1995), pp. 142–3.
55. Campbell (1982), p. 25.
56. Bailey (1982), p. 179.
57. Mike Petry, *Narratives of Memory and Identity: The Novels of Kazuo Ishiguro* (Frankfurt: Peter Lang, 1999), p. 39.
58. Lewis (2000), p. 37.
59. Lively (1982), p. 90.
60. King (1982), p. 24.
61. De Jongh (1982), p. 11.
62. Yoshioka (1988), p. 75.
63. Shaffer (1998), p. 21.
64. Shaffer (1998), p. 21.
65. Shaffer (1998), p. 23.
66. Mason, 'Interview' (1989), p. 337.
67. Shaffer (1998), p. 23.
68. Mason, 'Inspiring Images' (1989), p. 44.

69. Mason, 'Interview' (1989), p. 337; qtd in Shaffer, p. 24.
70. Shaffer (1998), p. 24.
71. Shaffer (1998), p. 24.
72. Shaffer (1998), p. 25.
73. Gabriele Annan, 'On The High Wire', *New York Review of Books* (7 December 1989), p. 3.
74. Shaffer (1998), p. 25.
75. Mason, 'Inspiring Images' (1989), pp. 42–5.
76. Shaffer (1998), p. 26.
77. Mason, 'Interview' (1989), p. 338; qtd in Shaffer, p. 27.
78. Lewis (2000), p. 27.
79. Lewis (2000), p. 29.
80. Lewis (2000), p. 36.
81. Milton (1982), p. 12.
82. Lively (1982), p. 90.
83. Yoshioka (1988), p. 79.
84. Lewis (2000), p. 35.
85. Lewis (2000), p. 35.
86. Shaffer (1998), p. 30.
87. Shaffer (1998), p. 31.
88. Shaffer (1998), p. 32.
89. Shaffer (1998), p. 33.
90. Shaffer (1998), p. 21.
91. Shaffer (1998), p. 35.
92. Mark Wormald, 'Kazuo Ishiguro and the Work of Art', in Richard J. Lane, Rod Mengham and Philip Tew (eds) *Contemporary British Fiction* (Cambridge: Polity, 2002), p. 231.
93. Wormald (2002), p. 232.
94. Wong (1995), p. 128.
95. Wong (1995), pp. 136–7.
96. Wong (1995), p. 138.
97. Wong (1995), p. 142.
98. Mason, 'Interview' (1989), p. 346.
99. Mason, 'Interview' (1989), p. 347.
100. De Jongh (1982), p. 11.

CHAPTER TWO

1. Nigel Hunt, 'Two Close Looks at Faraway', *Brick: A Journal of Review*, 31 (Fall 1987), p. 37.
2. Patrick Parrinder, 'Manly Scowls', *London Review of Books* (6 February 1986), pp. 16–17.
3. Geoff Dyer, 'On Their Mettle', *New Statesman* (4 April 1986), p. 25.
4. Kathryn Morton, 'After the War was Lost', *New York Times Book Review* (8 June 1986), p. 19.
5. Michele Field, 'This Britisher is Japanese', *Sydney Morning Herald* (12 March 1988), p. 74.
6. Anne Chisholm, 'Lost Worlds of Pleasure', *Times Literary Supplement* (14 February 1986), p. 162.
7. Christopher Tookey, 'Sydenham, mon amour', *Books and Bookmen* (March 1986), p. 33.
8. Rocio Davis, 'Imaginary Homelands in the Novels of Kazuo Ishiguro', *Miscelánea*, 15 (1994), pp. 139–54.
9. Bruce King, 'The New Internationalism: Shiva Naipaul, Salman Rushdie, Buchi Emecheta, Timothy Mo and Kazuo Ishiguro', *The British and Irish Novel Since 1960* (New York: St. Martin's, 1991), p. 207.
10. Gregory Mason, 'An Interview with Kazuo Ishiguro', *Contemporary Literature* 30 (1989), p. 340.
11. Mason, 'Interview', (1989), p. 341.

12. Norman Page, 'Speech, Culture and History in the Novels of Kazuo Ishiguro', Mimi Chan and Roy Harris (eds), *Asian Voices in English* (Hong Kong: Hong Kong University Press, 1991), pp. 166–7.
13. Mason, 'Interview', (1989), p. 345.
14. King (1991), p. 208.
15. Clive Sinclair 'The Land of the Rising Son', *Sunday Times Magazine* (11 January 1987), p. 37.
16. Mason, 'Interview' (1989), p. 342.
17. Mason 'Interview' (1989), p. 343.
18. Malcolm Bradbury, 'The Floating World', in *No, Not Bloomsbury* (London: Andre Deutsch, 1987), p. 364.
19. Bradbury (1987), pp. 364–5.
20. King (1991), p. 208.
21. Lewis (2000), pp. 62–3.
22. Lewis (2000), p. 63.
23. Lewis (2000), p. 64.
24. Lewis (2000), pp. 64–5.
25. Lewis (2000), p. 65.
26. Lewis (2000), p. 66.
27. Lewis (2000), p. 67.
28. Mason, 'Interview', (1989), p. 342.
29. Hunt (1987), p. 38.
30. Rebecca L.Walkowitz, 'Ishiguro's Floating Worlds,' *ELH*, 68 (2001), p. 1071.
31. Brian W. Shaffer, *Understanding Kazuo Ishiguro* (Columbia, SC: University of South Carolina Press, 1998), p. 42.
32. Shaffer (1998), p. 43.
33. Shaffer (1998), p. 44.
34. Shaffer (1998), p. 44.
35. Shaffer (1998), pp. 45–6.
36. Shaffer (1998), p. 48.
37. Shaffer (1998), pp. 49–50.
38. Shaffer (1998), p. 54.
39. Shaffer (1998), p. 56.
40. Tookey (1986), p. 34.
41. Shaffer (1998), p. 59.
42. Shaffer (1998), p. 59.
43. Shaffer (1998), p. 60.
44. Shaffer (1998), p. 61.
45. Tookey (1986), p. 34.
46. Mason, 'Interview', (1989), p. 344.
47. Cynthia F.Wong, *Kazuo Ishiguro* (Plymouth: Northcote House, 2000), p. 38.
48. Wong (2000), p. 39.
49. Margaret Scanlan, 'Mistaken Identities: First-Person Narration in Kazuo Ishiguro', *Journal of Narrative and Life History*, 3: 2 & 3 (1993), p. 144.
50. Wong (2000), p. 41.
51. Wong (2000), p. 43.
52. Wong (2000), p. 44.
53. Wong (2000), p. 45.
54. Wong (2000), pp. 46–7.
55. Wong (2000), p. 49.
56. King (1991), p. 207.
57. Peter J. Mallett, 'The Revelation of Character in Kazuo Ishiguro's *The Remains of the Day* and *An Artist of the Floating World*', *Shoin Literary Review*, 29 (1996), p. 12.
58. Page (1991), p. 166.

59. Scanlan (1993), p. 141.
60. Scanlan (1993), p. 142.
61. Scanlan (1993), pp. 142–3.
62. Scanlan (1993), p. 143.
63. Scanlan (1993), p. 144.
64. Scanlan (1993), p. 144.
65. Scanlan (1993), p. 144.
66. Scanlan (1993), p. 145.
67. Lewis (2000), p. 54.
68. Scanlan (1993), p. 151.
69. Lewis (2000), p. 54.
70. Mallett (1996), p. 18.
71. Scanlan (1993), p. 152.
72. Scanlan (1993), p. 152.
73. Gregory Mason, 'Inspiring Images: The Influence of the Japanese Cinema on the Writings of Kazuo Ishiguro', *East West Film Journal*, 3 (1989), pp. 42–5.
74. Lewis (2000), pp. 69–70.
75. Mason, 'Interview', (1989), p. 341.
76. King (1991), p. 208.
77. Mallett (1996), p. 12.
78. Tookey (1986), p. 34.
79. Mason, 'Interview', (1989), p. 339.
80. King (1991), p. 207.
81. Mason, 'Interview', (1989), p. 344.
82. Morton (1986), p. 19.

CHAPTER THREE

1. Michiko Kakutani, 'An Era Revealed in a Perfect Butler's Imperfections', *New York Times* (22 September 1989), p. 33.
2. Terrence Rafferty, 'The Lesson of the Master', *New Yorker* (15 January 1990), p. 102.
3. Galen Strawson, 'Tragically Disciplined and Dignified', *Times Literary Supplement* (19–25 May 1989), p. 535.
4. William Hutchings, 'English: Fiction', *World Literature Today* 64: 3 (1990), p. 464.
5. Merle Rubin, 'A Review of *The Remains of the Day*', *Christian Science Monitor* (13 November 1989), p. 13.
6. Geoff Dyer, 'What the Butler Did', *New Statesman and Society* (26 May 1989), p. 34.
7. Mark Kamine, 'A Servant of Self-Deceit', *The New Leader* (13 November 1989), p. 21.
8. Gabriele Annan, 'On The High Wire', *New York Review of Books* (7 December 1989), pp. 3–4.
9. Anthony Thwaite, 'In Service', *London Review of Books* (18 May 1989), p. 17.
10. David Gurewich, 'Upstairs, Downstairs', *The New Criterion* (December 1989), p. 80.
11. T. S. Eliot, 'The Love Song of J. Alfred Prufrock'; qtd in Thwaite (1989), p. 17.
12. Lawrence Graver, 'What the Butler Saw', *New York Times Book Review* (8 October 1989), p. 3.
13. Strawson (1989), p. 535.
14. Kamine (1989), p. 22.
15. Rafferty (1990), p. 103.
16. Graver (1989), p. 3.
17. Alice Bloom, 'Why the Novel (Still) Matters', *Hudson Review* 43 (1990), p. 161.
18. Kamine (1989), p. 21.
19. Rafferty (1990), p. 102.
20. Kamine (1989), p. 22.
21. Margaret Scanlan, 'Mistaken Identities: First-Person Narration in Kazuo Ishiguro', *Journal of Narrative and Life History* 3:2 & 3 (1993), p. 141.

22. Scanlan (1993), p. 146.
23. Scanlan (1993), p. 147.
24. Scanlan (1993), p. 151.
25. Deborah Guth, 'Submerged Narratives in Kazuo Ishiguro's *The Remains of the Day*', *Forum for Modern Language Studies* 35.2 (1999), p. 126.
26. Guth (1999), p. 130.
27. Guth (1999), p. 131.
28. Guth (1999), p. 131.
29. Guth (1999), p. 132.
30. Guth (1999), p. 133.
31. Guth (1999), p. 134.
32. Scanlan (1993), p. 151.
33. Guth (1999), p. 136.
34. Guth (1999), p. 137.
35. Kathleen Wall '*The Remains of the Day* and Its Challenges to Theories of Unreliable Narration', *Journal of Narrative Technique* 24 (1994), p. 18.
36. Wall (1994), p. 22.
37. Wall (1994), p. 23.
38. Wall (1994), p. 24.
39. Wall (1994), p. 24.
40. Wall (1994), p. 25.
41. Wall (1994), p. 26.
42. Wall (1994), pp. 27–8.
43. Wall (1994), p. 28.
44. Wall (1994), p. 30.
45. Wall (1994), p. 29.
46. Wall (1994), p. 29.
47. Wall (1994), p. 30.
48. Seymour Chatman, *Story and Discourse: Narrative Structure in Fiction and Film* (Ithaca: Cornell University Press, 1978), p.149; cited in Wall (1994), pp. 30–1.
49. Wall (1994), p. 31.
50. Wall (1994), p. 32.
51. Wall (1994), p. 34.
52. Wall (1994), p. 34.
53. Karl E. Jirgens, 'Narrator Resartus: Palimpsestic Revelations in Kazuo Ishiguro's *The Remains of the Day*', *Q/W/E/R/T/Y: Arts, Littératures & Civilisations du Monde Anglophone* 9 (1999), pp. 228–9.
54. Wall (1994), p. 36.
55. Wall (1994), p. 37.
56. James Phelan and Mary Patricia Martin, '"The Lessons of 'Weymouth'": Homodiegesis, Unreliability, Ethics, and *The Remains of the Day*', *Narratologies: New Perspectives on Narrative Analysis* (Columbus, OH: Ohio State University Press, 1999), pp. 90–1.
57. Phelan and Martin (1999), p. 91. Italics in original.
58. Phelan and Martin (1999), p. 92.
59. Phelan and Martin (1999), p. 104.
60. Phelan and Martin (1999), p. 105.
61. Phelan and Martin (1999), pp. 105–6.
62. Phelan and Martin (1999), p. 106.
63. Phelan and Martin (1999), p. 106.
64. Phelan and Martin (1999), p. 107.
65. Phelan and Martin (1999), p. 106.
66. Phelan and Martin (1999), p. 107.
67. Phelan and Martin (1999), pp. 107–8.

68. Andrew Teverson, 'Acts of Reading in Kazuo Ishiguro's *The Remains of the Day*', *Q/W/E/ R/T/Y: Arts, Littératures & Civilisations du Monde Anglophone* 9 (1999), p. 251.
69. Teverson (1999), p. 252.
70. Teverson (1999), p. 253.
71. Teverson (1999), p. 256.
72. Teverson (1999), p. 256.
73. Teverson (1999), p. 254.
74. Jirgens (1999), p. 221.
75. Gurewich (1989) p. 80.
76. Teverson (1999), p. 255.
77. Teverson (1999), p. 257.

CHAPTER FOUR

1. Norman Page, 'Speech, Culture, and History in the Novels of Kazuo Ishiguro', in Mimi Chan and Roy Harris (eds), *Asian Voices in English* (Hong Kong: Hong Kong University Press, 1991), p. 162.
2. John Sutherland, 'Why Hasn't Mr. Stevens Heard of the Suez Crisis?' *Where Was Rebecca Shot?: Curiosities, Puzzles, and Conundrums in Modern Fiction* (London: Weidenfeld & Nicolson, 1998), p. 188.
3. Meera Tamaya, 'Ishiguro's *Remains of the Day*: The Empire Strikes Back', *Modern Language Studies* 22 (1992), p. 51.
4. Kenzaburo Oe and Kazuo Ishiguro, 'The Novelist in Today's World: A Conversation', *Boundary 2: An International Journal of Literature and Culture* 18 (1991), p. 110.
5. John P. McCombe, 'The End of (Anthony) Eden: Ishiguro's *The Remains of the Day* and Midcentury Anglo-American Tensions', *Twentieth Century Literature: A Scholarly and Critical Journal* 48:1 (2002), p. 78.
6. McCombe (2002), pp. 78–9.
7. McCombe (2002), pp. 79–80.
8. McCombe (2002), pp. 93–4.
9. McCombe (2002), p. 81.
10. McCombe (2002), p. 81.
11. McCombe (2002), p. 82.
12. McCombe (2002), p. 82.
13. T. O. Lloyd, p. 341, qtd in McCombe (2002), p. 83.
14. McCombe (2002), p. 85.
15. McCombe (2002), p. 91.
16. McCombe (2002), p. 81.
17. McCombe (2002), p. 87.
18. McCombe (2002), p. 97.
19. G. Bo Ekelund, 'Misrecognizing History: Complicitous Genres in Kazuo Ishiguro's *The Remains of the Day*', *International Fiction Review* 32:1–2 (2005), p. 70.
20. Ekelund (2005), p. 71.
21. Ekelund (2005), p. 73.
22. Ekelund (2005), p. 70.
23. Ekelund (2005), p. 73.
24. Ekelund (2005), p. 73.
25. Ekelund (2005), pp. 70–1.
26. Ekelund (2005), p. 70.
27. Ekelund (2005), p. 71.
28. Ekelund (2005), pp. 73–4.
29. Ekelund (2005), p. 75.
30. Ekelund (2005), p. 76.

31. Ekelund (2005), p. 79.
32. Ekelund (2005), p. 83.
33. Ekelund (2005), pp. 83–4.
34. Ekelund (2005), pp. 85–6.
35. Ekelund (2005), p. 87.
36. Ekelund (2005), p. 90.
37. James M. Lang, 'Public Memory, Private History: Kazuo Ishiguro's *The Remains of the Day*', *CLIO: A Journal of Literature, History, and the Philosophy of History* 29:2 (2000), p. 144.
38. Lang (2000), p. 145.
39. Lang (2000), pp. 146–7.
40. Lang (2000), p. 147.
41. Lang (2000), p. 149.
42. Lang (2000), p. 150.
43. Lang (2000), p. 151.
44. Lang (2000), p. 152.
45. Michael Andre Bernstein, *Foregone Conclusions: Against Apocalyptic History* (Berkeley: University of California Press, 1994), p. 16; qtd in Lang (2000), p. 153.
46. Lang (2000), p. 153.
47. Lang (2000), p. 154.
48. Lang (2000), pp. 154–5.
49. Lang (2000), p. 158.
50. Lang (2000), pp. 156–7.
51. Lang (2000), p. 157.
52. Lang (2000), p. 160.
53. Lang (2000), p. 161.
54. Lang (2000), p. 161.
55. Lang (2000), p. 162.
56. Lang (2000), p. 163.
57. Gregory Mason, 'An Interview with Kazuo Ishiguro', *Contemporary Literature* 30 (1989), p. 337; qtd in Lang (2000), p. 164.
58. John Ash, 'Stick It Up Howard's End', *GQ* (August 1994), p. 43.
59. Susie O'Brien, 'Serving a New World Order: Postcolonial Politics in Kazuo Ishiguro's *The Remains of the Day*', *Modern Fiction Studies* 42:4 (1996), p. 788.
60. O'Brien (1996), p. 796.
61. O'Brien (1996), p. 788.
62. Allan Vorda and Kim Herzinger, 'An Interview with Kazuo Ishiguro', *Mississippi Review* 20 (1991), p. 140; qtd in O'Brien (1996), p. 789.
63. O'Brien (1996), p. 789.
64. O'Brien (1996), p. 790.
65. O'Brien (1996), p. 791.
66. O'Brien (1996), p. 792.
67. Pico Iyer, '"The Empire Writes Back"', *Time*, (8 February 1993), p. 58; qtd in O'Brien (1996), p. 793.
68. O'Brien (1996), p. 793.
69. O'Brien (1996), p. 788.
70. O'Brien (1996), p. 794.
71. O'Brien (1996), p. 795.
72. Salman Rushdie, 'What the Butler Didn't See', *Observer*, (1989), p. 53; reprinted as 'Kazuo Ishiguro', in Salman Rushdie, *Imaginary Homelands: Essays and Criticism 1981–1991* (London: Granta Books, 1991), pp. 244–6.
73. Andrew Teverson, 'Acts of Reading in Kazuo Ishiguro's *The Remains of the Day*', *Q/W/E/R/T/Y: Arts, Littératures & Civilisations du Monde Anglophone* 9 (1999), p. 254.
74. O'Brien (1996), p. 795.

75. O'Brien (1996), p. 796.
76. Molly Westerman, 'Is the Butler Home? Narrative and the Split Subject in *The Remains of the Day*', *Mosaic: A Journal for the Interdisciplinary Study of Literature* 37.3 (2004), p. 157.
77. Westerman (2004), p. 158.
78. Westerman (2004), p. 158.
79. Westerman (2004), pp. 158–9.
80. Westerman (2004), p. 159.
81. Westerman (2004), p. 159.
82. Westerman (2004), p. 159.
83. Westerman (2004), p. 159.
84. Westerman (2004), p. 159.
85. Wall (1994), p. 23.
86. Westerman (2004), p. 160.
87. Westerman (2004), p. 160.
88. Salecl (1996), p. 180: qtd in Westerman (2004), p. 160.
89. Westerman (2004), p. 160.
90. Westerman (2004), p. 161.
91. Westerman (2004), p. 162.
92. Westerman (2004), p. 161.
93. Westerman (2004), p. 162.
94. Westerman (2004), p. 163.
95. Homi Bhabha, *The Location of Culture* (London: Routledge, 1994), p. 70; qtd in Westerman (2004), pp. 163–4.
96. Bhabha (1994), p. 77; qtd in Westerman (2004), p. 163.
97. Westerman (2004), p. 164.
98. O'Brien (1996), p. 801.
99. Westerman (2004), p. 167.
100. Westerman (2004), p. 167.
101. Westerman (2004), p. 168.
102. Westerman (2004), p. 169.
103. Westerman (2004), p. 160.
104. Ryan Trimm, 'Inside Job: Professionalism and Postimperial Communities in *The Remains of the Day*', *Lit: Literature Interpretation Theory* 16.2 (2005), p. 138.
105. John J. Su, 'Refiguring National Character: The Remains of the British Estate Novel', *MFS: Modern Fiction Studies* 48.3 (2002), p. 567.
106. Oe and Ishiguro (1991), p. 115.

CHAPTER FIVE

1. Daniel Schacter, *The Seven Sins of Memory: How the Mind Forgets and Remembers* (Boston: Houghton, 2001).
2. Lillian Furst, 'Memory's Fragile Power in Ishiguro's *Remains of the Day* and W. C. Sebald's "Max Ferber"', *Contemporary Literature* 48.4 (2007), p. 533.
3. Furst (2007), p. 534.
4. Furst (2007), p. 535.
5. Furst (2007), p. 536.
6. Furst (2007), pp. 537–8.
7. Furst (2007), p. 538.
8. Furst (2007), p. 539.
9. Furst (2007), p. 539.
10. Furst (2007), p. 540.
11. Furst (2007), p. 541.
12. Furst (2007), pp. 541–2.

13. Furst (2007), p. 541.
14. Furst (2007), p. 542.
15. Furst (2007), p. 542.
16. Furst (2007), pp. 542–3.
17. Furst (2007), pp. 543–4.
18. Furst (2007), p. 545.
19. Furst (2007), p. 546.
20. Furst (2007), p. 546.
21. Furst (2007), p. 547.
22. Furst (2007), p. 548.
23. Furst (2007), p. 549.
24. Furst (2007), p. 542.
25. Furst (2007), p. 543.
26. M. Griffith, 'Great English Houses/New Homes in England? Memory and Identity in Kazuo Ishiguro's *The Remains of the Day* and V. S. Naipaul's *The Enigma of Arrival*', *Span* 36 (1993), pp. 448–503.
27. John J. Su, 'Refiguring National Character: The Remains of the British Estate Novel', *MFS: Modern Fiction Studies* 48.3 (2002), p. 555.
28. Su (2002), p. 553.
29. Su (2002), pp. 555–6.
30. Allan Vorda and Kim Herzinger, 'An Interview with Kazuo Ishiguro', *Mississippi Review* 20 (1991), p. 139; qtd in Su (2002), p. 563.
31. Su (2002), p. 563.
32. Su (2002), p. 564.
33. Su (2002), p. 565.
34. Su (2002), p. 565.
35. Griffith (1993), p. 491.
36. Su (2002), p. 566.
37. Su (2002), p. 567.
38. Su (2002), p. 567.
39. Su (2002), p. 568.
40. Su (2002), p. 569.
41. Su (2002), p. 569.
42. Su (2002), pp. 569–70.
43. Su (2002), p. 570.
44. Susie O'Brien, 'Serving a New World Order: Postcolonial Politics in Kazuo Ishiguro's *The Remains of the Day*', *Modern Fiction Studies* 42:4 (1996), p. 793.
45. Su (2002), p. 570.
46. Su (2002), p. 571.
47. Su (2002), p. 571.
48. Su (2002), p. 572.
49. Kwame Anthony Appiah, 'Liberalism, Individuality, and Identity', *Critical Inquiry* 27.2 (2001), p. 313.
50. Appiah (2001), p. 315.
51. Appiah (2001), p. 316.
52. Appiah (2001), pp. 316–17.
53. Appiah (2001), p. 316.
54. Appiah (2001), p. 319.
55. Appiah (2001), p. 319.
56. Appiah (2001), p. 320.
57. Appiah (2001), p. 331.
58. David Medalie, '"What Dignity is There in That?": The Crisis of Dignity in Selected Late-Twentieth-Century Novels', *Journal of Literary Studies* (2004), p. 2.

59. Medalie (2004), p. 4.
60. Aurel Kolnai, 'Dignity', in Robin S. Dillon (ed.) *Dignity, Character, and Self-Respect* (New York: Routledge, 1995), p. 56; qtd in Medalie (2004), p. 4.
61. Medalie (2004), p. 4.
62. Medalie (2004), p. 5.
63. Michael Meyer, 'Dignity as a (Modern) Virtue', David Kretzmer and Eckart Klein (eds), *The Concept of Human Dignity in Human Rights Discourse* (The Hague: Kluwer Law International, 2002), p. 203; qtd in Medalie (2004), p. 5.
64. Medalie (2004), p. 6.
65. Meyer (2002), p. 203; qtd in Medalie (2004), p. 6.
66. Medalie (2004), p. 6.
67. Medalie (2004), p. 7.
68. Medalie (2004), p. 8.
69. Medalie (2004), p. 11.
70. David Gurewich, 'Upstairs, Downstairs', *The New Criterion* (December 1989), p. 78.
71. Rob Atkinson, 'How the Butler Was Made to Do It. The Perverted Professionalism of *The Remains of the Day*', *Yale Law Journal* 10 (1995), p. 184.
72. Atkinson (1995), p. 185.
73. Atkinson (1995), pp. 185–6.
74. Atkinson (1995), p. 189.
75. Atkinson (1995), p. 191.
76. Atkinson (1995), p. 192.
77. Atkinson (1995), p. 194.
78. Atkinson (1995), p. 196.
79. Atkinson (1995), p. 197.
80. Atkinson (1995), p. 199.
81. Atkinson (1995), pp. 208–9.
82. Atkinson (1995), p. 200.
83. Atkinson (1995), p. 201.
84. Atkinson (1995), p. 209.
85. Atkinson (1995), p. 210.
86. Atkinson (1995), pp. 212–13.
87. Atkinson (1995), p. 218.

CHAPTER SIX

1. Brian W. Shaffer, *Understanding Kazuo Ishiguro* (Columbia, SC: University of South Carolina Press, 1998), p. 119.
2. Graham Swift, 'Kazuo Ishiguro', *Bomb* (Fall 1989), p. 23.
3. Richard Rorty, 'Consolation Prize', *Village Voice Literary Supplement* (October 1995), p. 13.
4. Pico Iyer, 'The Butler Didn't Do It, Again', *Times Literary Supplement* (28 April 1995), p. 22.
5. Alan Wall, *Spectator* (13 May 1995), p. 45.
6. Rorty (1995), p. 13.
7. Anita Brookner, 'A Superb Achievement', *Spectator* (24 June 1995), p. 40.
8. Richard Eder, 'Meandering in a Dreamscape', *Los Angeles Times Book Review* (8 October 1995), p. 3.
9. Lucy Hughes-Hallett, 'Feeling No Pain', *Sunday Times* Books (14 May 1995), p. 7.
10. Charlotte Innes, 'Dr Faustus Faces the Music', *Nation* (6 November 1995), p. 548.
11. Wall (1995), p. 45.
12. Amit Chaudhuri, 'Unlike Kafka', *London Review of Books* (8 June 1995), pp. 30–1.
13. Stanley Kauffmann, 'The Floating World', *The New Republic* (6 November 1995), p. 45.
14. Louis Menand, 'Anxious in Dreamland', *New York Times Book Review* (15 October 1995), p. 7.
15. James Wood, 'Ishiguro in the Underworld', *The Guardian* (5 May 1995), p. 5.

16. Kazuo Ishiguro, *The Unconsoled* (London: Faber & Faber, 1995), pp. 488–91.
17. Innes (1995), p. 547.
18. Brooke Allen, 'Leaving Behind Daydreams for Nightmares', *Wall Street Journal* (11 October 1995), p. A21.
19. Rachel Cusk, 'Journey to the End of the Day', *The Times* (11 May 1995), p. 35.
20. Shaffer (1998), p. 90.
21. Gary Adelman, 'Double on the Rocks: Ishiguro's *The Unconsoled*', *Critique: Studies in Contemporary Fiction* 42.2 (2001), p. 167.
22. Menand (1995), p. 7.
23. Vince Passano, 'New Flash from an Old Isle', *Harper's* (October 1995), p. 74.
24. Barry Lewis, *Kazuo Ishiguro* (Manchester: Manchester University Press, 2000), p. 108.
25. Cynthia F. Wong, *Kazuo Ishiguro* (Plymouth: Northcote House, 2000), p. 77.
26. Shaffer (1998), p. 99.
27. Wong (2000), p. 73.
28. Pierre François, 'The Spectral Return of Depths in Kazuo Ishiguro's *The Unconsoled*', *Commonwealth Essays and Studies* 26.2 (2004), p. 80.
29. Iyer (1995), p. 22.
30. Lewis (2000), pp. 104–5.
31. Michael Wood, 'The Discourse of Others', *Children of Silence: Studies in Contemporary Fiction* (London: Pimilico, 1995), p. 172.
32. M. Wood (1995), p. 172.
33. M. Wood (1995), p. 173.
34. Iyer (1995), p. 22.
35. Lewis (2000), p. 110.
36. Shaffer (1998), p. 99.
37. Wong (2000), p. 66.
38. Rorty (1995), p. 13.
39. Francis Wyndham, *New Yorker* (23 October 1995), p. 92.
40. Iyer (1995), p. 22.
41. Richard Robinson, 'Nowhere in Particular: Kazuo Ishiguro's *The Unconsoled* and Central Europe', *Critical Quarterly* 48.4 (2006), p. 111.
42. Robinson (2006), pp. 108–9.
43. Robinson (2006), p. 111.
44. Robinson (2006), p. 112.
45. Robinson (2006), pp. 112–3.
46. Robinson (2006), p. 115.
47. Robinson (2006), p. 116.
48. Merle Rubin, 'Probing the Plight of Lives "Trapped" in Others' Expectations', *Christian Science Monitor* (4 October 1995), p. 14.
49. Robinson (2006), p. 118.
50. Robinson (2006), p. 119.
51. Robinson (2006), pp. 119–20.
52. Kauffmann (1995), p. 45.
53. Shao-Pin Luo '"Living the Wrong Life": Kazuo Ishiguro's Unconsoled Orphans', *Dalhousie Review* 83.1 (2003), p. 58.
54. Luo (2003), p. 70.
55. Luo (2003), p. 73.
56. Luo (2003), pp. 73–4.
57. Luo (2003), p. 74.
58. Luo (2003), p. 60.
59. Luo (2003), pp. 76–7.
60. Luo (2003), p. 77.
61. Eder (1995), p. 7.

62. Paul Gray, 'Bad Dream', *Time* (2 October 1995), p. 82.
63. Allen (1995), p. A21.
64. Lewis (2000), p. 109.
65. M. Wood (1995), pp. 174–5.
66. Passano (1995), p. 73.
67. Brookner (1995), p. 40.
68. Kauffmann (1995), p. 44.
69. Menand (1995), p. 7.
70. Lewis (2000), p. 109.
71. François (2004), p. 79.
72. Sybil Steinberg, 'A Book About Our World', *Publisher's Weekly* (18 September 1995), p. 105.
73. Steinberg (1995), pp. 105–6.
74. Lewis (2000), p. 107.
75. Steinberg (1995), p. 106.
76. M. Wood (1995), p. 178.
77. Dylan Otto Krider, 'Rooted in a Small Space: An Interview with Kazuo Ishiguro', *Kenyon Review* 20 (1998): p. 148; qtd in Wong (2000), p. 67.
78. François (2004), p. 77.
79. Passano (1995), p. 73.
80. Cusk (1995), p. 35.
81. Kauffmann (1995), p. 44.
82. Allen (1995), p. A21.
83. Shaffer (1998), pp. 94–5.
84. Carlos Villar Flor, 'Unreliable Selves in an Unreliable World: The Multiple Projections of the Hero in Kazuo Ishiguro's *The Unconsoled*', *Journal of English Studies* 2 (2000), p. 163.
85. Villar Flor (2000), p. 166.
86. Steinberg (1995), p. 105.
87. Adelman (2001), p. 167.
88. Adelman (2001), p. 168.
89. Lewis (2000), p. 111.
90. Lewis (2000), p. 113.
91. Lewis (2000), pp. 114–5.
92. Lewis (2000), p. 115.
93. Lewis (2000), p. 117.
94. Lewis (2000), p. 120.
95. Wong (2000), p. 66.
96. Wong (2000), pp. 68–9.
97. Wong (2000), p. 69.
98. Wong (2000), pp. 69–70.
99. Wong (2000), p. 70.
100. Wong (2000), p. 74.
101. Wong (2000), p. 72.
102. Wong (2000), p. 78.
103. Wong (2000), p. 79.
104. Cusk (1995), p. 35.
105. Lewis (2000), p. 123.
106. François (2004), p. 77.
107. François (2004), p. 81.
108. François (2004), p. 82.
109. François (2004), p. 83.
110. François (2004), p. 84.
111. François (2004), p. 85.
112. François (2004), pp. 85–6.

113. François (2004), p. 87.
114. François (2004), p. 88.
115. François (2004), p. 89.
116. Hughes-Hallett (1995), p. 7.
117. Cusk (1995), p. 35.
118. Shaffer (1998), pp. 91–2.
119. Wyndham (1995), p. 90.
120. Villar Flor (2000), p. 160.
121. Wyndham (1995), p. 93.
122. Wyndham (1995), p. 94.
123. Kauffmann (1995), p. 45.
124. Hughes-Hallett (1995), p. 7.
125. Wyndham (1995), p. 94.
126. Steinberg (1995), p. 106.

CHAPTER SEVEN

1. Suzie Mackenzie, 'Between Two Worlds', *Guardian* (25 March 2000), p. 10.
2. Brian W. Shaffer, Rev. 'When We Were Orphans', *World Literature Today* 74.3 (Summer 2000), p. 595.
3. *Virginia Quarterly Review* '*When We Were Orphans* (Book Review)', vol. 77, issue 3 (Summer 2001), p. 100.
4. Joyce Carol Oates, 'The Serpent's Heart', *Times Literary Supplement* (31 March 2000), p. 21.
5. Michael Gorra, 'The Case of the Missing Childhood', *New York Times Book Review* (24 September 2000), p. 12.
6. Michiko Kakutani, 'The Case He Can't Solve: A Detective's Delusions', *New York Times* (19 September 2000), p. 7.
7. Alice McDermott, 'Whodunit?', *Commonweal* (3 November 2000), p. 25.
8. Gillian Harding-Russell, 'Through the Veil of Memory', *Queen's Quarterly* 109.1 (2002), p. 95.
9. Maya Jaggi, 'In Search of Lost Crimes', *Guardian* (1 April 2000), p. 8; see also Rosemary Hartigan, '*When We Were Orphans* (Book Review)', *Antioch Review* 59.3 (Summer 2001), p. 637.
10. Shaffer (2000), p. 595.
11. Jaggi (2000), p. 8; referring to Ishiguro's use of 'appropriations' as documented by Julia Llewellyn Smith in 'A Novel Taste of Criticism', *Times* (3 May 1995), p. 17 and Sybil Steinberg in 'A Book about Our World', *Publishers Weekly* (18 September 1995), pp. 105–6.
12. Benjamin Anastas, 'Keeping It Real', *Village Voice* 45.40 (10 October 2000), p. 62.
13. Kakutani (2000), p. 7.
14. Oates (2000), p. 21.
15. Ron Charles, 'The Remains of the Day with Parents', *Christian Science Monitor* 92.221 (5 October 2000), p. 15; see also *Virginia Quarterly Review* (2001), p. 100.
16. McDermott (2000), p. 25.
17. Barbara Hoffert, 'Review: *When We Were Orphans*', *Library Journal* 125.13 (August 2000), p. 157.
18. Gavin McNett, *Salon* (19 October 2000), http://dir.salon.com/story/books/review/2000/09/19/ishiguro
19. Andrew Barrow, 'Clueless in Shanghai', *Spectator* (25 March 2000), p. 44; see also Charles (2000), p. 15.
20. Barrow (2000), p. 44.
21. Brian Bouldrey. *San Francisco Chronicle* (24 October 2000), p. RV 5.
22. Henry Carrington Cunningham, III. 'The Dickens Connection in Kazuo Ishiguro's *When We Were Orphans*', *Notes on Contemporary Literature* 34.5 (2004), pp. 4–6.
23. Philip Hensher, 'It's the Way He Tells it', *Observer Review* (19 March 2000), p. 11.

24. Tova Reich, 'A Sleuth in Search of Himself', *The New Leader* 83.4 (Sep/Oct 2000), p. 43.
25. Hensher (2000), p. 11.
26. Gorra (2000), p. 12.
27. Candia McWilliam, 'Painful, Lovely, Limpid in Freezing Fog', *Financial Times* (Weekend, 8 April 2000), p. 4.
28. James Wood, 'The Unconsoled', *The New Republic* 223.16 (16 October 2000), p. 44.
29. Wood (2000), p. 45.
30. Harding-Russell (2002), p. 96.
31. Gorra (2000), p. 12.
32. Shaffer (2000), pp. 595–6.
33. William Sutcliffe, 'History Happens Elsewhere', *Independent on Sunday* (Sunday Review, 2 April 2000), p. 49.
34. Kakutani (2000), p. 7.
35. Wood (2000), p. 46.
36. Barrow (2000), p. 44.
37. Jaggi (2000), p. 8.
38. Anastas (2000), p. 62.
39. McWilliam (2000), p. 4: see also Barrow (2000), p. 44, McDermott (2000), p. 26, and Charles (2000), p. 15.
40. Oates (2000), p. 21.
41. Jaggi (2000), p. 8: see also Gorra (2000), p. 12.
42. McDermott (2000), p. 26.
43. James Francken, 'Something Fishy', *London Review of Books* (13 April 2000), p. 37.
44. Phil Whitaker, 'Return of the Native', *New Statesman* 129.4480 (3 April 2000), p. 58.
45. Oates (2000), p. 21.
46. Gorra (2000), p. 12.
47. Barrow (2000), p. 44.
48. Harding-Russell (2002), p. 95.
49. McDermott (2000), p. 25.
50. Bouldrey (2000), p. RV 5.
51. Boyd Tonkin, 'Artist of his Floating World', *The Independent* (Saturday, 1 April 2000), p. 9.
52. Gorra (2000), p. 12.
53. Oates (2000), p. 21.
54. Charles (2000), p. 15.
55. Gorra (2000), p. 12.
56. Francken (2000), p. 37.
57. Paul Gray, 'The Remains of Shanghai', *Time* (18 September 2000), p. 86.
58. Bouldrey (2000), p. RV 5.
59. Charles (2000), p. 15.
60. Gorra (2000), p. 12.
61. Reich (2000), p. 42.
62. Francken (2000), p. 37.
63. Mackenzie (2000), p. 10.
64. Tonkin (2000), p. 9.
65. Kakutani (2000), p. 7.
66. Charles (2000), p. 15.
67. Sutcliffe (2000), p. 49.
68. Jaggi (2000), p. 8.
69. Alexander M. Bain, 'International Settlements: Ishiguro, Shanghai, Humanitarianism', *Novel* 40.3 (Summer 2007), p. 242.
70. Shaffer (2000), p. 595.
71. Reich (2000), p. 43.
72. McDermott (2000), p. 25.

73. Reich (2000), p. 43.
74. McDermott (2000), p. 25: see also Oates (2000), p. 21.
75. Sutcliffe (2000), p. 49.
76. John J. Su, 'Refiguring National Character: The Remains of the British Estate Novel', *MFS: Modern Fiction Studies* 48.3 (2002), p. 568.
77. Mackenzie (2000), p. 10.
78. Oates (2000), p. 21.
79. Mackenzie (2000), p. 10.
80. Wood (2000), p. 48.
81. Shaffer (2000), p. 596.
82. Barrow (2000), p. 44.
83. Hartigan (2001), p. 637.
84. Wood (2000), p. 49.
85. Mackenzie (2000), p. 10.
86. Barrow (2000), p. 44.
87. Tonkin (2000), p. 9.
88. Reich (2000), p. 43.
89. Harding-Russell (2002), p. 100.

CHAPTER EIGHT

1. *Kirkus*, 73.1 (1 January 2005), p. 11.
2. Theo Tait, 'A Sinister Harvest', *The Telegraph* (13 March 2005), http://www.telegraph.co.uk/arts/main.jhtml?xml=/arts/2005/03/06/boish206.xml
3. James Wood, 'The Human Difference', *The New Republic* (16 May 2005), p. 36.
4. John Mullan, 'A Life Half Lived', *The Guardian* (18 March 2006), Books, p. 7.
5. Frank Kermode, 'Outrageous Game', *London Review of Books* 27.8 (4 April 2005), p. 21.
6. Sarah Kerr, 'When They Were Orphans', *New York Times Book Review* (17 April 2005), p. 16.
7. Siddhartha Deb, 'Lost Corner', *New Statesman* (7 March 2005), http://www.newstatesman.com/200503070047.
8. James Browning, 'Hello Dolly; When We Were Organs: Novelist Kazuo Ishiguro Pens a "1984" for the Bioengineering Age', *Village Voice* 50.13 (30 March 2005), p. 75.
9. Joseph O'Neill, 'Never Let Me Go', *The Atlantic Monthly* 295.4 (May 2005), p. 123.
10. Wood (2005), p. 38.
11. Claire Messud, 'Love's Body', *The Nation* (16 May 2005), p. 30.
12. Margaret Atwood, 'Brave New World', *Slate* (1 April 2005), http://www.slate.com/id/2116040/
13. O'Neill (2005), p. 123.
14. Kazuo Ishiguro, 'Future Imperfect', *Guardian* (25 March 2006), http://www.guardian.co.uk/books/2006/mar/25/featuresreviews.guardianreview36
15. Gary Rosen, 'What Would a Clone Say?' *New York Times Magazine* (27 November 2005), p. 4.
16. Daniel Vorhaus, 'Review of Kazuo Ishiguro, *Never Let Me Go*', *American Journal of Bioethics* 7.2 (February 2007), p. 99.
17. M. John Harrison, 'Clone Alone', *Guardian* (26 February 2005), p. 26.
18. Lev Grossman, *Time* (4 November 2005), p. 62.
19. Tait (2005).
20. Ruth Scurr, 'The Facts of Life', *Times Literary Supplement* (13 March 2005), pp. 21–2.
21. Tim Adams, 'For Me, England is a Mythical Place', *The Observer* (20 February 2005), p. 17.
22. Atwood (2005).
23. Peter Kemp, '*Never Let Me Go* by Kazuo Ishiguro', *Sunday Times* (20 February 2005), p. 41.
24. Atwood (2005).
25. Ishiguro (2006).
26. O'Neill (2005), p. 123.

27. Tait (2005).
28. Rebecca L. Walkowitz, 'Unimaginable Largeness: Kazuo Ishiguro, Translation, and the New World Literature', *Novel* 40.3 (Summer 2007), p. 216.
29. Walkowitz (2007), p. 235.
30. Walkowitz (2007), p. 224.
31. Walkowitz (2007), p. 224.
32. Walkowitz (2007), p. 225.
33. Walkowitz (2007), p. 226.
34. Walkowitz (2007), p. 226.
35. Walkowitz (2007), p. 227.
36. Walkowitz (2007), p. 227.
37. Walkowitz (2007), p. 228.
38. Walkowitz (2007), p. 228.
39. Bruce Robbins, 'Cruelty is Bad: Banality and Proximity in *Never Let Me Go*', *Novel* 40.3 (Summer 2007), p. 291.
40. Robbins (2007), pp. 292–3.
41. Robbins (2007), p. 293.
42. Robbins (2007), p. 294.
43. Robbins (2007), p. 294.
44. Robbins (2007), p. 295.
45. Robbins (2007), p. 296.
46. Robbins (2007), p. 298.
47. Robbins (2007), p. 298.
48. Robbins (2007), p. 299.
49. Robbins (2007), p. 299.
50. Robbins (2007), p. 300.
51. Robbins (2007), p. 300.
52. Robbins (2007), p. 301.

CONCLUSION

1. Natalie Reitano, 'The Good Wound: Memory and Community in *The Unconsoled*', *Texas Studies in Literature and Language*, 49.4 (2007), p. 362.
2. Leona Toker and Daniel Chertoff, 'Reader Response and the Recycling of Topoi in Kazuo Ishiguro's *Never Let Me Go*', *Partial Answers: Journal of Literature and the History of Ideas* 6.1 (2008), pp. 163–80.
3. Lisa Fluet, 'Ishiguro's Unknown Communities', *Novel: A Forum on Fiction*, 40.3 (2007), p. 285.
4. Earl G. Ingersoll, 'Desire, the Gaze, and Suture in the Novel and the Film: *The Remains of the Day*', *Studies in the Humanities* 28.1–2 (2001), pp. 31–47.
5. Jones, Edward T., 'On *The Remains of the Day*: Harold Pinter Remaindered', *The Films of Harold Pinter*, (Albany, NY: State University of New York Press, 2001), pp. 99–107.
6. A. O. Scott, 'Wallowing in Music for the Miserable, Then Splashing Down in a Giant Vat of Beer', *New York Times* (30 April 2004), p. 13.
7. Mick LaSalle, 'Merchant-Ivory's Final Film a Refined Delight. Naturally', *San Francisco Chronicle* (13 January 2006), p. E6.
8. Peter Bradshaw, 'The White Countess', *Guardian* (31 March 2006), p. 9.
9. Graham Swift, 'Kazuo Ishiguro', *Bomb* (Fall 1989), p. 22.
10. J. Hoberman, 'The Sorrow and the Ditty', *Village Voice* 49.17 (28 April 2004), p. C65.
11. Chu-chueh Cheng, 'Making and Marketing Kazuo Ishiguro's Alterity', *Post Identity*, 4.2 (Fall 2005), http://hdl.handle.net/2027/spo.pid9999.0004.202
12. Dylan Krider, 'Rooted in a Small Space: An Interview with Kazuo Ishiguro', *Kenyon Review* 20 (1998), p. 154.
13. Lawrence Graver, 'What the Butler Saw', *New York Times Book Review* (8 October 1989), pp. 3, 33.

Select Bibliography

NOVELS BY KAZUO ISHIGURO

A Pale View of Hills, London: Faber & Faber, 1982.
An Artist of the Floating World, London: Faber & Faber, 1986.
The Remains of the Day, London: Faber & Faber, 1989.
The Unconsoled, London: Faber & Faber, 1995.
When We Were Orphans, London: Faber & Faber, 2000.
Never Let Me Go, London: Faber & Faber, 2005.

SHORT STORIES

'A Strange and Sometimes Sadness', *Introduction 7: Stories by New Writers*, Faber and Faber, 1981, pp. 13–27.
'Waiting for J.', *Introduction 7: Stories by New Writers*, Faber and Faber, 1981, pp. 28–37.
'Getting Poisoned', *Introduction 7: Stories by New Writers*, Faber and Faber, 1981, pp. 38–51.
'A Family Supper', *Firebird 2*, ed. T. J. Binding, Harmondsworth: Penguin, 1983: pp. 121–31.
'The Summer After the War', *Granta* 7 (1983), pp. 119–37.
'October, 1948', *Granta* 17 (1985), pp. 177–85.
'A Village After Dark', *The New Yorker* (21 May 2001), pp. 86–91.
Nocturnes: Five Stories of Music and Nightfall, London: Faber & Faber, 2009.

FILMS AND SCREENPLAYS

A Profile of Arthur J. Mason, dir. Michael Whyte, with Bernard Hepton, Charles Gray, and Cheri Lunghi. United Kingdom: Skreba/Spectre, 1984, short film.
The Gourmet, dir. Michael Whyte, with Charles Gray and Mick Ford. United Kingdom: Skreba/Spectre, 1986, short film.
The Remains of the Day (with Ruth Prawer Jhabvala), dir. James Ivory, with Anthony Hopkins, Emma Thompson, and James Fox. United Kingdom: Merchant Ivory, 1993, 134 min.
The Saddest Music in the World, written by George Toles and Guy Maddin, dir. Guy Maddin, with Mark McKinney, Isabella Rossellini, and Maria de Medeiros. Canada: Rhombus Media, Buffalo Gal Pictures, and Ego Film Arts, 2004, 101 min. Original screenplay Kazuo Ishiguro.
The White Countess, dir. James Ivory, with Ralph Fiennes, Natasha Richardson, Vanessa Redgrave, Lynn Redgrave, and Hiroyuki Sanada. United Kingdom: Merchant Ivory, 2006, 136 min.
Never Let Me Go, screenplay by Alex Garland, dir. Mark Romanek, with Keira Knightley. United Kingdom: DNA Films, Fox Searchlight, Film4. In production.

OTHER WRITINGS

'I Became Profoundly Thankful for Having Been Born in Nagasaki', *Guardian*, (8 August 1983), p. 9.

'Introduction', Yasunari Kawabata, *Snow Country* and *Thousand Cranes*, Trans. Edward G. Seidensticker, Harmondsworth: Penguin: 1986, pp. 1–3.

Letter to Salman Rushdie, *The Rushdie Letters: Freedom to Speak, Freedom to Write*, ed. Steve MacDonogh, London: Brandon: 1993, pp. 79–80.

'Future Imperfect', *Guardian*, (25 March 2006), http://www.guardian.co.uk/books/2006/mar/25/featuresreviews.guardianreview36

SELECTED INTERVIEWS

Bryson, Bill, 'Between Two Worlds', *New York Times*, (29 April 1990), sec. 6, pp. 38–9, 44, 80.

Jaggi, Maya, 'Kazuo Ishiguro Talks to Maya Jaggi', *Wasafiri: Journal of Caribbean, African, Asian and Associated Literatures and Film*, 22 (1995), pp. 20–4.

Krider, Dylan Otto, 'Rooted in a Small Space: An Interview with Kazuo Ishiguro', *Kenyon Review*, 20 (1998), pp. 146–54.

Mason, Gregory, 'An Interview with Kazuo Ishiguro', *Contemporary Literature*, 30 (1989), pp. 335–47.

Oe, Kenzaburo, and Kazuo Ishiguro, 'The Novelist in Today's World: A Conversation', *Boundary 2: An International Journal of Literature and Culture*, 18 (1991), pp. 109–22. Reprinted as 'Wave Patterns: A Dialogue', in *Grand Street*, 10 (1991), pp. 75–91.

Shaffer, Brian W. and Cynthia F. Wong, *Conversations with Kazuo Ishiguro* (Jackson, Miss: University Press of Mississippi, 2008), 224 pp.

Sinclair, Clive, 'Kazuo Ishiguro', *The Roland Collection*, video interview, 1986.

Spiegel Online, Interview with Kazuo Ishiguro, (10 May 2005), http://www.spiegel.de/international/0,1518,378173,00.html

Vorda, Allan and Kim Herzinger, 'An Interview with Kazuo Ishiguro', *Mississippi Review*, 20 (1991), pp. 131–54. Reprinted as 'Stuck on the Margins: An Interview with Kazuo Ishiguro', *Face to Face: Interviews with Contemporary Novelists* (Houston: Rice University Press, 1993), pp. 1–36.

CRITICISM

Books Devoted to Kazuo Ishiguro

Lewis, Barry, *Kazuo Ishiguro* (Manchester: Manchester University Press, 2000), 191 pp.

Shaffer, Brian W., *Understanding Kazuo Ishiguro* (Columbia, SC: University of South Carolina Press, 1998), 146 pp.

Wong, Cynthia F., *Kazuo Ishiguro* (Plymouth: Northcote House, with British Council, 2000), 102 pp.

Selected books and Essays with Key Discussions of the Fiction of Kazuo Ishiguro

Adelman, Gary. 'Double on the Rocks: Ishiguro's *The Unconsoled*', *Critique: Studies in Contemporary Fiction* 42.2 (2001), pp. 166–79.

Appiah, Kwame Anthony. 'Liberalism, Individuality, and Identity', *Critical Inquiry* 27.2 (2001), pp. 305–32.

Atkinson, Rob. 'How the Butler Was Made To Do It. The Perverted Professionalism of "The Remains of the Day"', *Yale Law Journal* 10 (1995), pp. 177–220.

Cheng, Chu-chueh. 'Making and Marketing Kazuo Ishiguro's Alterity', *Post Identity* 4.2 (2005), http://hdl.handle.net/2027/spo.pid9999.0004.202

Ekelund, G. Bo. 'Misrecognizing History: Complicitous Genres in Kazuo Ishiguro's *The Remains of the Day*', *International Fiction Review* 32.1–2 (2005), pp. 70–90.

François, Pierre. 'The Spectral Return of Depths in Kazuo Ishiguro's *The Unconsoled*', *Commonwealth Essays and Studies* 26.2 (2004), pp. 77–90.

Furst, Lillian. 'Memory's Fragile Power in Ishiguro's *Remains of the Day* and W. C. Sebald's "Max Ferber"', *Contemporary Literature* 48.4 (2007), pp. 530–53.

Griffith, M., 'Great English Houses/New Homes in England?: Memory and Identity in Kazuo Ishiguro's *The Remains of the Day* and V. S. Naipaul's *The Enigma of Arrival*', *Span* 36 (1993), pp. 488–503.

Guth, Deborah. 'Submerged Narratives in Kazuo Ishiguro's *The Remains of the Day*', *Forum for Modern Language Studies* 35.2 (1999), pp. 126–37.

Ingersoll, Earl G. 'Desire, the Gaze, and Suture in the Novel and the Film: *The Remains of the Day*', *Studies in the Humanities* 28.1–2 (2001), pp. 31–47.

Jirgens, Karl E. 'Narrator Resartus: Palimpsestic Revelations in Kazuo Ishiguro's *The Remains of the Day*', *Q/W/E/R/T/Y: Arts, Littératures & Civilisations du Monde Anglophone* 9 (1999), pp. 219–30.

Lang, James M. 'Public Memory, Private History: Kazuo Ishiguro's *The Remains of the Day*', *CLIO: A Journal of Literature, History, and the Philosophy of History* 29.2 (2000), pp. 143–65.

Luo, Shao-Pin. '"Living the Wrong Life": Kazuo Ishiguro's *Unconsoled Orphans*', *Dalhousie Review* 83.1 (2003), pp. 51–80.

Mason, Gregory. 'Inspiring Images: The Influence of the Japanese Cinema on the Writings of Kazuo Ishiguro', *East West Film Journal* 3 (1989), pp. 39–52.

McCombe, John P. 'The End of (Anthony) Eden: Ishiguro's *The Remains of the Day* and Midcentury Anglo-American Tensions', *Twentieth Century Literature: A Scholarly and Critical Journal* 48.1 (2002), pp. 77–99.

Medalie, David, 'What Dignity is There in That?: The Crisis of Dignity in Selected Late-Twentieth-Century Novels', *Journal of Literary Studies* 20 (June 2004), pp. 48–61.

O'Brien, Susie, 'Serving a New World Order: Postcolonial Politics in Kazuo Ishiguro's *The Remains of the Day*', *Modern Fiction Studies* 42:4 (1996), pp. 787–806.

Phelan, James and Mary Patricia Martin. 'The Lessons of "Weymouth": Homodiegesis, Unreliability, Ethics, and *The Remains of the Day*', *Narratologies: New Perspectives on Narrative Analysis* (Columbus, OH: Ohio State University Press, 1999), pp. 88–109.

Reitano, Natalie, 'The Good Wound: Memory and Community in *The Unconsoled*', *Texas Studies in Literature and Language* 49.4 (2007), pp. 361–86.

Robbins, Bruce, 'Cruelty is Bad: Banality and Proximity in *Never Let Me Go*', *Novel* 40.3 (Summer 2007), pp. 289–302.

Scanlan, Margaret, 'Mistaken Identities: First-Person Narration in Kazuo Ishiguro', *Journal of Narrative and Life History* 3:2 & 3 (1993), pp. 139–54.

Sim, Wai-chew, 'Kazuo Ishiguro', *Review of Contemporary Fiction* 25.1 (2005), pp. 80–115.

Su, John J., 'Refiguring National Character: The Remains of the British Estate Novel', *MFS: Modern Fiction Studies* 48.3 (2002), pp. 552–80.

Sutherland, John, 'Why Hasn't Mr. Stevens Heard of the Suez Crisis?' *Where Was Rebecca Shot?: Curiosities, Puzzles, and Conundrums in Modern Fiction* (London: Weidenfeld & Nicolson, 1998), p. 188.

Teverson, Andrew. 'Acts of Reading in Kazuo Ishiguro's *The Remains of the Day*', *Q/W/E/R/T/Y: Arts, Littératures & Civilisations du Monde Anglophone* 9 (1999), pp. 251–8.

Toker, Leona and Daniel Chertoff, 'Reader Response and the Recycling of Topoi in Kazuo Ishiguro's *Never Let Me Go*', *Partial Answers: Journal of Literature and the History of Ideas* 6.1 (2008), pp. 163–80.

Walkowitz, Rebecca L., 'Ishiguro's Floating Worlds,' *ELH* 68 (2001), pp. 1049–76.

——, 'Unimaginable Largeness: Kazuo Ishiguro, Translation, and the New World Literature', *Novel* 40.3 (Summer 2007), pp. 216–39.

Wall, Kathleen, '*The Remains of the Day* and Its Challenges to Theories of Unreliable Narration', *Journal of Narrative Technique* 24 (1994), pp. 18–42.

Wong, Cynthia F., 'The Shame of Memory: Blanchot's Self-Dispossession in Ishiguro's *A Pale View of Hills*', *CLIO: A Journal of Literature, History, and the Philosophy of History* 24 (1995), pp. 127–45.

A Selection of Reviews of Kazuo Ishiguro's Novels

A Pale View of Hills

Bailey, Paul, 'Private Desolations', *Times Literary Supplement* (19 February 1982), p. 179.

De Jongh, Nicholas, 'Life After the Bomb', *Guardian* (22 February, 1982), p. 11.

King, Francis, 'Shimmering', *Spectator* (27 February 1982), p. 25.

Lee, Hermione, 'Quiet Desolation', *New Republic* (22 January 1990), pp. 36–9.

Lively, Penelope, 'Backwards and Forwards', *Encounter* (June–July 1982), pp. 86–91.

Milton, Edith, 'In a Japan Like Limbo', *New York Times Book Review* (9 May 1982), pp. 12–13.

An Artist of the Floating World

Dyer, Geoff, 'On Their Mettle', *New Statesman* (4 April 1986), p. 25.

Field, Michele, 'This Britisher is Japanese', *Sydney Morning Herald* (12 March 1988), p. 74.

Hunt, Nigel, 'Two Close Looks at Faraway', *Brick: A Journal of Reviews* no. 31 (Fall 1987), pp. 36–8.

Morton, Kathryn, 'After the War was Lost', *New York Times Book Review* (8 June 1986), p. 19.

Parrinder, Patrick, 'Manly Scowls', *London Review of Books* (6 February 1986), pp. 16–17.

Sinclair, Clive, 'The Land of the Rising Son', *Sunday Times Magazine* (11 January 1987), p. 37.

The Remains of the Day

Graver, Lawrence, 'What the Butler Saw', *New York Times Book Review* (8 October 1989), pp. 3, 33.

Gurewich, David, 'Upstairs, Downstairs', *New Criterion* (December 1989), pp. 77–80.

Kamine, Mark, 'A Servant of Self-Deceit', *New Leader* (13 November 1989), pp. 21–2.

Lee, Susanne Wah, 'Of Dignity and Servility', *The Nation* (18 December 1989), pp. 761–3.

Rafferty, Terrence, 'The Lesson of the Master', *New Yorker* (15 January 1990), pp. 102–4.

Rubin, Merle, 'A Review of *The Remains of the Day*', *Christian Science Monitor* (13 November 1989), p. 13.

Rushdie, Salman, 'What the Butler Didn't See', *Observer,* (21 May 1989), p. 53; reprinted as 'Kazuo Ishiguro', in Salman Rushdie, *Imaginary Homelands: Essays and Criticism 1981–1991* (London: Granta Books, 1991), pp. 244–6.

Strawson, Galen, 'Tragically Disciplined and Dignified', *Times Literary Supplement* (19–25 May 1989), p. 535.

The Unconsoled

Brookner, Anita, 'A Superb Achievement', *Spectator* (24 June 1995), pp. 40–1.

Cusk, Rachel, 'Journey to the End of the Day', *Times* (11 May 1995), p. 38.

Innes, Charlotte, 'Dr Faustus Faces the Music', *Nation* (6 November 1995), pp. 546–8.

Menand, Louis, 'Anxious in Dreamland', *New York Times Book Review* (15 October 1995), p. 7.

Passaro, Vince, 'New Flash from an Old Island', *Harper's* (October 1995), pp. 71–5.

Rorty, Richard, 'Consolation Prize', *Village Voice Literary Supplement* (October 1995), p. 13.

Wood, Michael, 'Sleepless Nights', *New York Review of Books* (21 December 1995), pp. 17–8.

Wyndham, Francis, 'Nightmare Hotel', *New Yorker* (23 October 1995), pp. 90–4.

When We Were Orphans

Bouldrey, Brian, 'A Life in Pieces', *San Francisco Chronicle* (24 October 2000), p. RV 5.

Carey, John, 'Few Novels Extend the Possibilities of Fiction. This One Does', *Sunday Times* (2 April 2000), Culture p. 45.

Gorra, Michael, 'The Case of the Missing Childhood', *New York Times Book Review* (24 September 2000), p. 12.

Harding-Russell, Gillian, 'Through the Veil of Memory', *Queen's Quarterly* 109.1 (2002), pp. 95–101.

Jaggi, Maya, 'In Search of Lost Crimes', *Guardian* (1 April 2000), p. 8.

Oates, Joyce Carol, 'The Serpent's Heart', *Times Literary Supplement* (31 March 2000), pp. 21–2.

Reich, Tova, 'A Sleuth in Search of Himself', *New Leader* 83.4 (Sep./Oct. 2000), p. 43.

Tonkin, Boyd, 'Artist of his Floating World', *Independent* (Saturday, 1 April 2000), p. 9.

Wood, James, 'The Unconsoled', *New Republic* (16 October 2000), p. 44.

Never Let Me Go

Atwood, Margaret, 'Brave New World', *Slate* (1 April 2005), http://www.slate.com/id/2116040/

Kakutani, Michiko, 'Sealed in a World That's Not as It Seems', *New York Times* (4 April 2005), p. E8.

Kemp, Peter, 'Never Let Me Go by Kazuo Ishiguro', *Sunday Times* (20 February 2005), p. 41.

Kerr, Sarah, 'When They Were Orphans', *New York Times Book Review* (17 April 2005), p. 16.

Menand, Louis, 'Something about Kathy: Ishiguro's Quasi-Science-Fiction Novel', *New Yorker* 81.6 (28 March 2005), pp. 78–9.

Messud, Claire, 'Love's Body', *The Nation* (16 May 2005), pp. 28–31.

Scurr, Ruth, 'The Facts of Life,' *Times Literary Supplement* (13 March 2005), pp. 21–2.

Wood, James, 'The Human Difference,' *New Republic* (12 May 2005), p. 36.

Index

Printed by Printforce, the Netherlands